THE
SELF-LOVE
HABIT

Transform fear and
self-doubt into **SERENITY,**
PEACE and **POWER**

Fiona Brennan

GILL BOOKS

Gill Books
Hume Avenue
Park West
Dublin 12

www.gillbooks.ie

Gill Books is an imprint of M.H. Gill and Co.

© Fiona Brennan 2021

978 0717 1 8875 8

Design origination by Graham Thew

Edited by Kristin Jensen

Proofread by Jane Rogers

Printed by CPI Group (UK) Ltd, Croydon, CRO 4YY

This book is typeset in Alda Regular, 10 on 16 pt.

The identities of the people in case studies in this book, both those who have told their own stories and those whose stories I have told, have been changed to protect the privacy of these individuals.

This book is not intended as a substitute for the medical advice of a physician. The reader should consult a doctor or mental health professional if they feel it necessary.

The paper used in this book comes from the wood pulp of managed forests. For every tree felled, at least one tree is planted, thereby renewing natural resources.

A CIP catalogue record for this book is available from the British Library.

5 4 3 2 1

For Mum, Dad and Orla.
Thank you for loving all of me, all my life.
My heart will always remain your home.

Foreword

Human beings are fairly complex compilations of stardust. How we navigate our worlds is influenced by our biology, past experiences, psychology, culture, and relationships. These influences are nuanced and layered, and they can often leave us feeling unable to get out of our own way. In the relentless war for our attention, the modern world has also designed a pretty extensive and subtle range of distractions, which even the most resilient of defences cannot protect against.

When I look back from a space of relative peace and contentment at my own journey, things that once seemed hazy now have clarity. One of the building blocks of my recovery came from the realisation that, although human beings are deeply complex and intricate, our needs aren't. Our culture often tricks us into believing we need certain things in order to be happy, and we find ourselves constantly chasing that moment of enlightenment. I spent fifteen years doing it – believing my happiness lay in achievement, material things, success and acceptance from others. I would set a goal, achieve it, and move on to the next one. Ironically, by chasing a certain life, I was missing out on living one. It always felt like there was something missing. It was an unquenchable thirst that I could never satisfy.

As I voyaged through the therapeutic process, it became pretty evident what that missing piece was: I never let myself experience pride; I had little to no compassion for myself; I had these unrelenting standards, and even when I managed to meet them, I brushed my accomplishments off. It was realising this that allowed for the rebuilding of my sense of self. This insight was important, but insight requires action.

The foundation of a strong sense of self is compassion. For me, it is the most basic of human needs. It is also a brilliant starting point for creating a more sustainable defence against the hostile elements of the modern world, so that we can embrace and enjoy the amazing and joyful stuff we all experience too. But the journey to building self-compassion doesn't mean we can bypass the inevitably difficult stuff that life throws at us. So much of the narrative within the wellness industry is about airbrushing out negativity, dismissing it as a bold child, and creating an almost synthetic positivity without any clear road map for how to actually get there. The reality is that it's often the darkness that can teach us the most about ourselves.

In Fiona's first book, *The Positive Habit*, she explored how the human condition relates to positivity and how positivity is much more than an inspirational quote or meme that we are force-fed in some Facebook thread. She looked at how we can hold our negative patterns to account. How we need to find ways to challenge them. How the neurological mechanisms that send us into a spiral of negativity are the very ones we can use to build a habitually more positive mindset. *The Positive Habit* provided a clear road map that was practical, tangible and, most important, impactful.

Fiona's writing doesn't come from a place of hierarchy. It feels like she is talking with you rather than to you, and that is very important. None of us have this mad world, or our mad heads, all figured out, but with Fiona it always feels like you are in safe hands – like she is shining a torch so that you can see your way in the dark. That is what resonates with me and hopefully it will resonate with you too.

Reading Fiona's second book, *The Self-Love Habit*, I am enlivened by the fact that she has continued this incredible, relatable style that made her first book such a success. Once again, the key here is the road map. Working on both a conscious and a subconscious level, Fiona explores four crucial habits for building the ability to accept and love yourself in a world that sometimes makes it hard to do so. Listen, open, value, and energise: these words don't mean a hell of a lot out of context, but once you start to delve into the content of each one, they really open up our reflective natures, which makes books such as this so important. Fiona's ability to disarm the ego and provide a window of self-awareness to the reader before rolling out the techniques and the rationale behind them is what makes her books so impactful. I don't feel condescended to, and, if I am honest, when I read books about the human condition I often find myself feeling that way.

This pandemic has tested us all – and continues to do so. Just when you think you have some form of control over your state of mind, you hit a wall. But it has also presented us with an opportunity. An opportunity to become better guardians of our own minds. To re-evaluate value systems and belief structures. To take personal responsibility for our own emotional wellbeing. To decide where and upon whom we want to place our precious presence and attention. But here's the thing: it takes work. It takes commitment. There are no shortcuts – you need to take the scenic route. It's longer and there are some crappy roads with potholes and hills, but, my God, it's worth it. This book can guide you on that scenic route and will act as the North Star if you are veering a little bit off course. In essence, what's important to remember is that, although the mind can be weakened, it can be strengthened. Life is not a straight line; trying to pretend it is lies at the root of a lot of our suffering.

I will finish by reiterating the key principles of the practice of mindfulness-based interventions. Nurture 'beginner's mind', or curiosity. Bring fresh eyes to this book. Open your mind to its content. Engage with it. Challenge it. Explore it. Knowledge and education diminish fear, and this book has those in abundance.

— NIALL BRESLIN, NOVEMBER 2020

INTRODUCTION

'Vivre sans aimer n'est pas proprement vivre.'

('To live without loving is to not really live.')

MOLIÈRE

EXTRACT FROM MY PRIVATE DIARY ENTRY, AGE 20. SUNDAY, 3 SEPTEMBER 1995, ISSY-LES-MOULINEAUX, PARIS.

I can hardly move. I am motionless. I feel lost and long for Mum. I know how pathetic this is. I mean, here I am in my worshipped blue studio in Paris, the dream I have been looking forward to for months and I feel totally empty and alone.

Things at home were so good before I left. I had so much fun that I almost wish none of it had happened. I spent the most loving and precious time with Mum, who could never have been more kind. All my friends were full of love and last but not least Ciaran came to see me coz he really wanted to! I find him so much fun, so kind and so sexy. I was so sad saying goodbye to him.

The tears of self-pity are rolling down my face. Have I made the right decision? I can't help thinking of my last disaster as an au pair. I am afraid and I feel trapped. I am here now miles away from the people I love. Why did I think I was able to deal with this? I think I am very tired and really need to relax. It physically hurts to be away from Mum, she means so much to me.

I am in a great city; I am determined to make a go of my acting career but I can't help feeling lost. Life is too precious to whittle away feeling sad. I have loved and I will keep on loving. People are the most important things in the world.

× × ×

Love and Fear

THERE ARE FEW certainties in life. Death is one, love is another. Despite humanity's desperate search for certitude and security, many of us invest too much of our lives in fearing death and doubting love.

In this book, I will do my utmost to trust your ability to love and be loved and to give you the courage to become comfortable with death so you can live fully. Many people look for security in all the wrong places and worry that they are not good enough. The etymology of the verb 'to worry' is Old English and it means 'to strangle'. If you feel anxious or overwhelmed, you may feel like you cannot breathe and are being psychologically choked.

Love is the antidote to fear. Love is life itself.

The primary focus of this book is self-love. When you love all the parts of yourself, you have the capacity, the compassion and the patience to love others. That well-known maxim, 'the whole is greater than the sum of its parts' (attributed to Aristotle), is true. For example, a family that strives to include each member is stronger, happier and more united as a result; or a sports team in which each member focuses on the overall effort rather than being a solo player is more successful. Clearly, it is easier to love the parts of yourself (and others) that you already like, for example being kind, generous and productive. My intention is that you begin to love the parts of yourself that you may hide from the world, the seemingly more 'difficult' parts that may lurk in the shadows, for example frustration, anxiety and anger. These are the parts that need your love, care and attention more than any other.

Loving all of yourself is not an indulgent or selfish act – ultimately, it is one of survival. It is the most selfless skill you will ever learn, and it definitely is a skill. It took me a long time to realise this on a cognitive level and longer still to live it. I have now made it my mission to share with you how to fall in love with yourself and ultimately with life. To do this, we must start with a still mind.

Have you ever experienced the immediate relief when an irritating background noise like a cooker fan or a radio is turned off? It is the absence of the sound that you enjoy. Peace ensues and you wonder why you had not turned it off sooner. Can you imagine being able to turn off unnecessary fear? Imagine living a life without self-imposed limitations. This is the transition you make when you choose to live through love. Your whole world opens to serenity. You no longer hear or feel the background hum of anxiety and your mind is clear. The realisation that you have a choice is your ultimate liberation. It is acting on that choice that makes all the difference.

Self-awareness and proactivity is love. Love is everything.

It is not a coincidence that you picked up this book. There is a reason that you selected it, so trust your instinct. You have my word that there is no concept or exercise in this book that I have not applied to alleviate my own anxiety and that of my clients. The four LOVE habits explored in this book will teach you the art of how to love yourself and others more deeply. They will transform your internal battles into inner peace and your external relationships into a source of endless joy. As Oscar Wilde said, 'To love oneself is the beginning of a lifelong romance.' So here we are, at the beginning.

Be Yourself

IF YOU HAVE ever felt anxious before an important event, a well-intentioned loved one may have said, 'Just be yourself.' But what if you genuinely do not know *who* that is? How can you just 'be' a stranger? What if the 'you' when you wake up in the morning seems like a different person from the one who goes to bed at night? Or different from the one who is at work or at home with your family or out with friends? What if you are confused by these disparate, often divided parts of yourself? How do you respond when the 'wrong' self turns up at the most inopportune of moments, for example the anxious part surfacing at an important meeting or when giving a speech? '*Véritable soi*' is a French phrase that originally comes from Latin and means 'true and genuine self'. This book will help you to live and breathe your one true self no matter where you are or whose company you are in.

The French philosopher Blaise Pascal wrote, 'All men's miseries derive from not being able to sit in a quiet room alone.' Could this be true? And if so, why are more of us not doing it? My diary entry above is an example of a lost young soul who was very much alone in a quiet room. I was unable to carry the burden of silence. Being myself, by myself, was too hard. The intensity of the emotions I felt, swinging from despair to determination in the blink of a tear, was exhausting. I was blinded by fear in the perceived absence of my mother's love and was unaware of my innate ability to love myself.

The two seemingly opposing emotions of love and fear have both played a crucial role in our evolution and survival. Love and fear are deeply and intrinsically interconnected – one cannot exist without the other.

Without experiencing the transformative energies of both fear and love, your development remains stagnant, stunted and small.

Your emotional comfort zone can become increasingly uncomfortable. Fear of being hurt and lack of confidence may lead you to shun new opportunities. You may unconsciously and automatically flee as soon as any fear emerges in order to protect yourself. For example, if you have been hurt by a partner in the past, you may remain single as it seems safer and you are less exposed to potential rejection.

Many of us will resist feeling our fear at all costs. We will distract ourselves, ignore, ruminate and attempt to anaesthetise the pain with food, alcohol or drugs. Fear itself is what we fear most. This resistance leads to either a low or high level of habitual anxiety, that background din that drains your energy. Recent data from the World Health Organization (WHO) shows that: 'The proportion of the global population with anxiety disorders in 2015 is estimated to be 3.6 per cent. As with depression, anxiety disorders are more common among females than males (4.6 per cent compared to 2.6 per cent at the global level).'[1] This estimate is based on diagnosed disorders, but the figure is likely to be far higher, with many people, especially men, staying silent. Undiagnosed day-to-day anxiety is rampant. I know this because I see it in my clinic, and I can't keep up with the clients who need my one-to-one help.

Fear is one of the most contagious emotions and is especially infectious in groups of work colleagues and families – when one person panics, their fear spreads like a virus. On a broader level, the media can inflict collective hysteria. The good news is that calmness and other positive emotions are equally infectious. A centred person has the ability to shift a crisis into a manageable event. Dr Brené Brown, the international bestselling author and researcher, defined calmness as 'perspective, mindfulness and the ability to manage emotional reactivity'.[2]

Resisting fear does one thing only: it creates more fear.

If I were to tell you that by accepting fear and yourself as you are, not how you think you should be, you will transform your life, would you believe me? It sounds too simple and also counter-intuitive. How can you accept something as debilitating as anxiety? I've seen many clients struggle with this principle and it is one we will return to often. In the seeds of acceptance, love emerges. Acceptance takes time, patience and love. Fortunately, we have an abundance of all three, so it is much more important to get it right than to get it quickly. When you have truly mastered the power of acceptance, you are liberated.

There is, of course, a wide spectrum of emotional states that dwell between love and fear. The subtle and nuanced rainbow of emotions that shapes your everyday world includes joy, happiness, calmness, serenity, irritability, frustration, anger and so on. Like most of us, you will sway unconsciously through this gamut of mental states, unaware that the two potent underlying energies of love and fear dictate your greatest decisions.

The Unconditioned Self

WHEN YOU LOOK in the mirror, what self do you see? Does the image reflect acceptance (love) or resistance (fear)? Can you look in the mirror and see beyond the immediately physical? Can you see past the lines on your face or the shape of your body? I would add to Pascal's quote above that much of our misery also comes from our inability to look at our own reflection *without judgement*. We are constantly looking to fix what is wrong with us, both externally and internally, and this creates a harsh, persistent message of 'I am not good enough as I am'.

Contrast this with how a toddler looks at him or herself in the mirror; often they will gaze with curiosity, warmth and joy. They are inquisitive, not critical, and accept all of themselves effortlessly. There is no internal critic questioning if their arms or belly look too chubby. They have not yet learned the cruel habit of self-comparison.

Next time you have the joy of being with a pre-school child, observe how comfortable they are in and with their own skin. Watch how they move their bodies like dancers, so at ease and full of grace. You and I were both this toddler once, totally at ease and comfortable in our skin. Can you remember that feeling of freedom?

In his 1762 book *The Social Contract*, Jean-Jacques Rousseau, the French enlightenment philosopher, wrote, 'Man is born free, but is everywhere in chains.' The Christian concept of original sin and the fall of man burdens humanity with guilt and shame for disobedience and for giving in to temptation in the Garden of Eden. With this theological backdrop, what chance did the notion of self-love have? How could we love ourselves in totality if we are identified as sinners before we can even talk?

Rousseau's concept of the 'noble savage' contradicts this notion. Essentially, he states that humans are born into nature pure, innocent and good and become corrupted by 'civilisation' and religion. The external influences cause catastrophic disharmony within the self and lead, over time, to becoming conditioned to loathe the more vulnerable parts of our nature. Rousseau also wrote, 'What wisdom can you find greater than kindness?' Imagine living free of guilt and being wisely kind and compassionate to the tender parts of yourself rather than harsh and unforgiving.

> **When you dwell in the province of self-love, life's greatest traumas become bearable and everyday mundanity is lifted into the sublime.**

In the extract from my diary above, I had just turned 20 and was clearly confused. I felt like an independent, mature adult embarking on a new adventure, but at the same time I felt like a homesick child. I had moved to Paris on my own with big plans to make it as an actress. I did not know a soul in the city, had little money and only school French. As an extrovert who depended totally on social interaction, how was I to survive alone?

I had no choice but to be with myself. There was a void in my young heart that literally hurt as I was in a strange city away from the people I loved. I did not know who my *véritable soi* (true self) was. I craved my mother's love in much the same way a child might on their first day of school. I yearned to return to a cocooned state of being. The threat of loneliness lingered deep in my heart and the hours, days, weeks and months stretched out ahead of me. Now, with the benefit of hindsight, I can see clearly that in my youth I was prone to being dramatic! It was my fuel. I believed my thoughts as facts, not rumours. I did not take the time to understand my fears. I thought that all love was conditional. Such can be both the folly and innocence of youth.

Imagine if your daughter, sister or friend was in the same position. What would you say to them? Would you tell them to come home? Would you fly over to be with them or would you encourage them to stay and ride out the storm, reassuring them that it would get better? In my case, I was an adult, albeit a young and anxious one. Even if my mother had dropped everything and run to my rescue in my little studio, would it have been the solution? Even then I knew it would not have been, and so did she.

As we mature, the relationship between a parent and child must evolve from the original dynamic of protector and protected to one of two balanced, emotionally self-reliant individuals, equals who operate on mutual respect and who have let go of any true or perceived pain from the past.

In my clinical work, I see many people aged 20, 30, 40 and beyond who remain stuck in old, static versions of the parent–child relationship. They are acting out their conditioned personal histories. This often leads them to be unintentionally consumed with blame and anger and they are often deeply repressed. They then unintentionally transfer this to their loved ones through guilt and irritation. For example, a person who cannot forgive an alcoholic parent transfers their unresolved fears to their non-alcoholic partner and becomes rattled each time their partner has a drink. Making insights through self-knowledge is imperative for your happiness and for those you love.

The Beholder

THE QUINTESSENTIAL QUESTIONS 'Who am I?' and 'What is the self?' have been debated by philosophers for centuries, from Socrates (Ancient Greece, 399 BC) to Philo of Alexandria (Judaism, AD 50) to St Augustine (Christian, AD 430) to Voltaire and Hume in the European Age of Enlightenment (eighteenth century). While this desire to explain our consciousness remains very much alive in philosophy and, indeed, psychology, the birth of modern neuroscience means that the brain can now be scanned for evidence of where human consciousness resides. Despite this, neuroscientists still have not been able to find it ... yet.

Our greatest power is invisible.

In his essay 'The Mystery of Consciousness', Sam Harris, the eminent American neuroscientist, states, 'The problem, however, is that no evidence for consciousness exists in the physical world.' The evidence is the experience. In lieu of science, the sceptics among us can perhaps learn something from spiritual leaders like Eckhart Tolle:

> There is one self that is the illusion, which is the identification with the mind and the ego, which is the unobserved mind that says 'what about me?' ... but I refer to who you are beyond the form, beyond the thoughts and emotions. You as the consciousness is the self. The self has no form ... you can never say 'there it is', because who is saying this? You are the consciousness! You are it![3]

Can you imagine this state of oneness? In Hindu philosophy, Ātman is the Sanskrit for 'universal self'. I refer to this presence throughout this book as 'the Beholder', the one who witnesses your thoughts, emotions and behaviours but is not defined by any of them. The Beholder is always with you – even now, it is the part of you that reads these words while your mind analyses the concepts we explore. Would you like to be totally in harmony with reality, even when – in fact, especially when – it is difficult? To accept life as it unfolds? To be free from a mind that is plagued by thoughts that never end? To live without an inflated ego that is either constantly seeking more power, wealth and acknowledgement or not feeling worthy and self-conscious?

Is this possible? Absolutely, yes, it is. It is my life's work and now this oneness can become yours. The four LOVE habits that you will learn have been created to capture fleeting moments of loving presence and to allow them to grow organically from moments to hours, weeks, months and years to a lifetime.

Although possible, this is not without effort.

Is there anything that is meaningful to you that you have gained without effort? Do you have a relationship with someone you love that requires no effort? Viewing effort and work as a positive in this process – or, indeed, in anything you do – is paramount. However, as I mentioned earlier, many of us look in all the wrong places to feel loved and secure. We look to convention.

The Conventional Calendar

'Have patience with all things, but, first of all with yourself.'

SAINT FRANCIS
DE SALES

AT THEIR FIRST CONSULTATION, my clients will often have a genuine sense of urgency that is palpable. They may have been waiting months for an appointment and are now really desperate to be free of the anxiety or issue they have sought my help for. I can relate to this need for things to happen *now*, but love cannot be rushed and fear needs time to be quelled.

So what causes impatience? There are many reasons, but one of the most toxic beliefs I encounter with clients that fuels impatience is that you must conform to the conditioned expectations of your family and society at key points in your life. However, it is more often your own conditioned expectations that you strive to meet. If you fail to do this according to the conventional calendar, you may constantly feel like a disappointment and like you are not good enough. While convention can give the illusion of security, it often does the opposite. You fail to feel accepted until you have ticked the next box. Love is therefore conditional and is always deferred.

A typical example of a conventional calendar, in chronological order, starting with childhood, is:

○ Do what you are told

○ Don't bring attention to yourself

○ Don't question authority

○ Do well in school

○ Get good grades in your final exams

- ○ Go to a good college
- ○ Study something that has good earning potential but is not what sets your heart on fire
- ○ Get a good job
- ○ Get married
- ○ Get a better job
- ○ Buy a house
- ○ Have a child
- ○ Have another one
- ○ And maybe another
- ○ Get promoted
- ○ Send your kids to good schools
- ○ Put off anything you want to do until you retire
- ○ Put your kids through college
- ○ Put the same suffocating social expectations on them
- ○ Retire with a good pension
- ○ Help to take care of your grandchildren
- ○ Die without too much difficulty and don't be a burden to your children

How many of the items on this list have you checked? It is not just family and society that create and maintain these expectations – we do it to ourselves. The roll call of assumptions about how your life 'should' play out leaves no room for the immense range of possibilities that do not follow this prescriptive path. For example, if you are not academic and do not fit in with the standard school system, you might believe that you are not smart enough to go to college. If you wish to pursue a more creative path, you may easily be talked out of it for fear of not having a secure income. How many latent artistic geniuses are sweating it out in offices until retirement?

When it comes to having children, there are many pressures: being single and not having met the right person at the right time; fertility issues; miscarriage; desperately wanting kids but being in a same-sex relationship and having to navigate the best way to make this happen; or perhaps one of the greatest social stigmas of all, especially for a woman – not wanting to have kids.

If you are in your twenties or thirties, you will be at the busiest box-ticking stage in your life. If you are in your forties, you may have ticked some of the boxes and still have some more to do, or maybe you have reached the stage where all the boxes are ticked and you realise that there is still something missing, a void in the empty nest or retirement years that you can't fill.

None of the things on this list is inherently negative – in fact, most of them are positive milestones in life (I've ticked a few myself) – but it is important to realise that *they are not the only options available*. They do not need to be followed in the order that society expects of us, or even followed at all. The fear of being left behind can keep you desperately propelling yourself forward in a bid to 'keep up' with the presumed and socially conditioned trajectory of your life rather than explore what you might really want. Even if you consider yourself to be 'a free spirit', you are likely to fall prey to these conditioned expectations. The energy you use not to conform can be equally exhausting.

The comparative culture of social media feeds on this insecurity, encouraging you to scroll through Instagram or Facebook. This can leave you feeling utterly deflated when you emerge from the digital fog. Social media does not take into account context and perspective. For example, a mum of three young kids will look enviously at her single friend's freedom to go for a run and a night out whenever she desires, while the same single friend looks at the pictures of her friend's three adorable children and worries that she will never have her own. The unfortunate compulsion to compare ourselves to others is nothing new, but the digital world amplifies this impulse and provides a constant platform for us to berate ourselves.

Part of you already knows that your 'achievements' – the house you live in, your salary, the car you drive (or do not drive), where you go on your next holiday – are not who you are or why people like you. You are not loved for having the perfect body or not. It may seem obvious, but part of you remains a servant to conditioned beliefs.

We are subconsciously hardwired to fit in and not stand out.

In the teenage years, being different in any way can be terrifying and the comparison habit can last a lifetime *if* you allow it to. However, I have yet to be at a funeral where the priest or a loved one gave a eulogy like this: 'We loved Peter or Sandra so much because they drove a brand new Mercedes, lived in a big house and worked 12 hours a day.'

It is often through the death of someone close or a collective experience such as the global coronavirus pandemic that a clearer perspective emerges of what is truly important. Without adversity, many of us whittle away our precious energy on ticking boxes. Most of us care way too much about what other people think of us. Even when you think you do not care, many of your choices are being guided by the primitive motive of trying to be included, to be a part of the pack.

> **The Self-Love Habit will help you to see this archaic impulse as something you can overcome by standing up, standing out and taking action.**

This can also translate into your political, social and civic responsibilities. One of the countless examples of injustices that need our attention is that in Ireland, we live in a 'developed' society where children are being made homeless every day. According to the Dublin Simon Community, statistics show that in November 2019, 10,448 people were homeless. One in three people seeking emergency services is a child. Stopping to have a chat to a homeless person, volunteering or donating are all ways that can help to alleviate some of the pain for those affected. Love teaches us to cut through divisive social chains, as referred to in Rousseau's *The Social Contract*.

The Self-Love Habit is first about becoming one with yourself, of feeling whole and complete, and then feeling connected to every individual. A homeless statistic is not just a number that you read – it could be yourself, your child or someone you love.

> **Love wakes us up to endeavour to help every human being to the best of our ability.**

Like all transformation, it begins and ends with self-knowledge.

× × ×

You Are Love

'Self-knowledge is no guarantee of happiness, but it is on the side of happiness and can supply the courage to fight for it.'

SIMONE DE BEAUVOIR

IF YOU ARE ASKED the question, 'Tell me about yourself,' what do you say? Imagine that you are not permitted to give any facts about where you live, how old you are or what you do for a living. The immediate impulse is to jump in with the facts that we believe define us. Our work, relationship status and number of children all act as acceptable codes of where we take our place in society. However, knowing and loving who you are in the deepest sense of the word is the essence of what this book is about.

Knowing yourself fully allows you to love yourself fully.

I recall quite vividly being about 18 years old and going for a walk on my own along a stunning coastline in Greece. I felt lost at the time, as too many late nights and too much alcohol were compounding my already low self-esteem. Suddenly, I felt that I was not on my own. Instead, I was with this lovely person (me) who I was content to be with and wanted to get to know better. A calming energy was assuring me that I was well then and that I would always be well if I listened to myself. This soothing part of me wanted me to stay. I did, but only for a short while and I quickly forgot my ability to self-soothe. As I mature, this energy has become a familiar warm glow that often comes to me as I nod off to sleep or walk by the sea. I do not actively create this feeling; it emerges all by itself. I have learned that it comes from stillness.

× × ×

Dare to Love Yourself!

THE WORD 'PHILOSOPHY' comes from Ancient Greek and literally means 'the love of wisdom'. Philosophers from the Age of Enlightenment, also known as the Age of Reason, such as Voltaire, Rousseau and Diderot, took a strong stance against the feudal system in which France was controlled by the Church and the monarchy. Their opposition helped to sow the seeds of the French Revolution and led to the separation of Church and State in France. They believed that society should be based on reason and the needs of the individual, that we are masters of our own fate. We can hear the echoes of Aristotle's and Socrates' philosophies here, as they also strove to set humankind free and enable us to think for ourselves rather than blindly accepting strict religious doctrine.

The phrase 'sapere aude' (dare to know) captured this growing sea change. A message of hope and self-agency was born – that you are in charge of your own happiness and, crucially, that you do not have to spend the rest of your life repenting for original sin.

Consider these two important questions:

1   Do you dare to know yourself?

2   Do you dare to see the goodness in yourself?

Interestingly, the study of philosophy has been mandatory in all French secondary schools since 1808. To this day, the French education system desires to produce enlightened citizens and has a thorough four-hour philosophy exam in the baccalaureate (the final exam in high school). Students write essays on questions such as 'Is it one's own responsibility to find happiness?' or 'Is man condemned to create illusions about himself?' In tackling such metaphysical questions, young adults develop the most useful intelligence of all: emotional intelligence. Pierre-Henri Tavoillot, head of the Philosophy Department at the Sorbonne University in Paris, proudly stated, 'If there is one reason to be optimistic about France, this is it.'[4]

I can't help wondering that if I, too, had pondered such questions in my Leaving Certificate, would I have been just a little bit better equipped to deal with the loneliness I felt in Paris? If developing emotional intelligence helps you to love yourself and to contribute to creating a more peaceful world, then surely this is a habit worth learning.

× × ×

Why Make Self-Love a Habit?

'Habits are the way you embody identity. True behaviour change is really identity change.'

JAMES CLEAR

WHEN YOU ARE learning a new habit, your brain uses a lot of energy to hard-wire the new behaviour into your neural structures. This way, it can transform a conscious activity in the prefrontal cortex and hippocampus regions of the brain into a subconscious pattern in the more primitive basal ganglia area of the lower brain. Wendy Wood, psychologist and author of *Good Habits, Bad Habits*, describes this process in more simple terms as 'the rudimentary machinery of our minds'.

Automating positive habits is a boon to the human brain, as it frees up your conscious mind to focus on new tasks and make decisions. If you drive, compare the nervous energy you spent when you first learned to drive (remembering which pedal and gear to use) with how you are now when you get behind the wheel. You can now drive a familiar route on autopilot, arriving at your destination safely and yet with no real memory of the journey. When a habit becomes automated, the conscious mind can roam freely to either solve problems or create new ones, which is why many people find the car to be a good place to think.

The flip side of the automation of habits is that negative habits are actually more automatic than positive ones and often occur before you have time to become aware of their destructive force. This is where the habit of rumination and catastrophising can kick in.

Imagined worries become as gripping as real ones.

The Self-Love Habit will train you to automate the process of being an emotionally intelligent individual. Positive behavioural habits will become your default state. By developing a loving presence, all your encounters become ones where you listen to understand, are open to reality, value the other and inject a loving energy into the exchange.

Subconsciously you know how to love, but the habit of showing love is one that few of us have consciously learned. The difference may appear subtle, but the impact is immense. For example, many people only find the right words to express their love to a parent when the parent is on their deathbed or vice versa, when a parent will express deep feelings of love for their child in their final hours. Many of my clients who were fortunate enough to be present when their parents passed have told me that they never realised how deeply they were loved until that moment.

Doubts and grievances melt away in the final prized moments of our lives.

Death wakes us up to the importance of speaking our truth. We finally find the courage to say what we want to say before it is too late. Establishing self-love as a habit now means you do not wait until your or a loved one's dying hours to enjoy deep, honest and loving relationships. And that includes your relationship with yourself.

In one 2011 psychological study,[5] it was estimated that 40 per cent of what we do on a daily basis is an automatic subconscious habit, including our behaviours, thoughts and emotions. Are you in the habit of giving and receiving love? Many of us struggle to form new positive habits not because we are incapable of making the change, but because the new behaviour does not match our old identity. For example, I may want to lose weight, but in my mind I identify myself as someone who has always been overweight.

In his book *Atomic Habits*, James Clear outlines what he calls 'The Four Laws of Behavior Change' that apply if you want to change a negative habit to positive one:

1 Make it obvious.

2 Make it attractive.

3 Make it easy.

4 Make it satisfying.

It is my mission to help you change the negative unconscious habit of living through fear into the positive conscious habit of living through self-love. I have incorporated these four 'laws' throughout the book as an underlying methodology. Once you begin to feel the reward of living a more loving life, any old habits of stress and anxiety will melt away into the past – where they belong.

✕ ✕ ✕

How to Use this Book

YOU MAY HAVE read hundreds of self-help books or maybe this is your first. Either way, you will have doubts about whether what is proposed will really work. I appreciate that, I really do. It would be a mistake for you not to question what you read. While a healthy level of scepticism is normal, I want to gently highlight at this stage that two common beliefs have the potential to block your progress. These are:

✕ 'This won't work for me.' This is true *if* you believe it. For the duration of the process, trust me and trust yourself. It will work if you allow it to.

✕ 'I already know this' or 'This is obvious.' Perhaps, but knowing something intellectually and living and breathing it are two different things.

If and when these thoughts arise, remember that they are normal, then consciously choose to gently let them go.

There are a few other essential points that will help you to engage fully with the book:

✖ Remember, the Self-Love Habit is unique because it works on both a conscious and subconscious level. Listen to the audios every day.

✖ Give the book your full loving commitment and keep an open mind.

✖ If I repeat myself, it is intentional, as neuroplasticity and habit-building work on repetition.

PART ONE

Part One is broken into three chapters. Below is a brief summary of what we will cover.

THE JOURNEY TO SELF + LOVE

✖ What is self-love?

✖ How to understand yourself better

✖ Hypnotherapy – what it is and what it is not

✖ The connection of self-love and the relationship you have with your body

✖ The science of self-love and falling in love

✖ Practical exercises on all of the above

THE DIVIDED SELF

✖ What are the different parts of yourself?

✖ Examination of the two main players: Part A: The Beholder (the unconditioned, conscious mind – love) and Part B: The Shadow Self (the conditioned subconscious mind – fear). For clarity, I will often simply refer to these as Part A and Part B. These two parts often experience the most conflict. For example, A says 'I am going to start exercising', but B turns on Netflix. Another brief example might be that A wants to leave her job, but B is afraid to do so. These are relatively common experiences and many of my clients have been consumed by such inner battles that express themselves as anything from mild irritation to a full-blown war.

✘ The four main blocks to self-love (read on to find out what they are!)

✘ Understanding the purpose of the Shadow Self

✘ The inflated ego and how to tame it

✘ Practical exercises on all of the above

THE UNITED SELF

✘ How to unite Parts A and B – love and fear

✘ How to live and breathe your ideal self

✘ The malleable self – understanding your past, present and future selves

✘ How looking at the world from different perspectives will help you to unite your orphaned parts

✘ Practical exercises on all of the above

PART TWO: THE FOUR LOVE HABITS

When you are feeling more unified, whole and complete, we will move on to the second part of the book, which introduces the four LOVE habits. These four key habits are formed and expressed through four active verbs and are designed to be highly practical and easy to recall. You can apply them to any situation, person or place to achieve the happiest outcome for yourself and everyone around you. They contain the requisite emotional intelligence to help you transform all areas of your life from the influence of fear into one of love.

These four habits are contained in the easy-to-remember acronym LOVE. You won't forget that!

L – Listen. Listening to your heart and other people in a way that seeks first of all to understand.

O – Open. Opening to compassionate presence, vulnerability, honesty and relinquishing the ego.

V – Value. Valuing yourself and others, learning to appreciate gratitude, trust and respect.

E – Energise. Energising, evolving and transforming yourself and the world with a loving presence.

Please note that these four habits must be learned and practised in the order in which they are presented. Do not be tempted to skip forward.

As you practise them and they become embedded in your subconscious, you will begin to be able to choose the most useful habit for your current situation. For example, when you feel hurt that someone has let you down, it may serve you best to be open to compassion both for yourself and for the person you feel hurt by.

THE LOVE INTERVIEWS

Between each habit, there is an exclusive interview with a highly acclaimed wellness expert. These are all well-known people from Ireland and beyond (see below) who have experienced the journey to living a more loving and present life.

I carefully selected people who I believe can really help you to learn the art of how to love. The interviews are direct transcriptions of the conversations I had, and I would like to acknowledge each of them and thank them for their time. They are:

- ✕ **Dermot Whelan**, comedian, radio presenter, media and meditation expert
- ✕ **Roz Purcell**, bestselling author and wellness entrepreneur
- ✕ **Dr Rick Hanson**, neuropsychologist, senior fellow of the Greater Good Science Center at UC Berkeley and *New York Times* bestselling author
- ✕ **Alison Canavan,** international speaker, author, integrative mindfulness health coach and HeartMath facilitator

While each interviewee answered the same eight questions, their answers are unique. Many of the feelings they share are similar to the ones I have heard many times in my clinic and also felt myself. You learn a lot about yourself through the insights into the private inner worlds of others. The knowledge that you are not alone is incredibly reassuring.

There is a final, fifth interview that I conducted with Tomi Reichental, a Holocaust survivor who has made Ireland his home since 1959. This interview follows a different format because the horror of what Tomi went through is more than most of us can comprehend. He was imprisoned at the age of nine in the Bergen-Belsen concentration camp and 35 members of his family were murdered by the Nazis. This is one of the most uplifting interviews I have ever conducted, and it will give you some powerful insights.

× × ×

Exercise: LOVE Interview with You

Before you read the LOVE interviews, it is important that you interview yourself as this book is for you. You will be asked to answer the same questions again at the end, after you have read the book and listened to your love to rise and sleep audios. It will be interesting to see what shifts for you.

There is no time like the present, so grab a pen and your journal and let your answers flow!

1   Einstein said of himself, 'There is a grotesque contradiction between what people consider to be my achievements and the reality of who I am.' In other words, he felt a divide between how he was publicly perceived and how he privately felt. Do you relate to this statement?

2   Do you find it easy or difficult to hold on to a separate sense of self that is not identified with your ego?

3   Do you believe human beings are born naturally loving themselves?

4   What is/are the main reason(s), in your opinion, why somebody would NOT love themselves?

5   Do you think it is necessary for people to love themselves before they can fully love others?

6   Do you love yourself? And if so, have you always loved yourself? If not, why not?

7   What one thing would you say to your eight-year-old self that you think they needed to hear?

8 Vietnamese Buddhist monk Thích Nhất Hạnh once said, 'Only love can save us from climate change.' In essence, he suggests that if we are too consumed with our own suffering, we cannot help Mother Earth. Do you agree?

✕ ✕ ✕

The Power of Simple

The Self-Love Habit is practical, simple and it works.

The four LOVE habits enable you to quickly access a straightforward tool to ground you in the now and help you not to spiral into future concerns or past regrets. Even if you are a very busy person, you can take the time needed to implement the self-care practices in the Self-Love Habit.

Many people reading self-help books start off with the best of intentions, yet they often skip the writing/exercise parts with the intention of returning to do it, but they never do. This can be counterproductive in that, rather than boosting their self-esteem, 'failing' to do these exercises becomes yet another reason for them to be hard on themselves: 'I'm useless, I can't even follow a self-help book properly.'

Let this book be different. Know that I commend you for any and all efforts you make. Throughout our lives, far too much attention is paid to what we do not achieve rather than to what we *do*. Always acknowledge your progress. By taking this self-compassionate approach, you will benefit from the full potential of the book and the audios.

I implore you to listen to the morning meditation and sleep time hypnotherapy that accompany this book for at least 66 days. They are effortless yet life-changing. I've had thousands of clients from my online programme, *The Positive Habit,* and readers of my first book, who, just by listening to my hypnotherapy audios, have transformed anxiety into calmness and insomnia into deep sleep. Repetition is essential to make an imprint on your subconscious mind. Like a child, it needs consistent reassurance and love.

The following symbols will act as a visual reminder of when you need to engage in any of the practical tasks at hand.

✕ ✕ ✕

The Self-Love Habit Tools

 AUDIO
MEDITATION

There are two audios included with this book. You can download the app from thepositivehabit.com. Remember to insert the password LOVE.

> *Your mind is most malleable when you first wake up and just before you go to sleep at night.*

1 'Love to Rise' (7 minutes) – listen every morning as soon as you can; the earlier, the better.

2 'Love to Sleep' (26-minute guided hypnotherapy and binaural sleep-time beats) – listen last thing at night, with or without headphones. Make sure to have your phone switched to the 'do not disturb' mode.

The Self-Love Habit works on both a conscious and subconscious level.

For a significant shift to happen in you, it is *essential* that you listen to both of the audios. This is where the loving shift happens on a subconscious level, reinforcing all that you are reading. Repetition changes the neural networks in your brain as the suggestions become firmly etched into your mind.

Do not skip this essential part of the Self-Love Habit.

Listen to the morning and night-time audio every day for 66 days (and longer if you wish). You will find a chart at the back of the book where you can tick off the days you have listened. When you reach the state of living from love entirely, you will need to sustain it; in the conclusion, I will show you how.

For the purpose of the audio, please allow my voice to be your voice. This will really help you to establish the habit of self-love.

 ## BE A FRIEND TO YOURSELF

Friendship and love are deeply intertwined. Interestingly, in Latin they share the same root: '*am*'. For the duration of this book and beyond, I want you to imagine that each word you read, each exercise you complete and each time you listen to the 'Love to Rise' and 'Love to Sleep' audios, you are treating yourself as you would a best friend, someone you love deeply and wish to help.

Being a good friend to yourself is the highest form of love.

When you see the friendship symbol, it is my gentle reminder and a visual cue for you to love yourself as your best friend.

 THE DAILY PROMISE TECHNIQUE

What does a promise mean to you? Would you make a promise to a child with no intention of keeping it? What happens when a promise is made and then broken? Has this happened to you? If so, how do you feel around this person?

You are not responsible if other people do not keep their promises. Your responsibility is to be impeccable with your own word, to trust yourself. I suggest you carefully consider what you can commit to that is realistic and honest before making any promise. With that in mind, I want you to consider making the following promise to yourself. It is designed to be attainable and realistic, and above all does not put any pressure on you.

> 'I promise to accept all parts of MYSELF today to the best of my ability.'

That's it. Full stop. I am keeping this simple because I want to make sure that you do not break this self-promise. It is an essential key to the Self-Love Habit. Acceptance is love in action. Notice the words contained in the sentence above, 'to the best of my ability'. We cannot attain perfection and there will be moments when you do not accept yourself.

However, you can do your best to be kind to yourself when you need it most.

There is no part of you that needs to be got rid of or that needs to be fixed. Acceptance, as previously stated, is the beginning of deep inner transformation. Any time you feel fear, anxiety or irritation, repeat to yourself, 'I accept all parts of myself today.' I assure you that you will find that your uneasiness and intolerance will almost immediately soften.

TWO-MINUTE MIRROR EXERCISE

How often do you check your emotional and spiritual wellbeing when you look in the mirror? Most likely not very often! When we look in the mirror, most of us are at best checking our appearance or at worst criticising it and looking for faults.

This symbol means that I will ask you to spend at least two minutes a day looking at your own reflection. This is something you can do last thing at night or first thing in the morning (or both, should you so desire).

> *I recommend that you set the timer on your phone for two minutes when you first start this exercise to help ensure you spend the full amount of time required.*

Making – and above all, maintaining – eye contact with yourself is a profound way of getting to know yourself better and becoming more at ease with and comfortable in your own skin. Your confidence grows and your ability to maintain eye contact with others increases. It takes courage to look into your own eyes without judgement because the default instinct is usually to focus on your perceived flaws.

However, no matter how uncomfortable it becomes, when you stay with the discomfort, it will dissolve. The soul mirror work will help you to accept and love all the parts of yourself, creating an inner glow that shines on the outside. Others are immediately attracted to your inner state of contentment.

 ## FIVE HUGS A DAY

Human touch is essential for our wellbeing. Without it, we wither. One of the hardest strains on mental health for many people during the Covid-19 social distancing measures was the lack of human touch. A thousand words cannot replace a warm embrace.

If you grew up in an affectionate family, you may be a frequent 'hugger' and find it easy to give and receive physical affection. If, however, affection was rare or entirely absent when you were a child, it is understandable that it may not come naturally and may even feel uncomfortable. If so, you will need to introduce hugging slowly into your life. Start with one a day with a family member or a pet and work your way up. Once after an emotional session I hugged my client. She cried and said that in all her 45 years, her mother had never held her like that.

When you hug, try to hold it for at least 15 seconds and do not break away suddenly. There is an art to hugging and science shows that the longer we linger, the more we increase our oxytocin levels (oxytocin is also known as the love hormone). It is especially important to hug children and teenagers (even if they balk), as oxytocin promotes attachment and solidifies our relationships. I will come back to oxytocin later in the section on the science of love.

LOVE LETTERS

When was the last love letter you wrote? If you are over a 'certain age', you may recall that writing letters was one of the main forms of communication. Sadly, it is a dying art, but let's revive it!

When you put pen to paper, the energy of the words you choose is different and your true, authentic self emerges. You can feel very connected to the person you are writing to and a feeling of love lingers for both yourself and the recipient.

This is a sixth tool in the second part of the book, where I will ask you to write four love letters, one for each of the four LOVE habits.

x x x

The Self-Love Quiz

Answer 'yes' or 'no' to these questions and make a note of your score out of 20. Give yourself one point for each 'yes' answer. Do not think about your answers. Move quickly through the questions and let your instincts guide you.

8·3·21

1   Can you sit peacefully in silence alone, without distractions?   /

2   Can you sit peacefully in silence with others?   /

3   Do you cope well with uncertainty?   ○

4   Do you accept yourself just the way you are?   ○

5   Do you feel comfortable maintaining eye contact with yourself in a mirror?   /

6 Do you feel at ease making eye contact with others? |

7 Do you listen to your (gut and heart) instinct? ◯

8 Do you have an inner voice that is kind to you? 1

9 Are you patient with yourself when learning something new or adapting to change? |

10 Do you feel comfortable feeling vulnerable? ◯

11 Do you take care of your mind and body on a daily basis? |

12 Do you say no to other people if you feel tired or overwhelmed? |

13 Do you value yourself? |

14 Do you trust yourself to make good decisions? ◯

15 Are you at ease with your body and physical appearance? |

16 Do you feel connected to family and friends? /

17 Do you let go of the hurt from the past? |

18 Do you feel you have enough energy to help others? /

19 Do you mainly live in the present moment? ◯

20 Do you love yourself? |

Score = 14/20

The higher the number of 'yes' answers, the more you love yourself. However, remember that scores are neither 'good' nor 'bad', but are just a useful tool to show where you are right now. In fact, the questions that you answered 'no' to are the most interesting, as they provide insights into where you need to pay attention. For example, the question on vulnerability is an area I need to continue to work on. Accepting where you are at this moment is exactly where you need to be, as outlined in the daily promise technique.

You will take this quiz again at the end of the book to help you evaluate your progress.

Your mind is very powerful, and you are already a fully conscious, loving being. All you need to do is believe this with total conviction. So let's fully embark on our voyage together. I'm in if you are!

PART ONE

THE JOURNEY
TO SELF + LOVE

'L'amour est l'emblème de l'éternité. Il brouille toute notion de temps, efface tout souvenir d'un début, annule toute peur d'une fin.'

('Love is the emblem of eternity; it confounds all notions of time, erases all memory of a beginning, all fear of an end.')

MADAME DE STAËL

IN THIS CHAPTER, I will help you to start your journey to knowing and loving yourself more deeply. In order to do this, we need to explore what love is and who you are. We will also examine the science of love and how to self-generate it at a biological level. You will also examine how you feel towards your body and if you love it. I will explain what hypnotherapy actually is, what it is not and why it is important. Hypnosis and positive visualisation will help to transform the neural pathways in your brain to operate from love rather than fear. In addition, you will learn how to create calmness by activating your vagus nerve. Feeling calm helps you to feel safe, and in order to love, it is essential to feel secure. I will also provide powerful exercises to help you gain invaluable perspective on your life and relationships.

As you read, I will give you friendly reminders to keep practising your self-love tools and in particular to listen to your 'Love to Rise' and 'Love to Sleep' audios.

× × ×

What Is Love?

I ONCE MET a man in Athens wearing a T-shirt that read, 'The only solution is love.' His T-shirt did not identify the problem, only the solution; but then, it did not need to. When love is absent, conflict reigns. War and suffering, both inside ourselves and in the world at large, are rampant. Love is the reason we get up in the morning. It is the essence of our survival. Love is life and life is love.

Love is both mercifully simple and incredibly complex. It can seem both tangible and intangible. It gives and it takes. It is multi-layered and multifaceted. It can fill you up and it can leave you empty. It can heal and it can hurt.

Having examined several concepts of 'the self' in the introduction, let's now turn to look at 'love'. We have identified that the unconditioned self, also known as 'the Beholder', is pure presence. This non-judgemental presence creates energy. On that basis, the following equation may help us to grasp the ethereal energy we call love.

The Beholder (conscious presence) + Energy = Love

There is no greater gift that you can give to yourself, others and the whole planet than your conscious attention. Or as Matt Haig puts it in his book *Notes on a Nervous Planet*, 'The answer to making our minds and our planet healthier and happier is essentially the same one.'

Not so long ago, I had a charming, intelligent client who had been struggling with self-hatred and anxiety for years. He was incredibly proactive, participating in therapy diligently and making significant progress, until one day he turned to me in a session and said, 'You speak so often of self-love, but I genuinely don't know what that means. I can understand it intellectually, but it is such an alien feeling. It sounds selfish and I have no idea *how* to love myself.'

This client is far from alone. In addition, I have heard many people express two main concerns:

1   Self-love is selfish – they feel guilty practising it, as if they had no right to love themselves.

2   If you are open to it, *how* do you love yourself?

Regarding the first concern, the misleading phrase 'he or she loves him/herself' often conjures up an image of a self-centred person with an overinflated ego who never considers how other people are feeling. We may have an image of a vain person who suits themselves or perhaps posts endless pictures of themselves on social media boasting about their latest achievement. This is a common misconception and leads to the belief that to love yourself is an audacious, narcissistic act. In fact, the very opposite is true. The person who is at the whim of their ego, does not appear to consider other people and feels the need to post 'look at me' pictures is deeply insecure and is often suffering from self-loathing.

Self-love is a private affair that does not require public recognition.

On the other hand, when you love yourself, you do not necessarily retire to the background. Instead, you have a *quiet confidence* whether you are the centre of attention or not. Once you are past the first hurdle (loving yourself is selfish), we can continue. Thankfully, in recent years there is a growing recognition that loving yourself is *the* cornerstone of positive mental health. It is becoming more generally accepted as a positive skill worth acquiring.

The second issue of how to actually love yourself is not a skill we are taught at school and is rarely something that parents impart to their children, having never learned it themselves. This is what this book is about: to show you how to love yourself in a very real and practical way. You already know how to love and care for other people and it is time now to practise the same skill towards yourself.

How **to love yourself lies in the subtle art of turning this innate caring tendency internally so that you can sustain it externally.**

Most of us need to work on the skill of acceptance. Although you know how to love your family and friends, you may struggle to accept them exactly as they are and not how you wish them to be. You may unintentionally use control as a mechanism to protect those you love and in doing so create disharmony.

When you see someone you love struggling emotionally or mentally, your first instinct may be to try to 'fix' them or the situation that is causing them to suffer. For example, if your child is feeling lonely and you suspect that he/she is being left out at school, you may want to rush in and complain to the teacher before you understand the situation in its totality. Your desire to make the child feel better overrides everything else. Taking the time to get a full picture and being at ease with your child's loneliness is what will grow their confidence, which is the very thing that will help them to integrate into a group. You love them regardless. This child will be more likely to grow up accepting and loving all the parts of themselves. This takes a huge amount of practice, so please do not be hard on yourself if you are getting frustrated with someone you love.

If we are not trying to fix the situation, we often ignore it, using distraction as our prime tool. For example, a young child falls in the park and you try to distract them by saying, 'Look at the ducks in the pond.' Imagine that *you* were to fall and your partner ignored the shock you felt and your bloody knee and asked you to look at the ducks!

By witnessing distress (in ourselves and others) without the need to distract, we eventually learn how to be at ease with emotional pain. Through the four LOVE habits, you will learn on a conscious, subconscious and experiential level to accept and love yourself. This love is abundant. You create it and therefore you can rely on

it to never run dry. It is the energy we need to save both ourselves
and our precious planet.

✕ ✕ ✕

What the World Needs
Now Is Love, Sweet Love

AS A SPECIES, we have the ability to be brutally cruel to one another
and also to the planet. Man's inhumanity to man is not new, nor
is our abuse of the environment. Now, more than ever, time is
running out for humankind and planet Earth due to the speed of
climate change.

While we may acknowledge 'Mother Nature' as our collective
mother and most of us claim to love her, our actions speak louder
than our words. According to EarthDay.org, if we do not change
our behaviour, what we have to look forward to is:

> more droughts and heatwaves, which can have
> devastating effects on the poorest countries and
> communities. Hurricanes will intensify and occur more
> frequently. Sea levels could rise up to four feet by 2100 –
> and that's a conservative estimate among experts.[6]

Zen master and global spiritual leader, poet and peace activist Thích
Nhất Hạnh clearly takes both climate change and humanity's role
in it seriously. He says, 'Only love can save us from climate change.'[7]
He poses the pertinent question that if people cannot save them-
selves from their own suffering, then why would they care about
Mother Earth?

If we truly want to save the planet, and most of us do, we must first save ourselves through love.

Only when we care properly for ourselves can we extend this care and love to the universe. When we are calmer, more centred and healthy in body and mind, we are much more likely to look after our environment and make consciously positive choices such as recycling, reusing, conserving energy and resources, becoming vegan, travelling less, etc.

Self-interest, greed, ignorance, corruption, vested interests and economic and political systems that are not aligned with a global green and human agenda lead to wholesale destruction of the environment, abuses of human rights and economic inequality as the de facto state of being. If 'thinking globally, acting locally' is to be implemented, then change starts within the individual. Becoming whole and at one within ourselves allows us to extend this to the rest of humanity and to the natural world. The inter-connectedness of all humanity becomes patently clear. In short, your rubbish is my rubbish and vice versa.

A positive example of a change in the collective mindset is when, in the 1950s and 1960s in America, there was a dramatic decrease in racist attitudes. In 1942, only 35 per cent of white Americans would accept the idea of sharing public transport with the Black community, but by 1963 this figure had increased to 78 per cent.[8]

Sadly, we see that fear is once again a driving force in American politics. The fact that the #BlackLivesMatter hashtag even exists today says it all. Malcolm Gladwell, in his recent book *Talking to Strangers*, tells the tragic story of Sandra Bland, a 28-year-old Black American woman who hung herself in a prison cell after being arrested by a white policeman after a routine traffic stop quickly escalated due to the assumptions that he made because she was a stranger from out of state and Black.

Gladwell's central message in the book is that we rush in far too quickly when we encounter a stranger. He says of the Sandra Bland case, 'If we were more thoughtful as a society – if we were willing to engage in some soul-searching about how we approach and make sense of strangers – she would not have ended up dead in a Texas jail cell.'

In order to ensure that all your encounters with people, whether they are strangers or not, come from a place of tolerance, acceptance and love, you need to understand who and what is determining your life and no longer remain a stranger to yourself.

× × ×

Whose Life Are You Living?

IMAGINE THAT I am sitting opposite you. I look you straight in the eye and ask you to take a moment to answer the following questions as honestly as you can without reflecting on them but simply answering 'yes' or 'no'.

1 Do you have the courage to live a life true to yourself, not the life others expect of you? *Yes – leaving Barclays & CFC, staying single.*

2 Do you wish you did not work so hard? *No. I wish I didn't try as hard.*

3 Do you have the courage to openly express your feelings? *Yes*

4 Do you keep in touch with your friends? *yes*

✱ 5 Do you wish you could let yourself be happier? *yes*

Bronnie Ware, a hospice nurse, regularly saw patients die. Therefore, by the nature of her job, she experienced how people face the final days of their lives. Moved by her experiences, Ware wrote the best-selling, now classic, book, *The Top Five Regrets of The Dying*. The catchy title intrigues everyone because we all want to know what the regrets are so that we can face our own death without having made the same mistakes.

The top five regrets are affirmative statements to the five questions above that you have just answered. For Bronnie's patients, how-ever, these were just sad and final facts that began with 'I wish' and ended in a full stop. The dying are highly aware of the value of each precious moment.

How did you answer the first question and would this change in light of Bronnie Ware's research, which identified it as the top regret in her study of the terminally ill? Do you sacrifice what you want to keep other people happy? Are you living your life defined by a conditioned code that you are afraid to break? Bronnie Ware's research on regrets illustrates that 'it all comes down to love and relationships in the end'.[9] In order for you to be true to yourself, to work less, to keep in touch with friends and to allow yourself to be happier, you must learn the art of self-love. From that, all else flows. The most powerful and relaxing method I know to etch this pathway of self-love into your malleable subconscious is through hypnotherapy.

Hypnotherapy and the Habit of Self-Love

'You use hypnosis not as a cure but as a favourable condition in which to learn.'

MILTON ERICKSON

THE TERM 'HYPNOSIS' is loaded with misconceptions, yet it is an everyday occurrence. Neither macabre nor manipulative, when applied therapeutically as a tool it is in fact magical. Let me clarify. Do you know that feeling you have when you are lost in an activity such as watching a film, immersed in a good book, lost in music or in awe of a beautiful scene in nature? You become incredibly present. Everything but the activity fades into the background and you have a single focus. Your mind and body connect, your thoughts cease, you are not aware of time passing; you are effectively in a trance. Hypnosis is the same thing. Your brain operates from both the alpha brain wave (relaxed yet alert) to the delta brain wave (deep dreamless sleep) and both states are optimum for positive change. You have quietened the conscious mind to reach beyond thought, opening the subconscious to reprogramme the brain for health and happiness.

Milton Erickson, known as the 'father of hypnotherapy', highlights in the quote above that the hypnotic state creates a favourable condition in which to learn and change. You now have the space and peace that are necessary for change. Erickson specialises in non-direct suggestions. For example, 'close your eyes and relax' is a command, whereas 'if you close your eyes, you may experience a pleasant and deep sense of comfort as you begin to relax' is an indirect suggestion that is more likely to be accepted. The conscious mind is less likely to analyse an indirect suggestion than a direct one. All decisions are ultimately up to you and as a result, all change comes from your desire to change.

Hypnotherapy is a delightful daydream that becomes your reality.

A classic research study, 'Hypnotherapy: A Reappraisal' by Alfred A. Barrios and the American Psychological Association, concluded that the reason hypnosis is so effective in facilitating therapy is that 'the incongruent perceptions, beliefs, and attitudes are kept from interfering with the suggestion (and thus with the conditioning).' The study also demonstrated that there are remarkable results for recovery rates for clients when comparing hypnotherapy to other modalities:

× **Psychoanalysis:** 38 per cent recovery after 600 sessions
× **Behaviour therapy:** 72 per cent recovery after 22 sessions
× **Hypnotherapy:** 93 per cent recovery after six sessions

Theory is one thing, experience quite another. You can read and research any topic endlessly, but it is unlikely to really resonate with you until you have truly felt it yourself. Childbirth is a concrete example of this. While many women (myself included before my son was born) spend hours poring over books on childbirth and take prenatal classes, it is not until they have actually given birth that they know what it feels like. However, your subconscious mind does not know the difference between imagination and reality, so your body will respond in the same way whether the event is 'real' or imagined. Virtual reality (VR) games illustrate this well. A good friend of mine is so terrified of heights that when she was asked to jump off a high plank in a VR game, she went rigid with fear (while sitting safely on her sofa), her throat constricted, her breathing became shallow and her palms got sweaty.

> **Hypnotherapy uses the power of the imagination in a purely positive and holistic manner.**

With hypnotherapy, no VR headset is necessary, as your mind is powerful enough on its own to create the chemicals you need for peace and happiness. For example, hypnobirthing, where women train their brain before childbirth to deliver their babies calmly and consciously, has proved so successful that in 2016 the NHS trained more of their midwives to practise it. Janet Cairns, Head of Midwifery at Hull University, said, 'We know hypnobirthing has many benefits and can reduce the need for surgical intervention during labour.'[10]

Many of my clients who suffer from anxiety spend hours imagining the worst-case scenarios happening to them. They visualise their children in car accidents, their partner leaving them or their boss firing them, torturing themselves with thoughts that are not true. On a biological level, their bodies respond to each thought as a genuine threat to their safety and that of their loved ones and the stress hormone cortisol rushes through their system. While cortisol has a necessary short-term function related to survival and enabling 'flight or fight' responses, having it coursing round your nervous system on an ongoing basis is damaging to both physical and mental health. Hypnotherapy reduces the production of cortisol and calms the mind down, which has immense positive physical effects.

What makes hypnotherapy truly transformational is that it bypasses the self-critical mind and ego through relaxation, allowing the subconscious to listen to and implement your conscious desires.[11] This can be particularly helpful not just in the realm of our emotional world, but also on a practical level.

× × ×

Hypnotherapy for Healthy Habits

HAVE YOU TRIED but failed to create healthier habits for yourself in the past? Perhaps at New Year you vowed to become healthier, slimmer and happier, only to revert to your old ways by February? If so, you are not alone. The failure rate for New Year's resolutions is estimated to be around 80 per cent,[12] so please do not be hard on yourself. This negative loop of starting and not maintaining positive self-care habits is not your fault.

Relying on willpower is the main reason for failure. Expecting Part A (your conscious mind) to do all the heavy lifting and ignoring Part B (your subconscious mind), which is where your habits, beliefs and emotions actually live, is unlikely to work. Imagine having an issue with a friend but constantly talking about it to another person and hoping that it will somehow be resolved. You need to communicate with the person directly to understand their position. In this case, you need to access your subconscious, and hypnotherapy is how you do that.

Instead of putting pressure on yourself to make a change, use compassion and patience. For example, let's say you want to be more confident, but the harder you try, the more nervous you become. Taking the time to deal with the fears and misconceptions that

Part B holds will gradually bring your subconscious mind on board. The aim is not to have a battle between the parts of yourself, which only further divides the self. Instead, as you become more unified, so, too, does your behaviour. You begin to act according to your conscious desires (in this case, with more confidence), with no battle and greater ease.

> *The Self-Love Habit aims to ensure that your conscious mind (A), which is doing the reading right now, and your subconscious mind (B), which listens to the audios, are both being gently guided in the same direction.*

 ## BE A FRIEND TO YOURSELF

Care for yourself as you would a friend, a child, a parent, a pet – someone you love deeply.

Imagine that you are in charge of looking after a vulnerable person, a child or an animal. You would ensure they get good food, exercise and loving attention, wouldn't you? Now imagine that B (your subconscious mind) is that vulnerable person and you know that you would treat it in the same way, with care and respect. In effect, you become a good parent, finding a way that works even when your subconscious is demanding, difficult, unreasonable, afraid or oversensitive. Your firm but gentle approach will eventually work and your subconscious will align with your conscious mind. You are no longer divided. We will fully explore this in Chapter 3: The United Self.

 ## THE DAILY PROMISE
TECHNIQUE

The daily promise technique, 'I promise to accept all the parts of MYSELF today to the best of my ability', as highlighted in the introduction, will really help you when you feel an internal battle kicking off. I use this all the time and it can shift a potential 'bad day' into an uncomfortable moment that passes almost as quickly as it came.

× × ×

Let Go of Time and Embrace
Units of Energy Instead

MANY CLIENTS SAY they do not have time to tend to their needs, especially if they have a full-time job and/or a family to care for. This is understandable, but bear with me as I explain how the more you care for yourself, the more energy you have.

Imagine that the 24-hour clock measures not seconds, minutes and hours, but units of energy – *your* energy – and you only have a certain amount of it each day. You become less clock-obsessed and more focused on what matters, in the first instance by preserving and using your energy wisely. Everything else comes after that. For example, imagine that you rush back from the supermarket with a mountain of shopping to unload, but you are dying to pee and also thirsty; in short, your body is crying out to be cared for. Do you think to yourself, 'I'll go to the loo after I have unloaded all of this' but then find you go straight into making lunch for the family and eventually realise an hour later that you still need to pee and are parched? If this sounds familiar, then you need to reconsider your priorities.

Tending to your needs first, especially the most basic ones, is not a luxury. It is essential. I have learned that looking after my energy is the only way I can bring positive energy to others. I need to have the mental resilience to behold the pain of my clients and to know that both they and I will be stronger and not weaker because of it. It also helps me to have fun, to laugh and to spend time with family and friends.

Nobody is going to give you more time – you must claim it by looking after yourself properly.

The one thing we all have in common is that we have 24 hours a day and a certain amount of energy. It is true that some of us have more energy than others, which depends on your age, health and circumstances. Knowing how much energy you have available and doing your best to maintain it without comparing yourself to others is crucial. If you are tired at 10 p.m., then acknowledge and accept that. Do not compare yourself to your best friend, who can dance until 2 a.m.!

✕ ✕ ✕

Design Your Day

IN HER BOOK *Super Attractor*, Gabrielle Bernstein outlines a simple method she calls 'Design Your Day'. Basically, you ask yourself these four questions first thing in the morning:

1 How do you want to feel today?

2 Who do you want to be today?

3 What do you want to receive today?

4 What do you want to give today?

I find this exercise really helpful and suggest that you try it by using a journal to record your answers. Try to be specific, as it can help to shape your day, especially if you are working towards a goal. You are effectively co-creating with the universe by consciously choosing how you wish to feel and be and what you wish to receive and give. However, I often find myself simply answering with one word: love. I want to feel loved, I want to be loved, I want to receive love and I want to give love. Everything else will manifest from there.

Another simple question I ask myself each morning is, 'How can I make the most of this beautiful day?' One way I know I can make the most of my day, and ultimately my chance at a long and healthy life, is to care for and love my body. So I get specific – I write down 'do my yoga' or 'go for a run'. According to one study at the Dominican University of California, you are 42 per cent more likely to achieve your goals if you write them down.[13]

✕ ✕ ✕

How to Love Your Body

'I first came to Fiona for emotional eating. I always hated my body and was desperate. We never really spoke about food or what I weighed. At first I was frustrated, as we didn't seem to be focusing on the problem. One year later, I looked into a shop window and saw this beautiful, slim person looking back at me. I honestly did not recognise this healthier, happier me!'

JANE, 37, ACCOUNTANT, CLIENT

WHAT KIND OF RELATIONSHIP do you have with your body? Do you love it? Do you hate it? Many of us are so out of alignment with our bodies that we struggle to accept them as 'good enough', never mind love them. If you have a negative relationship with your body, then learning the art of self-love is particularly pertinent.

While the term body dysmorphia disorder (BDD) may sound dramatic, it is simply suffering from obsessive thoughts about a body flaw, imagined or otherwise. According to the Anxiety and Depression Association of America, BDD affects 1.7–2.4 per cent of the population,[14] which is as many as one in 50 people. Negative thoughts and feelings about body shape, size and so on are highly prevalent – just listen to a group of women chatting and you will hear many self-deprecating comments about their bodies. Men also have negative thoughts and feelings about their body, but they tend to be less publicly self-critical.

Such feelings generally start in the pre-teen or teenage years (as young as 11) and affect both boys and girls equally. Unkind comments made by other kids can have a lasting effect. Repetitive negative thoughts about our bodies provide the perfect ammunition to use against ourselves and block self-love. If you feel your body is too fat, too thin, the wrong shape or size, not toned enough or not attractive enough, then the only way you are going to move forward is by accepting yourself just as you are right now.

Apply the daily promise to the different parts of your body that you deem not good enough. Start to see the power of your body and how hard it works for you each day. Your body will start to flourish with the love you show it and will sustain positive habits such as eating well and exercising daily.

Mind and body exercises such as yoga and tai chi are incredibly powerful for releasing blocked emotions and developing a closer relationship with your body. As much as we try to cognitively bury the past, the body holds on to the memory. Trauma is a residue of past experiences that have not been released. If you become overwhelmed by physical sensations such as finding it hard to breathe or sweating, it would be incredibly beneficial for you to start a yoga practice. I have been doing it for years and I know deep down that it is what helps to keep me both physically and mentally fit.

> **When you change your awareness,**
> **you change your biology.**

Your body is a powerful healer and it knows instinctively what is best for all the parts of yourself. Your mind is your body and your body is your mind. They are not merely connected – they are one and the same. If one suffers, so does the other. If I am stressed, my shoulders will tense and my digestion will be sluggish. If I have menstruation cramps, I will feel more irritable.

Ask your body these two questions every day:

1 Are you holding on to any unnecessary tension?

2 What do you need right now to feel better?

The first question immediately helps to dissolve tension. Awareness alone is enough to release much of the unnecessary tension, as you will feel your shoulders drop, your jaw soften and your breath deepen.

The second question is like the one you would ask a child who is tired after a busy school day. Is it best that he/she does their homework straight away or do they need some downtime? Your self-care routine needs to change according to the circumstances. Knowing how to pause and tenderly ask yourself what you need right now to feel better is one of the most self-loving questions. Remember to close your eyes and take some deep belly breaths before you ask either question, then simply listen for the answer – the wisdom resides in your body. (Belly breaths are deep, full, slow breaths in through the nose and out through the nose. Aim for the breath to expand your belly with the inhale and contract with the exhale. Your shoulders should remain still. Watch a small child breathe and you will notice that their belly moves, not their shoulders.)

Let's now look more closely at the positive influence that love plays on a biological and scientific level.

× × ×

The Science of Self-Love

LOVE UNDER THE MICROSCOPE is far from an intangible feeling, but rather is a complex of neurobiological processes that can be studied scientifically. Human beings move between physiological states that are determined by a primitive interplay of hormones and the autonomic nervous system (ANS). In fact, we are constantly moving between approach and avoidance, between love and fear.

Feeling safe is the foundation for feeling love physically.

Oxytocin is a hypothalamic nonapeptide hormone, perhaps more commonly known as the 'love hormone' or the 'cuddle hormone', and it plays an essential role in our ability to feel safe. The primary function of oxytocin is therefore to promote the survival of the species.

Oxytocin is also a stress-buffering hormone that is made primarily in the hypothalamus area of the brain and is released into the bloodstream at the posterior pituitary. It is also released into our nervous system and has facilitated our transition from reptile to mammal. Dr Sue Carter, a biologist and a pioneer in the study of love, writes, 'We are here today because of oxytocin.'[15]

Unlike many other species, a human infant is entirely dependent on the care of its parents and in particular its mother; the baby must form an attachment to its mother, otherwise it will not survive. Oxytocin has a key role to play here, as it is predominantly released during childbirth, breastfeeding and sexual activity. This insight might help to explain that if you argue or lose contact with your mother, it can shake you to the core and undermine your feeling of safety. It also helps me to understand why I was so full of fear in Paris, living on my own for the first time, away from my mother.

Oxytocin is so positively potent that it will heal a physical wound if applied directly. The same is also true of an emotional wound.

There is no more powerful healer than human touch.

According to Dr Carter, the most reliable way to boost oxytocin is through physical exercise. Unlike many other hormones, oxytocin is actually made in the brain and facilitates the flow of oxygen to it. Fresh air and daily exercise are therefore not luxuries but necessities for your physical and emotional survival and wellbeing. Low oxytocin levels generally predict difficulties with being adaptable in life, and adaptability is a key part of emotional resilience.

✕ ✕ ✕

Polyvagal Theory

'If you want to make the world a better place, help people to feel safe.'

DR STEPHEN PORGES

IN 2019, I had the privilege of studying with Dr Stephen Porges, the world-renowned American scientist and professor of psychiatry at the University of North Carolina at Chapel Hill who developed polyvagal theory. This theory examines the relationship between the ANS and social behaviour and has revolutionised our understanding of the vagus nerve, which is the longest of the cranial nerves in the human body, starting at the base of the brain and running into our digestive system. It controls the parasympathetic nervous system (also known as the rest and digest system) and acts as a lever of calmness when you know how to activate it, primarily, although not uniquely, through deep diaphragmatic breathing. This is when inhalation is deep and fast while exhalation is long, slow and measured. Feeling safe is dependent on a relaxed autonomic state in which you are mobile yet without fear.

Being alert but relaxed is the optimum state to live and love from.

Neuroreceptors in your brain are constantly evaluating your environment for cues about safety or danger, which come predominantly from how you feel that other people are relating to you. Human beings need others to co-regulate on a biological level and the way we do this is through the facial muscles around our eyes. The lines and wrinkles that many of us want to get rid of when we smile or frown are in fact one of our most vital communication tools. The next time you are at a conference or event and the speaker appears to be nervous or on edge, give them a big smile and watch their confidence grow. The muscles in this area are called the orbicularis oculi. I am not sure if I was more impressed with Dr Porges's ability to pronounce this or his ground-breaking research!

Polyvagal theory allowed us, for the first time, to understand the function of the vagus nerve, which has two branches: one that leads to the mammalian brain (prefrontal cortex) and one that runs to the reptilian brain (the oldest part of the brain). When the reptilian branch is activated it can cause relaxation to the extent that the subject becomes totally limp, just as a reptile would at times 'play dead' in the wild in order to survive.

Dr Porges's discovery that the vagus nerve has two branches helps us to understand why someone confronted by a sudden danger, such as assault or rape, sometimes will not fight back but will simply freeze with fear. This understanding is monumental in the healing process, as they may have spent years questioning why they did not fight back and may feel guilty or useless because of it. Yet this was not their fault or possibly even their choice, but rather the oldest part of their brain being triggered to 'play dead' to protect them.

Contrary to what we may believe, feeling safe is not simply the removal of threat. On the ANS level, we need to feel the cues of safety in our environment. When we are triggered into fear, our bodies can react in ways we do not understand. Dr Porges gave a personal example of this in a story of how he experienced his own physical reaction to trauma. A few years ago he went for an MRI scan (the scanner is a big tube-like structure and can be claustrophobic) and felt very calm (no threat) and self-assured as he entered the machine. However, within a few moments he experienced blind panic and demanded to get out of the scanner immediately, as his environment had not provided him with the cues to make his body feel safe.

Our bodies have their own histories, regardless of what the mind perceives. Many people experience this when, for example, they are on a plane and tell themselves to feel calm while their body has already started to panic. The more closely you are connected to and aware of your body and the hidden emotions that live within each muscle, the more you can help yourself to manage traumatic reactions to current or past stimuli. For example, many people suffer panic attacks in busy, noisy public spaces with no conscious understanding of why they happened. In such cases, the ANS has become overwhelmed, causing an involuntary physical reaction in the body. The answer is not to avoid these places, but to empower yourself with the knowledge that you can breathe deeply *before* you begin to panic rather than becoming frightened by it when it is too late to control it.

Deep, fast inhalation and long, slow exhalation will activate your vagus nerve and parasympathetic nervous system to feel calm and safe. The knowledge that on a scientific level you are in charge of how calm you feel, no matter what situation you find yourself in, is worth remembering.

You create your state. You choose your response. You generate love.

The Brain Chemistry of Self-Love

DAVID HAMILTON, organic chemist and author of the bestseller *I Heart Me: The Science of Self-Love*, spent four years in the pharmaceutical industry developing drugs to treat cardiovascular disease and cancer. He became disillusioned when he saw only minute differences in the effectiveness of the drugs yet at the same time saw the power of the placebo effect. He has since made it his life's work to help people use the power of their minds to be happy and healthy. Hamilton identifies three stages in self-love, which move from:

1 'I am not enough' – the most common negative thought we can have; to

2 'I have had enough' – the realisation that something needs to change; to

3 'I am enough' – when someone has developed self-love and has a healthy level of self-esteem.

Which stage are you at? Wherever you are now, it is my intention that you will reach a place of self-belief where you know that you are more than enough.

Hamilton believes the phrases 'self-love' and 'inner self-esteem' are interchangeable. Internal self-esteem comes from you and does not depend on the opinion of others or on your achievements. By contrast, external self-esteem relies on factors outside yourself, for example your career or status in the community, which you believe you need to feel valued.

In order for you to create the chemistry of self-love, we need to examine what Hamilton refers to as the four components of emotion (Figure 1).

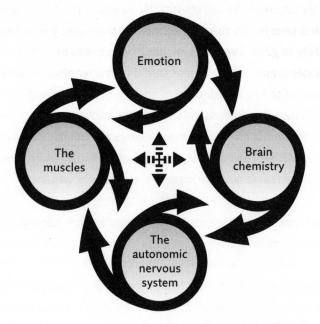

Figure 1 (*Source:* drdavidhamilton.com)

1 The emotion itself is the first component, whether it is happiness or sadness, fear or love.

2 Each emotion has a brain chemistry pattern that it creates and it can shift quickly between emotional states, which can be exhausting. Consider a day where you feel many different emotional states, both high and low – the laboratory in your mind has been working hard. You have more energy when your emotional state is consistently calm.

3 The third component is the ANS, which, as already stated, is the physical response you have to an emotion. For example, if you feel shame or embarrassment you might blush or if you are nervous you might sweat. If you respond to these ANS responses (the blushing or sweating) with resistance, it will only intensify the uncomfortable sensations – if you worry what people will think when you are blushing, you are more likely to go an even deeper shade of red. However, if you blush or sweat and simply do not care if other people notice (which, most of the time, they don't), the uncomfortable response will ease naturally. So if you find yourself sweating or blushing, accept the thoughts and emotions, accompanied by some deep breaths, and this will reactivate your parasympathetic system, which will help you to feel calmer and safer.

4 The fourth component in Hamilton's model is the role your muscles play in emotions, which for the most part is involuntary. For example, when someone smiles at you, you will more than likely smile back. If you feel stress, your muscles will tense in your upper back and shoulders. Becoming aware of how stiff or relaxed your body feels can be a useful indicator of your emotional state.

If you want to feel happy, smile, and the feel-good hormone, serotonin, is released. If you want to feel safe and loved, go for a run, have sex or embrace a loved one, as they all help you to generate that all-important oxytocin. In my first, bestselling, book, *The Positive Habit*, I demonstrate how to self-generate positive emotions in more detail and teach you how to cultivate six super-positive emotions; love, calmness, confidence, gratitude, hope and happiness.

While learning to create and soak in positive emotions is a crucial skill, so, too, is processing negative and uncomfortable ones as they arise. As a child you literally do not have the brain capacity to do this as the prefrontal cortex, the more rational and newer part of the brain, does not fully develop until we are 25 or so. Younger people process information through the amygdala, the primitive alarm bell of the mind.[16] This is why we need to be especially compassionate and patient with younger people. If you are 25 or younger, please cut yourself some slack and take solace in the fact that the ability to link actions to consequences naturally increases as we mature.

> **Processing emotion at the time we feel it clears it from the body and opens us up to embodying love and unblocking pain.**

The following technique is a practical way to help you to process emotion at the time you feel it and serves as an act of love for yourself and your relationships.

× × ×

Emotional Tidy-as-You-Go Method

THE FRENCH PROVERB *'mieux vaut prévenir que guérir'* translates as 'prevention is better than cure', and this applies to both your physical and your mental health.

Think of your home and how much easier it is when you tidy things up as you go, be it unloading the dishwasher, putting rubbish in the bin or putting shoes and clothes away. It might never be perfect, but that is not the aim. Tidying little and often really does help to keep the space functioning, and, more important, you will not feel overwhelmed by mess.

Your mind is in effect your inner home.

Keep your mind tidy and anything is possible.

By being super alert, relaxed and aware of your mind, you can deal with negative thoughts and tensions within yourself and your family, friends and colleagues as they arise and *before* they become toxic emotions, beliefs and/or disputes. So much of emotional intelligence is actually emotional awareness. By pre-empting patterns of conditioned responses, you transform conflict into compassion.

When a negative thought or emotion emerges, follow these three steps:

1 Observe the thought without identifying with it. Imagine that the thought is a wave in the sea. You are looking at the sea but not actually swimming in it. In other words, *you are not the thought* but rather the Beholder who simply observes it.

2 Ask yourself, 'Is this true or simply a rumour in my mind?'

3 Breathe into the thought, accept it and release it by showing it kindness. *You do not have to believe the thought.* I find it useful to literally smile at the thought. It passes much more quickly.

TIDYING YOUR RELATIONSHIPS

Apply this method to avoid a build-up of tension with other people, especially those closest to you. Imagine that someone makes a comment or is irritable with you.

1 Witness their irritability in the same way that you can see it in yourself. There is no need to identify with it or take it personally, even when it is directed towards you. The Beholder is again simply witnessing.

2 Ask the person what you can do to help them. What do they need from you right now to feel better? Have you misunderstood one another? If they are being unfair, calmly state how you feel. Always put the emphasis on your feelings, not theirs. For example, say 'I feel that was unreasonable' as opposed to 'You are being unreasonable.'

3 Breathe into the tension, accept that it happens in all relationships and show both yourself and the other person kindness. Smile. It will pass.

> **Use the emotional tidy-as-you-go method to cleanse your mind, heart, soul and your relationships each day.**

Do not wait for unresolved or petty grievances to build up between you and your friends or loved ones. Have you ever claimed that you have let something go, for example the time your partner forgot to call to say they would be late for your birthday dinner, only to bring it up later in an argument that has nothing to do with the lateness incident? I know I have. Most of us recognise the words 'and another thing ...' that get spat out in an argument. It is always with the best of intentions that we try to let things go, but often we are only pushing them under an emotional rug. Eventually you can't even walk on the rug and all the dirt comes out. Please note that this does not mean that you choose to fight every battle – if you can genuinely let something go, then do.

When you non-confrontationally, consciously clear the air at the time a misunderstanding or tension arises, you are being truthful, open and honest. Honesty breeds trust and trust makes us feel safe, and when we feel safe, we are open to love.

× × ×

Falling in Love

THE OFT-REPEATED CLICHÉ about lovers spending hours gazing into each other's eyes is probably true. Zick Rubin, American social psychologist, lawyer and author who is credited with completing the first empirical measurement of love, found that in general, we maintain eye contact 30–60 per cent of the time with most people in our lives. However, when we are with the person we love, this increases to 75 per cent of the time.[17] Steady and frequent eye contact cements love, which is why I ask you to do the mirror work. It truly is a powerful part of establishing the Self-Love Habit.

The initial stages of romantic love can be both exciting and intense as you get to know your partner. A melting pot of similarities and differences emerges, yet often both parties temper their preferences to suit the other in an earnest desire to ensure the relationship is a success. But if you are not careful, the desire to please may eventually turn into resentment. Compromise, although essential, is often the most challenging part of cohabitation and one party can often make so many compromises that they end up losing themselves entirely.

A genuine fear that many people have is being seen as selfish. The truth, however, is that unless you remain true to yourself, you are not being selfish enough.

Plato wrote, 'The god of love lives in a state of need,' and this is chemically true. When you first fall in love, there is literally a chemical explosion in your brain that moves into your body and can cause you to feel weak, excited, ecstatic and petrified all at the same time! According to Dr Helen Fisher, biological anthropologist and research professor at Rutgers University, there are three stages to romantic love – lust, attraction and attachment – and each stage has its own chemical properties (Figure 2).[18]

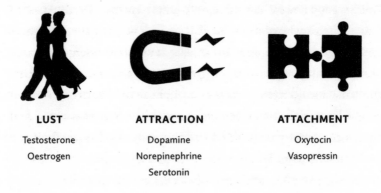

LUST	ATTRACTION	ATTACHMENT
Testosterone	Dopamine	Oxytocin
Oestrogen	Norepinephrine	Vasopressin
	Serotonin	

Figure 2 (*Source:* Tito Adhikary, SITNBoston)

The first and second stages of lust and attraction are highly addictive states due to the release of dopamine (the reward chemical) and serotonin (the happy chemical found in most antidepressants). This cocktail of chemicals and hormones may help to explain why many relationships end after two to three years. As the novelty factor wears off, the couple feel more relaxed in each other's company, irritations can arise and sexual passion can fade.

Dr Fisher also discovered that the brain area most linked with addiction, the nucleus accumbens, becomes activated in the brains of people who are in the early stages of romantic love. This activation is incredibly primitive and is associated with craving, which is why when lovers are apart, it can cause physical withdrawal symptoms. If you have a friend who has recently fallen in love and now you rarely see them, go easy on them.

Long-term relationships dwell in the third stage of love, which is defined by attachment. The reward-seeking hormones (dopamine) found in the second stage have decreased and the bonding ones, such as oxytocin and vasopressin, are more active.

There is good news when it comes to long-term love. Dr Fisher asked older couples who claimed to still be in love with their partners and who had been together for at least 21 years to undergo the same brain scan as that given to younger couples. Fisher discovered that the same brain activity was present in both the younger 'loved-up' couples and in the older 'companionative' couples. However – and this is the great part – the older couples had sustained all the positive aspects of being in love but had left behind the anxiety-activated, yearning, addictive ones that can cause problems.[19]

When you shift from the early stages of lust, desire, craving and addiction into the secure attachment that comes with a long-term functioning relationship, you move into a sustainable situation, a place where two people can love each other while at the same time maintaining their own sense of self.

When you reach this stage, there is room to breathe and be loved and accepted for who you are.

In a dysfunctional relationship, one of the parties may be constantly disappointed by their partner and thus seek to control and change them into their desired version. When we cannot tolerate ourselves, we will often look to another to remove or distract us from our own inner discontent. The parts of your partner, or indeed any person, that you find difficult to tolerate are often reflections of those parts of yourself that you actively dislike or have unconsciously ignored. When a relationship breaks up, people often remark that they grew apart. For *any* relationship to endure, the parties must grow together and this means that we need to make the time to let the partner, parent, child or friend develop and then accept them as they are, even if they make decisions we might not agree with as they transition through life. You are on the road to becoming romantically enlightened.

✗ ✗ ✗

Enlightened Romance

THE EUROPEAN AGE OF ENLIGHTENMENT, or Age of Reason, of the late seventeenth and eighteenth centuries was a time of growing belief in people's ability to use reason and logic to rise above the restrictive and authoritative doctrines of Church and State. Coupled with this was the development of a humanitarian desire to eradicate injustice and suffering.

Philosophers such as Voltaire, Hume and Rousseau believed that knowledge could only come from experience and reason based on verifiable scientific evidence rather than religious mysticism. They shared the aspiration that through education, people of all ages and nationalities would eventually unite behind the same shared scientific truths; that a mutual moral code would open the door to an enlightened and ordered society based on equity and logic.

However enlightened the philosophical giants of this period may have been, they may have missed the greatest human aspiration there is: to love and be loved.

Human beings yearn for more than reason, science and logic to motivate them to rise in the morning.

The Romantic movement of the late eighteenth century to the mid-nineteenth century was a revolt against the scientific rationalism of the Enlightenment. Emphasis was instead put on the importance of emotional sensitivity and individual subjectivity. For the Romantics, imagination, rather than reason, was the most important creative faculty, emotions were emphasised over rationalism and the inner plight of the individual was prioritised over the need for collective change.

The Romantic movement also focused on the divine spirit in nature. Poets such as William Wordsworth, William Blake and Percy Bysshe Shelley transformed the mundane into the sublime, while J. M. W. Turner painted perfect visions of the natural world. As Wordsworth wrote, 'Nature never did betray the heart that loved her.'

Romantic poetry, philosophy and literature have had the biggest influence on how we view romantic love today and this is echoed in film, literature and music. It is the most common theme in all art forms. One of the outcomes of this is the belief that there is a soulmate for you in this world and in order to be happy, you must find them so that you can strive to live in a state of blissful passion. No pressure!

We can learn much from the ideas of the Enlightenment and Romanticism about how to love ourselves and others.

Logic and imagination can live together in harmony, romance and independence support

each other, and loving yourself helps you to contribute at a societal level.

✕ ✕ ✕

Romantic Realism

ALAIN DE BOTTON, the contemporary British philosopher, refers to romantic love as 'romantic fatalism'. In *Essays in Love,* he writes, 'We are all too often forced to share a bed with someone who cannot fathom our soul.' He discusses how we hold on to conditioned beliefs that one day we will meet the partner of our dreams and then we will find 'a perfect creature to soothe our relentless yearnings'.

De Botton's theory on love owes much to Aristotle, the ancient Greek philosopher who placed more emphasis on reason and logic than romantic aspirations. While reason and logic are not sexy, they are attractive on a long-term basis. Accepting our partner as they are, not as we wish them to be, provides us with the emotional freedom to encourage and bring out the best in them. We relinquish the pressure on them to conform to an idealised version that we have created in our mind and we are also free from constant disappointment when they do not meet our 'unfair' expectations.

As you move through the stages of falling in love with yourself and of uniting the parts of yourself, you, too, will begin to let go of what you believe you 'should' be. In much the same way that you can save a relationship with a romantic partner, you can save the relationship with yourself. The daily promise technique, 'I promise to accept **all** the parts of MYSELF today to the best of my ability', is grounded in this philosophy.

The term 'romantic realism' appeals to me as I am a bit of a romantic at heart. If I hear a soppy song on the radio, especially one from the early stages of my relationship, I may shed a nostalgic tear. I choose to hold on to the positive memories of romantic love and at the same time allow my husband to be exactly as he is without the desire to shape or control him according to what I think he should be. But it was not always like this. I used to waste hours arguing with him, both in person and in my mind, that 'he should be more this or that'. Over the years, as I began to work on my relationship with myself, my marriage also became much happier and more loving. We have been together for 24 years and I still feel a rush of excitement when I hear his key in the door.

× × ×

Love Your Own Business

'Imaginer c'est choisir.'

('To imagine is to choose.')

JEAN GIONO

WHEN YOU LOVE YOURSELF fully and unconditionally, you will always have an inner sanctuary, a safe place you can retreat to when life becomes hectic. This space is private and nobody else needs to visit. The only way you can authentically create this internal space is through self-knowledge. You are the only person who knows intrinsically what you need to feel safe, calm and loved and the only person you can ever fully know *is* yourself. Without this inner safe haven, many people spend their time desperately trying to understand and control other people rather than looking inward.

In her book *Loving What Is*, Byron Katie, an American speaker and author who teaches a method of self-inquiry known as 'The Work', claims there are only three types of business:

1   Your own business

2   Other people's business

3   God's business

The first of these is the only one that should concern you. Katie writes, 'There would be no war if we all sat down and looked at ourselves', which is useful when I find myself getting caught up in business that is not mine. It is a clear reminder to step back.

Jean-Paul Sartre, the French existentialist writer, was one of those who practised self-scrutiny and appears to have stuck to his own business. Existentialism is a philosophy that espouses free will and the freedom of the individual. Sartre was one of only two people ever to refuse to accept the Nobel Prize for Literature. In a statement to the *Swedish Press* magazine on 22 October 1964, published in the French newspaper *Le Monde*, he claimed, 'It is not the same thing if I sign Jean-Paul Sartre or if I sign Jean-Paul Sartre, Nobel Prize winner. A writer must refuse to allow himself to be transformed into an institution, even if it takes place in the most honourable form.'[20]

And yet, so many of us do become transformed into institutions as we lose our individuality, whether it is through marriage, the company we work for or the college we attend. Our identity can become almost tribal as we over-identify with the group we are part of; this brings to mind 'ultra' football fans who will view the opposing team's fans as the enemy. Similarly, fundamentalism, whether expressed in religious or national terms, is dangerously exclusive when it becomes institutionalised. Institutions that support existential individualism provide a positive environment that incorporates belonging and freedom, for example a marriage where the couple support each other but allow the other their private space. As Khalil Gibran puts it in his book *The Prophet*, 'But let there be spaces in your togetherness.'

Humankind needs to belong to a group and at the same time remain independent of it.

The rather dramatic exercise below will help you to continue the lifelong journey of self-knowledge and to gain some powerful insights into what is truly important to you. As you will see, your relationship with your own mortality is deeply rooted in your ability to live fully in the present.

x x x

Exercise: 365 Days to Love!

This imagination exercise will help you to affirm what you wish for yourself now, not in the future, but rather in this moment, the only one you ever have.

Imagine that you have been told with 100 per cent certainty that you have 365 days left to live on this planet. You will get to live each day in the fullness of your health, but in 365 days you will die. One year, 12 months, 52 weeks, 365 days – that's it.

The purpose of the exercise is not to induce anxiety about your impending death, but to help you wake up to life. It will sharpen your mind immediately and clarify your true desires about how you wish to live. In this scenario, please imagine that you are at peace and have

accepted your fate – your only desire is to make the most of each
precious day.

> *Do not skip forward, promising yourself that you will get*
> *back to it later!*

Give yourself the necessary time to consider the questions below and
then answer them honestly with the understanding that you have 365
days left. Focus on the answers first; you will complete the affirmations
later. I started the first few to help you by example.

1 What do you most value in your life now?

    × **Fiona's example:** I value taking care of my mind and body.

    × **Daily affirmation:** I vow to take care of my mind and body.

2 How would you like to feel when you wake up each morning?

    × **Fiona's example:** Grateful, refreshed and joyful about the day
       ahead.

    × **Daily affirmation:** When I wake up, I feel grateful, refreshed and
       joyful about the day ahead.

3 How would you like to feel when you go to sleep?

    × **Answer:**

    × **Daily affirmation:**

4 What way do you want to greet your loved ones?

    × **Answer:**

    × **Daily affirmation:**

5 What tone of voice do you wish to use?

    × **Answer:**

    × **Daily affirmation:**

6 How do you want to feel when you look in the mirror?

 × **Answer:**

 × **Daily affirmation:**

7 Who are the people you most want to spend time with?

 × **Answer:**

 × **Daily affirmation:**

8 Do you want to spend time in nature?

 × **Answer:**

 × **Daily affirmation:**

9 Do you want to laugh more?

 × **Answer:**

 × **Daily affirmation:**

10 Do you want to try things you have never done before?

 × **Answer:**

 × **Daily affirmation:**

11 Do you want to stop 'sweating the small stuff'?

 × **Answer:**

 × **Daily affirmation:**

12 Do you need to worry about money?

 × **Answer:**

 × **Daily affirmation:**

13 Will you make more of an effort to see your friends?

 × **Answer:**

 × **Daily affirmation:**

14 What kind of energy do you choose to bring into a room?

    × **Answer:**

    × **Daily affirmation:**

15 Can you forgive yourself for past mistakes?

    × **Answer:**

    × **Daily affirmation:**

16 Can you accept other people as they are?

    × **Answer:**

    × **Daily affirmation:**

17 What do you wish to be remembered for?

    × **Answer:**

    × **Daily affirmation:**

Perspective is a wonderful thing, as is hindsight. Most people spend their lives seeking certainty, but the only real certainty we have is death. We just usually do not know when it will come.

According to the Central Statistics Office, the most recent figures for life expectancy at birth in Ireland are 78.4 years for men and 82.8 years for women.[21] For the sake of argument, let's imagine that you will live until the age of 75, which gives you 900 months to live. You sleep for 300 of these. I am 44, so based on the maths above, I have roughly 372 months left. If you feel like it, you could calculate how many months you have left.

Turn aspirations into affirmations.

In doing this exercise, you begin to truly live each day as if it were your last. Repeat the affirmations every day for the duration of the time you read this book, either last thing at night before you listen to your 'Love to Sleep' audio or in the morning after listening to the 'Love to Rise' audio.

Now that you have started your journey into self-love and self-knowledge, you are ready to progress to the next chapter, which looks at what causes inner conflict. In this exploration of the divided self, you will seek to understand the parts of yourself that may have unintentionally been sent into exile. Together we will bring your Shadow Self out of the darkness into the light and replace fear with curiosity as we move towards the ultimate unification of your heart and soul.

THREE KEY POINTS TO REMEMBER

1   The equation for love is:
    The Self (conscious presence) + Energy = Love

2   Hypnotherapy will change the neural pathways in your brain from fear into love.

3   The vagus nerve is your very own calmness lever. Simply breathe deeply any time you want to feel calmer and more loving.

× × ×

The Self-Love Habit Tools

This is a gentle reminder to incorporate the following daily mindfulness tools into your every day. They are designed to be easy habit-building tools to make love your priority.

AUDIO MEDITATION

Listen to the 'Love to Rise' and 'Love to Sleep' audios every day. Record your progress in the chart at the back of this book.

BE A FRIEND TO YOURSELF

Cultivate the voice of your inner critic to become your inner companion.

THE DAILY PROMISE TECHNIQUE

Practise the daily promise technique: 'I promise to accept all the parts of MYSELF today to the best of my ability.' Write it down, if you have not already, on a sticky note and put it on the mirror where you brush your teeth. Repeat this promise every day and again if and when a fearful or negative thought emerges.

THE TWO-MINUTE MIRROR

Spend at least two minutes a day looking into your own eyes. Look beyond the physical, without judgement. Maintain eye contact until a feeling of calmness or ease emerges. This is something you can do last thing at night or first thing in the morning or both should you so desire.

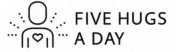

FIVE HUGS A DAY

Don't forget to get your full five-a-day quota!

THE DIVIDED SELF

'On commence toujours par le simple, puis vient le complexe, et par une illumination supérieure on revient souvent à la fin au simple. Tel est le cours de l'intelligence humaine.'

('One always begins with the simple, then comes the complex, and by superior enlightenment one often reverts in the end to the simple. Such is the course of human intelligence.')

VOLTAIRE

IN THIS CHAPTER we will cover the importance of the conflict between the two parts of yourself: the Beholder (the true, unconditioned self – Part A) and the Shadow Self (the conditioned self – Part B); the four blocks to self-love; and why understanding the purpose of the Shadow Self will help you to accept, love and, above all, learn from your 'darker' side. We will also examine the role of the ego and in particular the perils of an inflated one.

× × ×

Part of Me

HOW DECISIVE ARE YOU? Reflect for a moment on a time when you had to make an important decision in your life. Examples may include deciding which college to attend, which house to buy, whether or not to live abroad, whether to apply for a new job or aim for a promotion, whether or not to start your own business, whether to get married or stay single, whether or not to try to have a child or a second child, which school to send your child to, whether to endure invasive treatment if you got ill or let nature take its course, or whether to put a parent into a nursing home or to take care of them yourself.

As you ponder these life-changing, pivotal choices that most of us have encountered at some stage (and many of which are referred to in the introduction as part of the conventional calendar), you may recall that at the time, part of you felt one way and another part felt entirely differently. There may have been a divide in your mind, an uncertainty; two different voices with two conflicting opinions, one part of you desperate for a change and another full of doubt. In the end, one of these voices prevailed. Recognising the impact of these conflicting parts and whether the decisions were driven by fear or made from a place of love is central to taking full responsibility for running your life.

**In these monumental moments, the severed
self is apparent and magnified; indecision and
procrastination have nowhere to hide.**

Sadly, fear often reigns in the decisions we make, but living in internal conflict is brutal and unnecessary.

In this chapter, I will illustrate that the division of the self is not just present in making major life decisions, but is a consistent weight that is present in almost every thought we have and every action we take. We battle with ourselves over routine daily habits such as whether to go to the gym, have a second piece of toast, visit our mother after work or come home and watch a movie. Who are these two disparate parts, antagonising each other like tired siblings in the back of a car? A fatigued mind finds it hard to be a loving one.

**Imagine the peace of mind, ease in yourself and
renewed energy you would gain if these parts
were to stop quarrelling, then listen and unify.**

For much of my earlier life, I suffered such internal strife. I was proud of my public persona while I desperately hid my private self, assuming that if people saw 'that' part of me I would be rightly shunned. I felt, at heart, unlovable.

Like many, I thought I was alone, but after listening to thousands of clients, I saw a pattern emerge that this disparate feeling is more 'normal' than abnormal. In fact, I have yet to meet a client who does not feel this division on some level. Mostly it is deep, unintentionally destructive, relentless and exhausting – and, mercifully, avoidable. What is rather ironic is that I love my clients for all the parts that they try to hide from the world. I feel blessed that they allow me to see their vulnerable selves. When you show your vulnerable side, people relate to you in a profound way. Your vulnerability allows them to feel safe, to be at ease with themselves.

In this chapter, we will examine the four major blocks to self-love that cause us to feel divided. They are:

1 Childhood conditioning

2 Shame

3 Perfectionism

4 Distraction

In my work with clients, I regularly hear the following phrases: 'I feel like I am two different people', 'I have lost myself' and 'I don't know who I am any more.' This split identity creates anxiety and uncertainty, which become intensified when we are expected to perform, for example when giving a presentation at work or when meeting our new girlfriend's or boyfriend's parents for the first time. The fear that the 'wrong' part will manifest itself is debilitating and erodes our self-esteem. At its very worst, the split self can leave us questioning our own sanity, and because we fear that nobody will understand us if we try to explain how we feel, we say nothing.

It is important to highlight that the divided self is *not* a serious psychiatric health issue such as dissociative identity disorder (formerly referred to as multiple personality disorder), schizophrenia or borderline personality disorder. It is a common state of affairs that most of us experience on a sliding scale, in particular when we are required to make a difficult decision, change a habit and/ or are suffering from anxiety and stress.

As you continue to read *The Self-Love Habit*, listen to your 'internal voice' and identify if it is a monologue or a dialogue. Observe when it changes. If it is a dialogue, does it shift from mild debate to major conflict depending on the situation? If it is a monologue, does it relentlessly analyse your every move and criticise (the 'inner critic')?

Shakespeare used the technique of asides and soliloquies to expose the private inner thoughts and 'voice' of his characters to his audience. In doing so, the 'hidden' self is revealed and it is not always pretty. We hear Hamlet berate himself, 'Remorseless, treacherous, lecherous, kindless villain! Why, what an ass am I!'

The next time you make a mistake, observe the way you speak to yourself. Is it critical? It is important to be able to observe the divided self without judgement.

✗ ✗ ✗

Understanding the Divided Self

RECALL THE TWO parts of yourself:

A. The Beholder: The unconditioned conscious mind.

B. The Shadow Self: The conditioned subconscious mind.

These two selves can also be identified in the following way:

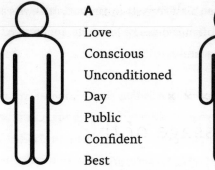

A	B
Love	Fear
Conscious	Subconscious
Unconditioned	Conditioned
Day	Night
Public	Private
Confident	Vulnerable
Best	Shadow

At first glance it may appear that A is positive and B is negative, but on closer investigation this is not the case, as both parts are necessary and learning how to accept, understand and then embrace them is a crucial skill. When a new client comes to see me, they are usually hopeful that I will be able to get rid of Part B, as if I am a surgeon removing an ingrown toenail or a cancerous cyst. It may also be why you are reading this book; the client, like you, no longer wants internal conflict or to feel anxious. I can help you, as I have helped myself and many others, to live in peace, but not in the way that you might imagine. I do not 'cut out' any part of my clients' selves, but I do help them to accept, understand and then embrace all the parts of themselves. I will help you to do the same.

The most important thing to remember when it comes to Part B, or indeed any part of you, is that *each part of you has the desire to protect you*. You are naturally programmed to survive, so even when it appears that you are sabotaging your own progress, please remember that the part that is holding you back is not intentionally trying to jeopardise your ability to live in peace. It is confused and believes that it is protecting you, comforting you and keeping you safe, for example if you wish to be more sociable but turn down an invite to a party because you feel anxious. I will expand on this below.

Understanding our primitive thirst for self-preservation allows a deeper inner connection, allowing you to be less judgemental and easier on yourself. The battle ends.

× × ×

The Message of the Shadow Self/Part B

'The shadow may carry the best of the life we have not lived. Go into the attic, the basement, the refuse bin. Find gold there. Find an animal who has not been fed or watered. It is you! This neglected, exiled animal hungry for attention is a part of yourself.'

MARION WOODMAN

Humanistic psychologists Carl Rogers and Abraham Maslow believed that human beings are, at heart, good. They understood that in order to heal emotional pain, we must try to understand negative behaviour and not judge it. Humanism is, in many respects, the parent of the positive psychology movement. Both focus on our ability to be our own agents of change and both share the desire to help us to 'self-actualise' in humanistic terms or to 'flourish' in positive psychology terms.

If you are plagued with negative thoughts, suffer from anxiety, have low self-esteem or obstruct healthy behaviours, if you are caught in obsessive-compulsive behaviour and/or if you are having conflict with your family or friends, there is one question you need to ask:

> **What is the message my Shadow Self wants me to hear?**

Whether it is binge eating or shouting at your loved ones, the unwanted behaviour makes total sense to your subconscious Shadow Self. For example, a person with social anxiety may also suffer from stomach pain. Every time they are about to go out, their stomach flares up, providing the more socially acceptable excuse not to attend the event: 'I'm not feeling well.' Similarly, someone who drinks too much on a Friday night to escape the thoughts of a job they hate is acting logically on a subconscious level, as the alcohol numbs the pain, if only temporarily.

Please look at your own behaviour or emotions that fit this pattern. How is your Shadow Self protecting you? Let go of recriminations and judgements and instead take a humanistic, loving approach to yourself by trying to understand the motivation behind the undesirable behaviour.

There are four common obstacles to self-love that keep inner conflict alive. Becoming aware of these blocks will help you to hear the murmurs of Part B (the subconscious) as they slowly emerge from the shadows into the full light of love.

The Four Major Blocks to Self-Love

1. CHILDHOOD CONDITIONING

'The precursor of the mirror is the mother's face.'

DONALD WOODS
WINNICOTT

AS PREVIOUSLY STATED, David Hamilton, author of *I Heart Me: The Science of Self-Love*, uses the terms 'self-esteem' and 'self-love' interchangeably. This is logical; after all, if you have a low opinion of yourself, it is likely that you are not loving towards yourself. So where does self-esteem come from? According to Professor Ulrich Orth of the University of Bern, who studied 9,000 people born between 1970 and 2001, the data illustrates that the more loving and warm the home environment in their childhood years (aged 0–6), the more likely it was that the subject enjoyed high levels of self-esteem in their adulthood.[22] By the same token, if you were valued as a child by your parents, you are more likely to value yourself as an adult. The foundations and neural pathways to self-love have been laid and it is therefore more likely that you will follow this route. However, the study also shows that the correlation between healthy self-esteem and a loving home environment as a child starts to wane after the age of 27. It would appear that life events/patterns after this age, such as the responsibility of becoming financially independent and forming romantic relationships, can shake our sense of self. If you grew up in a very protective environment, becoming an independent adult can be hard. Striking the balance between fostering independence and protecting children is a challenge for all parents.

If you are a parent, no doubt you try to do your best and your parents will probably have done the same. Our best, however, is always subject to context. For example, a parent who grew up in a war-torn country will likely be affected by trauma. If the suffering remains unspoken and unprocessed, it is highly likely to 'leak' into the next generation. This is known as intergenerational trauma. Boston-based Dutch psychiatrist and pioneering post-traumatic stress disorder (PTSD) researcher Bessel van der Kolk, the author of the *New York Times* number 1 bestselling book, *The Body Keeps the Score: Brain, Mind, and Body in the Healing of Trauma*, writes, 'One does not have to be a combat soldier, or visit a refugee camp in Syria or the Congo to encounter trauma. Trauma happens to us, our friends, our families, and our neighbours.' Research by the Centers for Disease Control and Prevention in the US[23] has shown that one in five Americans was sexually molested as a child, one in four was beaten by a parent to the point of a mark being left on their body and one in three couples engages in physical violence. A quarter grew up with alcoholic relatives and one out of eight witnessed their mother being beaten or hit.

Regardless of what has happened in our past, if we find the courage to speak about traumatic events, we will learn from them, we will become stronger and with time we will uncover the meaning in our suffering. You must refuse to allow your past to subconsciously dictate the trajectory of your life. As Mr Rogers, the children's TV presenter and icon of kindness, says in the movie based on his life, *It's a Beautiful Day in the Neighborhood*, 'Anything mentionable is manageable.'

The 'perfect' childhood is a myth. Some backgrounds are certainly more secure and loving than others, but none is perfect. It is not necessary for a child to suffer terrible adverse experiences to develop low self-esteem. Often it is simply the child's perception of and sensitivity to their caregivers that can cause self-doubt, for example feeling abandoned on the first day of play school.

Donald Winnicott (1896–1971), Britain's first ever child psychoanalyst, dedicated his life to helping parents raise happy children, with the belief that society would eventually become a safer place. He famously coined the phrase 'the good enough parent'.[24] Perfection and pressure are the antithesis of positive parenting. Winnicott believed that infants must be allowed to express their initial rage at the world and be met with unconditional acceptance. This gives children the knowledge that they can cry and still be loved.

Although society has moved away from the 'children should be seen and not heard' mentality, the dominant mentality now in parents is to train children to 'be good'. A quiet, shy child who sits in the corner will often be complimented by adults for 'being good.' But what is behind their silence? According to Winnicott, when a parent demands compliance too soon from an infant, a 'false self' is born. The public persona of the child displays the 'good' behaviour expected by parents, while the underlying 'true' self, in order to receive love, suppresses natural feelings of anger, sadness and the need for adventure. As you grow up, this can create a tension within yourself as your 'true' hidden self strives to express itself.

Tolerating defiance is an act of love for both children and adults.

Winnicott's solution is for parents to let go of their demands and allow the young child to express itself in the knowledge that even when they are angry, they are loved. As with many aspects of parenting, this can be easier said than done!

When a client shares with me their hurt, pain, disappointment and sometimes downright acrimony towards their parents, they often feel guilty afterwards. It can be quite illuminating to hear a person say, 'My mother ruined my life' in one breath and in the next defend her, saying, 'Honestly, she wasn't that bad really, she did her best.' You may be familiar with saying something negative about a loved one to a friend and if they repeat it back to you, you will defend your loved one. Hearing others criticise our family members does not usually sit easy with us, and neither should it. As a species we are primed and conditioned to love our parents and to seek their approval, regardless of our age. The process of examining one's childhood should have nothing to do with apportioning blame or feeling guilty, but rather trying to understand one's parents with compassion. They are human beings, after all, and therefore flawed.

× × ×

Exercise: Become the Loving Link

In her recent book, *The Book You Wish Your Parents Had Read (And Your Children Will Be Glad That You Did)*, psychotherapist Philippa Perry takes a humanistic approach to child rearing. Children are not wild beasts that must be tamed, but little people who depend on a parent not to pass on their own childhood emotional baggage. She writes, 'We are but a link in a chain stretching back through millennia and forwards until who knows when. The good news is that you can learn to reshape your link, and this will improve the life of your children, and their children, and you can start now.' It is reassuring to know that it is never too late to try to understand your own past and to start to reshape your link with your children and future generations.

To help you become a more loving and present link in your family's chain, ask yourself whether you hold on to any anger or resentment towards either or both of your parents. If this is the case, then a reflective journalling exercise I created to help my clients understand the world through their parent's eyes will help you to move on, let go and find inner peace.

> **Warning: this exercise may cause tears and even anger, but that is okay. Tears are always a sign of progress, so let them come.**

Write down, first from your mother's perspective, what you know factually about her life and also what you imagine to be true. In short, put yourself in her shoes.

✗   Before you were born, what was her own childhood like? Describe the relationship she had with her parents and siblings. Can you imagine what it was like for her growing up?

✗   Describe her life as a young adult, meeting your father and their relationship, if they had one.

✗   From her perspective, describe the first year of your life and what was going on for her. What challenges did she face?

✗   Describe what it was like being your mother through your childhood and teenage years. Please do not be hard on yourself – your role is to try to understand, not to judge.

✗   Describe your relationship with your mother now. If she is dead, are there any unresolved issues that you can put down on paper? What would you say to her if she were still alive?

Now do the same exercise but with your father.

Having completed this reflective journalling, can you see any patterns emerging that might inform how you react to situations and people in your life as an adult? Can you understand more clearly the impact your parents' lives have had on your own sense of self? Often how we feel about ourselves and our level of self-esteem is a mirror of how our parents feel or felt about themselves and the level of belief they had in you.

How high is your self-esteem?

Morris Rosenberg was an American sociologist who developed the Rosenberg Self-Esteem Scale, which has become the most widely used reliable empirical method to gauge an individual's self-esteem. It consists of 10 questions with results rated between 0 and 30. The higher the score, the higher the level of self-esteem.

Below is a list of statements that concern general feelings you may have about yourself. Please read the statements and tick how strongly you agree or disagree with them.

Before you start, take a deep breath and centre yourself. Tick the relevant response that occurs to you as soon as you read the statement without analysing your response.

		Strongly agree	Agree	Disagree	Strongly disagree
1.	On the whole, I am satisfied with myself.		✓		
2.*	At times, I think I am no good at all.			✓	
3.	I feel that I have a number of good qualities.	✓			
4.	I am able to do things as well as most other people.	✓			

5.* I feel I do not have much to be proud of.				✓	
6.* I certainly feel useless at times.				✓	
7. I feel that I am a person of worth, at least on an equal plane with others.	✓				
8.* I wish I could have more respect for myself.			✓		
9.* All in all, I am inclined to feel that I am a failure.				✓	
10. I take a positive attitude toward myself.	✓				

14 8 2 13

Scoring: Give the following scores for each statement that has no asterisk beside it.

Strongly agree = 3

Agree = 2

Disagree = 1

Strongly disagree = 0

Items with an asterisk are reverse scored, that is:

Strongly agree = 0

Agree = 1

Disagree = 2

Strongly disagree = 3

Add together the total number from each statement to get your overall score. Note: The scale ranges from 0 to 30. 27

Scores between 15 and 25 are within normal range. Scores below 15 suggest low self-esteem.

Whether your self-esteem is low, high or average, rest assured that it is where it needs to be right now. Awareness is the first step to progress. Self-esteem can be vastly improved through consistent self-love.

The second block to self-love is shame, which we will look at next.

'If you put shame in a petri dish, it needs three ingredients to grow exponentially: secrecy, silence, and judgement. If you put the same amount of shame in the petri dish and douse it with empathy, it can't survive.'

BRENÉ BROWN

2. SHAME

Shame is a suffocating emotion and is poisonous to self-love and love of others. Encompassing both self-disgust and self-reproach, it often leads to defensive behaviours that compound the problem. For example, someone who is highly self-conscious will often radiate an awkward energy that keeps others at a distance. This can then lead to over-sensitivity and compulsively finding fault in others. After social encounters, the person in question often feels guilty and ashamed of their behaviour and so the loop of isolation continues.

Allowing others to love you takes great faith in yourself.

Accepting love for who you are right now and not how you perceive others want you to be is an essential skill that will save you from prolonged and unnecessary pain. Shame is a self-reflexive emotion, meaning that we feel it in relation to how we perceive others see us. We pick up on their behaviour towards us and the language they use about us and we use this as a lens to examine ourselves. Self-reflexive emotions such as guilt, envy, jealousy and gratitude are more subtle in nature and can take us by surprise. For example, seeing your partner chatting with an attractive person can trigger jealous emotions you may not have realised were lurking under the surface.

Shame resilience theory (SRT) was developed by Dr Brené Brown, researcher and international bestselling author. Dr Brown is famous for her work on how to become comfortable with being vulnerable and SRT is founded on research, predominantly with women. Dr Brown states that the main triggers for carrying shame are 'appearance and body image, sexuality, family, motherhood, parenting, professional identity and work, mental and physical health, aging, religion, speaking out, and surviving trauma'.[25]

Often where there is shame, guilt is lurking close behind. Healthy remorse is a good sign of emotional intelligence when you have done something wrong, but to feel ashamed and guilty for being human, having weaknesses, making mistakes, putting on weight, being a parent, being a boss, being an employee, having a past and speaking your mind is not. The truth is that shame is often rooted in unresolved issues from childhood. For example, someone who was abused as a child will often carry the shame of the trauma, blame themselves and feel guilty that they are somehow responsible.

**You do not have to do anything wrong
to experience the toxicity of shame.**

Can you recall being worried as a child about how your parents or teacher would react to something you may have done wrong? Do you remember the fear of getting into trouble or making a mistake? Where did you feel it in your body? Is this feeling familiar to you today? How do you feel if you have to tell your boss that you have not had enough time to complete a task? Often the fear of being found out for a mistake we have made is far greater than the consequences of telling the truth. For example, a child who breaks her mother's favourite vase by accident is so full of fear that she hides the evidence. That child then spends each day dreading the inevitable moment when the mother notices the vase is missing and her dishonesty rather than the broken vase becomes the focal point. It can take immense courage to be honest and in doing so show your vulnerability. Yet when we are brave and honest, the reaction we anticipated is often far less serious or extreme. People appreciate honesty.

Brené Brown's work in shame resilience theory suggests there are four steps that we can take to overcome shame. These are:

1 Recognising the personal vulnerability that led to the feelings of shame

2 Recognising the external factors that led to the feelings of shame

3 Connecting with others to receive and offer empathy

4 Discussing and deconstructing the feelings of shame themselves

If you carry any shame, can you find it in your heart to let it go? Can you free yourself of guilt? To know that you can do something wrong and still be loved is human understanding and compassion at its best. When you free yourself or another from shame, there is a true liberation wherein love and self-love can blossom without the toxic facade of perfection and comparison.

3. PERFECTIONISM

'Perfectionism is self-abuse of the highest order.'

ANNE WILSON SCHAEF

Recently I had a new client, Alison (name changed), who displayed many of the symptoms of being a perfectionist: burn-out, constant anxiety and not being able to delegate. In a session I noticed she was distracted by my bookcase, so I asked her if she liked books, to which she enthusiastically answered, 'Yes, I used to read all the time, but not any more. I don't have the time.' I then asked her if the books were in perfect order on the shelf in terms of size, colour or alphabetically, to which she answered, 'No.' I asked her if she believed that this would take away from the power and the insights that the books had to offer. 'No, of course not,' she said.

If perfectionism was a friend, then he/she would be a toxic one, not a real friend. Perfection, the false friend, promises to help you achieve everything you want in life but suggests that anything less than perfect is because of your laziness. Perfectionism likes nothing better than to compare you to other people as you scroll through social media or mingle at a party, highlighting all your flaws. It does not matter if you have become the CEO of your company or have come first in a triathlon, you are still not good enough as you are. Maybe if you lost more weight or had more friends you would be more worthwhile, but not now, never now, and so you end up in a state of perennial striving.

The impact of perfectionism on your life can be either that you overachieve and run the risk of burnout or that you underachieve and procrastinate constantly. In the first case, the fear is that you must excel or you will not be accepted and ultimately loved. In the second, if you try to achieve something and fail you will feel ashamed, so subconsciously you believe that it is safer not to try. Most of us sit in the middle of these two extremes. Either way, fear is the motivator and rejection is often what we are most afraid of.

To help us identify whether you are a perfectionist and what type (one who overachieves or one who underachieves), please consider the three following scenarios.

- ✕ **Scenario 1:** You have completed a project for work or college on time and met the deadline. While it is not 'perfect', it is completed to the best of your ability given the timeframe and resources. Do you ask for more time or submit it as it is now?

- ✕ **Scenario 2:** You have exams in six months. Do you create a study plan and follow it or wait until the last few weeks or days to start?

- ✕ **Scenario 3:** You come home from work and the house really needs to be tidied and cleaned, but you are tired from the day at work. Do you tidy and clean until it is 'perfect' and then relax or do you have a rest first and then tackle the chores?

SCENARIO 1 ANALYSIS

If you decide to ask for more time, you are displaying perfectionist tendencies. The question remains, will you ever be happy with the final result? Often when we try to make something better, we wipe out much of the creativity that went into the original piece of work and actually lessen its impact and relevance.

If you decide to hand the project in on time with the work you have done, you will make it easier for yourself, your boss and your colleagues. Contentment, not perfection, comes from knowing when you have done your best and when it is time to let go. I have had to apply this when writing this book!

SCENARIO 2 ANALYSIS

If you procrastinate when it comes to study – or anything that requires dedicated effort, for that matter – you are likely to be a perfectionist who underachieves. You will probably spend the months leading up to the exams in a state of flux, knowing that you 'should' be studying but constantly putting it off. Eventually, with the pressure piling up, you do your best to cram six months of work into a month or less. The result, even if you get a good one (and many crammers do in exams), is less important as true success is positive mental wellbeing, being kind to yourself and distributing the workload evenly.

If you start to study with the full six months to go and space it out, doing more as the exam approaches, you will be showing kindness towards yourself and are likely to be in a better place mentally for the exam.

SCENARIO 3 ANALYSIS

I have seen many clients, women in particular but not exclusively, who cannot rest until their house is 'perfect', which means they never rest. Fearne Cotton, in her book *Calm: Working through Life's Daily Stresses to Find a Peaceful Centre*, writes, 'I am a neat freak. When my husband leaves cupboard doors open after he's made a cup of tea, I want to throw every single tea bag into the street in a fit of rage.' This makes me smile because I can relate to the obsessive need for a neat space. However, it is far more important that your mind is tidy, calm and ordered and that you have a sense of space and peace. No matter how clean your home is, it can never give you the sense of inner calm that you are looking for.

Calmness comes through stillness, not activity.

Fabrice Midal, author of international bestseller *The French Art of Letting Go*, explains that when we allow ourselves to be all the things we dislike about ourselves and when we let go of epic self-expectation, we can find true liberation. On perfectionism, Midal says that 'our obsession with perfection leads us to harass ourselves psychologically in a way that would be punishable by law if we did the same to someone else'.

Your 'inner judge' is unfortunately a harsh dictator who insists that no matter what you do, it is not enough. In order to succeed, you remain in the striving state of lack, a sorry state that can make your skin crawl, your confidence crumble and your sleep restless.

The *Harvard Business Review* conducted a meta-analysis of 95 studies from the 1980s to the present day that examined the relationship between perfectionism and productivity in the workplace. The research included nearly 25,000 working-age individuals and concluded, unsurprisingly, that perfectionists work longer hours and do not know how to switch off.[26] As a result, perfectionists have higher rates of stress, anxiety and ill health. If an individual is suffering from burnout, they are not going to be very effective or make clear decisions. Ironically, their work becomes far from perfect. Either way ...

Perfection does not exist.

There are, of course, many excellent standards of work, master-pieces and incredible achievements, but if you look closely enough, you will always find imperfections. The natural world is a good example – the raw wilderness, randomness and imperfection makes it beautiful. Or take Renaissance artist Michelangelo's most famous statue, *David*, which was carved from a block of marble that had been rejected by other sculptors who claimed the quality of the marble was too poor to create a masterpiece.[27] *David* now takes pride of place in the Galleria dell'Accademia in Florence, with mil-lions of people flocking to see its perfect imperfection each year.

You, too, are perfectly imperfect. We all are in our own unique way. This enlightened principle will help you to remove one of the major obstructions to self-love.

Alison, the perfectionist we met earlier, has now set many boundar-ies in work, has delegated tasks to her team and does not recognise the overworked, overwhelmed person she was when we first met. She has also returned to her love of reading.

4. DISTRACTION

'The cure for loneliness is solitude.'

MARIANNE MOORE

When our internal battles become too intense, many of us slide unconsciously from inner war to distraction. For example, imagine you are on your commute home from work and your inner critic is giving you a hard time for not performing well at work that day. The word 'should' is foremost in your mind: I 'should' have contributed more, I 'should' have been more assertive, I 'should' have got a better outcome. The constant self-recrimination is so exhausting that by the time you arrive home you are too tired to cook, so you order a takeaway, turn on Netflix, maybe drink some wine and/

or eat some chocolate. Soon the critical voice has been drowned out. What a relief ... until a feeling of dread creeps in as the credits of the series you were binge watching roll by. You reluctantly yet exhaustedly go to bed and *bang*, the critical voice is back stronger than ever, accompanied by a pounding heart and a mind that will not let you sleep.

Instead of resisting, fighting with and eventually ignoring the initial critical thoughts you had on the commute home, it is far more advisable to accept them and do your best to understand them so that you can sleep peacefully. Distracting yourself from negative emotions will only serve to intensify them later. As Marcus Aurelius, the Stoic philosopher and Roman emperor, said in his book *Meditations*, 'Nowhere you can go is more peaceful – more free of interruptions – than your own soul.'

Distracting ourselves through activity is not the answer, as it ignores our primeval need for stillness, for just being. Solitude does not equal loneliness or emptiness, although we may be conditioned to believe so and thus fear it.

So why do you distract yourself from the peace of 'your own soul'? One answer may be that as soon as you feel even a hint of boredom, as in having nothing to do, you fear the onset of loneliness. To pre-empt this, you will find endless activities to keep you 'occupied'. While many of us do like being on our own in a quiet house, we often fill the time with distractions: we work, comfort eat, scroll through social media, shop online, have an extra glass of wine – anything but just *be* in stillness.

The unoccupied mind can become a torture too hard to bear.

One study highlights this all too clearly. In the study, conducted by Timothy Wilson, a social psychologist at the University of Virginia in Charlottesville, hundreds of people were asked to sit alone in a lab room for 15 minutes with no distractions apart from the choice of being able to give themselves an electric shock. The results were astonishing. Even though many participants had previously stated that they would pay money to avoid the pain of an electric shock, 67 per cent of men and 25 per cent of women chose to inflict it on themselves rather than just sit there quietly and think. One man was even reported to administer it to himself 191 times![28]

Do you personally feel lonely often, sometimes or rarely? Have you ever noticed that you can feel lonely even when you are surrounded by others, for example at a party, a work night out or a family gathering? Paradoxically, many of our most desperately lonely moments are felt when we are in the company of other people, including those we love most. Loneliness has little to do with being on your own and more to do with feeling disconnected even when you are in company.

When we fail to connect with ourselves, we struggle to connect to others.

Having a preoccupied mind means being cut off from the moment. We have all had the experience of chatting to a friend but literally having no idea what they have just said because our mind was elsewhere. You may be doing your best to follow them and are even making the right sounds at the right time to show this. However, desperately trying to catch up can put tremendous pressure on your nervous system, leaving you exhausted. Being on the receiving end – that is, speaking to a friend who is visibly struggling to remain present – can leave us feeling disconnected and lonely.

True connection can only occur when both parties are fully present.

You can't control how conscious or present someone else is, but your inner stillness and calm attention can subtly and slowly influence the other person and bring them back to the moment. We will practise this later on in the first LOVE habit, Listen.

In order to really know yourself you need to spend quiet time, alone in peace, away from all distractions. Ironically, the more often you do this, the less lonely you become. Listening daily to the 'Love to Rise' and 'Love to Sleep' audios along with establishing the four key habits of Listen, Open, Value and Energise (LOVE) are a practical way to help you to turn towards all the parts of you with love. Together, we will transform any unwanted feelings of isolation into a deep inner connection to your Beholder, the loving presence within. As you will find out in the next section, the mistake many of us make is in believing that we are our ego, our personality.

x x x

You Are Not Your Ego

'The ego is the true location of anxiety.'

SIGMUND FREUD

WHILE THE WORD 'ego' from the Latin simply means 'I' or 'the self', modern interpretations from Freud and Jung to Eckhart Tolle have given it a strong negative charge. In *A New Earth*, Tolle writes, 'The ego is an imposter that pretends to be you.' In its purest form, the ego is your likes and dislikes and it determines many of your choices, from the style of your clothes to the music you like. It is a culturally conditioned preference, neither negative nor positive. An *inflated ego*, on the other hand, identifies with and believes your thoughts.

You are not your likes and dislikes, you are not your thoughts, you are not your ego.

Freedom emerges from identification with the Beholder (full conscious presence), not the ego. When you identify with presence you are not at the mercy of the ego, which desires to keep you living in the past or future.

The interviews included in this book provide an enlightening insight into four well-known people who are externally 'successful', yet who remain free from an enlarged ego. This in itself is refreshing and a testament to their strength of character. I once had a client who worked behind the scenes in the music industry and the stories he told me were, well, terrifying. The musicians almost always started out as lovely people and were grateful for their success, but for some of them, as their status grew they became increasingly demanding and unreasonable. For example, if a flight they wanted to get on was fully booked, they would shout at my client, 'Just tell them who I am!'

But you do not have to be famous or powerful to develop an inflated ego. Some of the signs that an ego is getting out of control are:

1 Always wanting to get your way

2 Feeling envious of other people's success

3 Feeling jealous or left out of other people's relationships

4 Being super competitive and not content even when you do win

5 Becoming defensive if someone challenges you

6 Measuring yourself on your latest achievement

7 Not listening to others, just waiting to speak

8 Consistently bringing conversations back to yourself

How many of these can you identify with? I have felt the cold discomfort that many of these signals applied to me at various stages in my life and I continue to work hard to overcome them. It can be difficult to come to terms with aspects of ourselves that we do not admire. Indeed, many of us have moments when we behave like petulant children demanding to get our own way, or we may suffer from jealousy, do not listen properly to others or want to be the centre of attention. Shy people are not immune to this and may also have an inflated ego; they bring attention to themselves by saying nothing. Your job is not to judge yourself, but to become aware of these moments and generate presence in the moment. Resist the ego's desire to pull you out of the moment into the past (rumination) or future (fear).

How quick are you to defend yourself if someone is critical or unkind to you? Think of minor incidents, like genuinely forgetting to put out the bins, to ones where you have been accused of something you did not do. Things like being falsely accused of bullying at work or of being dishonest can be a true test of our resolve to remain calm in the face of injustice.

Is that so?

Hakuin Ekaku was a Zen master and was greatly revered by the inhabitants of his village as a truly spiritual man. Many of the villagers looked to their master for guidance. One day a young and beautiful girl in the village announced with great fear to her parents that she was pregnant. So great was her shame and so mighty the anger of her parents, who demanded to know who the father was, that the young girl crumbled and said it was Hakuin. Her parents were furious and angrily confronted the master. Hakuin's response was simply, 'Is that so?'

Hakuin's reputation was destroyed and he became the object of much gossip. When the infant was born the parents wanted nothing to do with the child and brought it to the Zen master, ordering him to take care of what they deemed was his responsibility. The master accepted the baby and simply responded to their demands with the response, 'Is that so?'

For many months, the Zen master lovingly nurtured the baby. No one came to him for guidance any more, so he had all day to spend with the baby. One day, the young girl missed her baby so much and was so racked with guilt that she confessed that Hakuin was not the father, that it was actually the son of the village butcher. The parents were so full of shame and remorse that they went to the master and begged his forgiveness. Hakuin simply handed back the happy, loved infant with the response (I think you know where this is going), 'Is that so?'

When you are at peace with yourself, you have no need to defend your behaviour. You can stand tall and be proud of who you are. Replace accusation and defensiveness with love and inevitably something positive will emerge, like the happy baby in the story.

fearing conflict => facing conflict => not needing conflict

The exercise below will help to challenge some of the negative beliefs your ego may be clinging to. By challenging them you begin to understand them, and when you understand them you can begin to let them go.

× × ×

Negative Thought Identifier

TAKE A MOMENT now to pause and identify the three most repetitive negative thoughts you have about yourself each day. You may need to scan through your day to complete this exercise in self-observation.

The three most common negative persistent thoughts that I hear in my work are: *- I don't work hard enough*
- I'm selfish
- I'm not present enough

- ✗ 'I am not good enough.'

- ✗ 'I am lazy.'

- ✗ 'I am stupid.'

A close fourth is 'I am ugly/fat.' Negative thoughts about not having enough energy or time are also common. It is heart-wrenching to hear amazing, kind, active, intelligent people speak about themselves in this derogatory way.

Did you hear these critical thoughts or something similar as a child, either said directly to you or perhaps said about you by other family members? Much of our sense of self comes from such phrases. But remember, they are just words. Together, we will dispel limiting beliefs that hold you back.

> **Positive mental health stems from consistent and loving self-awareness.**

Take a normal day and observe your thought patterns.

1 How often do you have these negative thoughts?

2 What triggers them to arise? Is it the time of day? A particular place? A particular person? Are you tired or hungry when they pop into your mind?

3 Does it feel as though these thoughts are automatic and out of your control?

Negative thoughts are sometimes not immediately apparent. For example, 'I am lazy' could manifest as constant pressure to tick things off your 'to-do' list or 'I am stupid' may appear as, 'I won't

bother looking for a new job because I probably wouldn't get it.'
The most common one, 'I am not good enough,' can rear its head
in every aspect of your life.

> **Often the roots of many of our negative
> thoughts come from a feeling of not deserving
> to be loved.**

Now that you have identified and noticed the patterns, each time
you hear that thought you need to counteract it, as it is not true.
Do not believe your negative thoughts. When you practise this,
such thoughts will, with time, disappear.

So, turn the three examples above into:

✗ 'I am good enough.'

✗ 'I am full of energy.'

✗ 'I am smart.'

✗ ✗ ✗

Positive Thought Enhancer

YOU WILL, I hope, have heard some positive feedback during your
childhood. Like negative thoughts, many of the positive beliefs you
have about yourself also stem from your early years and these need
to be reinforced.

Observe your positive beliefs and *write them down*, remembering
that they are *not* the totality of your strengths, but just the surface
of your true potential. Often we are so set in what we believe we
are good at that we dismiss our full potential. For example, 'I am

not sporty' or 'I am not good at maths' are fixed mindset beliefs that are a hangover from the messages you received as a child and you do not question them – that is, you did not, *until now*. When you love someone, you do everything in your power (within reason) to bring out the best in them and that includes supporting them in new endeavours. It is time to give yourself that same chance.

In the next chapter, we will examine how to unite the parts of yourself. You are not the good or the bad things that happen to you. You are not a negative or a positive thought. You are not a happy emotion or a sad emotion. One part of you is not unlovable and the other lovable. You are whole and unified. You are love itself.

THREE KEY POINTS TO REMEMBER

1 Most of us have two major conflicting parts of ourselves: the true self (A) and the Shadow Self (B). Understanding the purpose of the Shadow Self will help you to live in peace.

2 The four blocks to self-love are childhood conditioning, shame, perfectionism and distraction.

3 The inflated ego cannot survive when you are present. Recognise the signs when your ego emerges and attempts to take control.

× × ×

The Self-Love Habit Tools

This is a gentle reminder to incorporate the following daily mind-fulness tools into your every day. They are designed to be easy habit-building tools to make love your priority.

AUDIO MEDITATION

Listen to the 'Love to Rise' and 'Love to Sleep' audios every day. Record your progress in the chart at the back of this book.

BE A FRIEND TO YOURSELF

Cultivate the voice of your inner critic to become your inner companion.

THE DAILY PROMISE TECHNIQUE

Practise the daily promise technique: 'I promise to accept all the parts of MYSELF today to the best of my ability.' Write it down, if you have not already, on a sticky note and put it on the mirror where you brush your teeth. Repeat this promise every day and again if and when a fearful or negative thought emerges.

THE TWO-MINUTE MIRROR

Spend at least two minutes a day looking into your own eyes. Look beyond the physical, without judgement. Maintain eye contact until a feeling of calmness or ease emerges. This is something you can do last thing at night or first thing in the morning or both should you so desire.

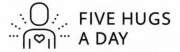

FIVE HUGS A DAY

Don't forget to get your full five-a-day quota!

THE UNITED SELF

'Liberté, égalité, fraternité'

IN THIS CHAPTER we will start to unite the parts of you by further examining the ideal self, the orphaned self and the malleable self. We will also look at how consciously choosing positive lenses in which to look at the world helps you to become a unified person. When you change your perspective, the world changes.

The French declaration of 'liberty, equality, fraternity' comes directly from the philosophy of the Age of Enlightenment and was frequently referred to during the French Revolution as the essence of what people were fighting and dying for – the right to freedom, to be treated equally and to share a common brotherhood of love. From 1793 onwards, in Paris and other cities, some people painted 'Unity, indivisibility of the Republic; liberty, equality or death' on the front of their houses.[29] However, officials asked them to remove the graffiti and the phrase fell into disuse under the Empire. It re-emerged under the Third Republic and today is woven into the very fabric of the nation and its people. While liberty, equality and fraternity is not always practised in France or elsewhere, it remains an aspiration and a call to action.

The Self-Love Habit is not aspirational – it is both actionable and achievable. You can create freedom in your own mind, treat everybody equally and show kinship towards fellow human beings. You can choose to be a unified, balanced person. You can choose to live at ease with all your parts, your circumstances and the people in your life. However, in order to make such a choice, you must be aware that you do actually have a choice in the first place.

This chapter addresses the choice that is always available to you to love and live in peace, no matter what adversities you encounter. We will explore the concepts of the ideal self, the malleable self and the orphaned parts of ourselves. The united self is about bringing these various parts of ourselves back together. Like a jigsaw with all the pieces, you feel complete.

× × ×

The Ideal Self

'The ideal is within you, and the obstacle to reaching this ideal is also within you. You already possess all the material from which to create your ideal self.'

LEO TOLSTOY

DISAPPOINTMENT is a hard burden to carry. The parent who says those dreaded words, 'I am disappointed in you', to their child leaves the child frozen in feelings of inadequacy. Even an expression of anger or annoyance would be better than one of disappointment because this instils an inert despair in a young mind. Later, in adulthood, many will go on to inflict this judgement of disappointment upon themselves through their internal voice: 'I thought you would be doing better than you are now, what's wrong with you?'; 'What a mess, surely you can do better than this?' It is easy to see how such thoughts destroy motivation and lead to frustration and despair.

The divide between our real self as we are now and the idealised version of ourselves can feel painfully real. Many of us perceive our ideal self as the perfect version of ourselves, a remastered version that meets everybody's expectations of us, whether they be our parents, children, friends, colleagues or broader society. As a consequence, the ideal self always lives in the future while the real self is a present, inferior version that we are disappointed with.

The advertising industry is geared towards deceiving you into believing that if you buy certain products or brands, you will achieve your ideal-self status. It attempts to manipulate intrinsic human weakness by telling us that we must not be content with who we are now if we are to be successful in the future. As an industry, it attempts to keep you living in a perpetual state of striving for the ideal self, which is always just out of reach. Clearly this is a never-ending trap, so let's consider a radical proposition:

What if you are already your ideal self?

The ideal self is not a fixed destination but a movable feast, a living, breathing organism that lives in the now *if you choose to let it*. The ideal self learns and changes over time. It is not a series of completed accomplishments.

The ideal self is proactive, not perfect.

Carl Rogers, known as the father of psychotherapy, believed that our happiness lies in the congruence of the real self and the idealised self and that we are driven by the basic motive to self-actualise, that is, to reach our full potential. In order to do this we need to feel loved, especially in childhood. Rogers proposes five characteristics commonly found in those who are on the path to self-actualising. Take a moment and consider how many of these relate to you:

1 **Being open to experience:** This is the ability to be at peace with both negative and positive emotions. Emotions are processed and not denied.

2 **Existential living:** The ability to live in the moment without judgement.

3 **Trusting your own feelings:** Listening to your gut.

4 **Being creative:** Stepping outside your comfort zone.

5 **Living a fulfilled life:** Being happy and satisfied with your life as it is now but also looking for new challenges.[30]

I hope you can identify with these characteristics, as they encapsulate much of what we are covering in this book. Accepting and loving your real self exactly as you are now allows you to live and breathe your ideal self. Ironically, relinquishing pressure allows your ideal self to breathe. One of the greatest misconceptions of our time is that the more pressure you put yourself under, the more success you will enjoy.

Replace pressure with acceptance.

You already have within you all it takes to be ideal, whole, complete and unified. The closer both the real ideal selves are, the more unified you become (Figure 3).

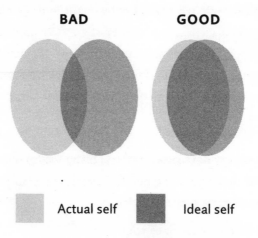

BAD   **GOOD**

Actual self   Ideal self

Figure 3 (*Source:* simplypsychology.org)

Exercise: Become Your Ideal Self

How close are you to living as your ideal self? How big is the gap between how you see yourself now and how you wish to be? Seeing the best in yourself will give you the energy to be your ideal self today and not at some point in the future that never arrives.

Take a moment to journal how your ideal self lives and breathes by answering the following questions. I have included my own answers as a guide to help you.

× How does your ideal self feel ...

  × When it wakes up in the morning?
    Energetic, positive and grateful.

  × Last thing at night before it drops off to sleep?
    Calm, safe and grateful.

  × When it looks in the mirror?
    Proud, connected, content, non-judgemental.

  × About the future?
    Excited and optimistic, emotionally resilient for change and challenges.

× How does your ideal self handle challenging relationships?
  With compassion and patience.

× What energy does your ideal self bring into every room it enters?
  Fun, positive, calming and loving.

× What kind of work does your ideal self do?
  Helping people to live and breathe their ideal selves without pressure and through self-love.

× How does your ideal self switch off?
Easily and often, through reading, hypnotherapy, yoga, meditation, walking by the sea.

× How does your ideal self cope when life does not run smoothly?
With the courage, patience and love to deal with the negative emotions and anxiety that may arise.

× How does your ideal self commit to its dreams?
Each day as a habit by being proactive and focused and mentally through the power of visualisation.

× How often does your ideal self laugh?
Very often.

The answers to these questions will give you a clear indication of how wide the gap is between your ideal and real self. What areas need your attention to start to close the gap? Do you notice how they correspond to the exercise we did in the last chapter, '365 Days to Love'? Your ideal self is aware of how finite life is.

To help close the gap, let's turn the answers into affirmations. Put them somewhere you will see them every day to act as a reminder. For example, my affirmations are:

× I wake up every morning energetic, positive and grateful.

× I go to sleep each night calm, safe and grateful. I sleep the whole night through.

× I am proud, connected and loving when I look in the mirror.

× I am excited, optimistic and emotionally resilient for change and challenges in the future.

× I handle difficult relationships with patience and compassion.

- ✗ I bring fun, calm, positive and loving energy into every room I enter.

- ✗ I help people to be their ideal selves without pressure and through self-love.

- ✗ I switch off easily and often.

- ✗ I commit to my dreams each day as a habit. I am proactive and focused and I mentally visualise my dreams.

- ✗ I laugh very often.

Affirmations really do work, so read your list out loud as you look in the mirror. If you have the courage, say them to someone you love and trust. Do this every day.

✗ ✗ ✗

The Orphaned Selves

'The sun was rising in all its splendid beauty; but the light only seemed to show the boy his own lonesomeness and desolation, as he sat, with bleeding feet and covered with dust, upon a door-step.'

CHARLES DICKENS, *OLIVER TWIST*

IN THE CLASSIC Victorian novel *Oliver Twist*, Oliver, a young orphan, escapes the harsh conditions of the workhouse for what he hopes will be a better life and ends up being exploited by a pickpocketing gang in London's criminal underworld. Oliver is starving not only for food, but for love and care his entire life.

As children we often see ourselves, other people and the world around us in black and white terms, as either good or bad. If you were generally deemed 'good', you may have difficulty accepting the 'bad' parts of yourself. If you were generally seen as 'bad', you may struggle to see the good in yourself. We all have a mixture of positive and negative emotions and it is unfair to define a child using only one of them. This can also be couched using words such as being the 'easy' or 'difficult' one. The underlying message is that one is 'good' and one is 'bad' and this label can stick with a person for their whole life.

Remember, any repetition in a self-help book is not a mistake, so indulge me as I reiterate that you need to stop judging yourself and others as either 'good' or 'bad'. The parts you find harder to love, that can cause you to be angry, jealous, anxious or sad, are not 'bad'. They are craving to be heard, understood and loved.

Almost all of us have parts of ourselves that have been abandoned, forgotten about and are starved of our love. We are built to survive, so as children, when we experience emotional pain that we do not comprehend, we block it out. We play to escape whatever is causing us stress. The world of our imagination tries to provide a safe haven. For example, a child who hears her parents fighting in the next room may play with her dolls and imagine them having a nice tea party. If we are born into adverse conditions we normalise them, believing this is the way of the world. This in itself is a survival mechanism.

It is not 'bad' to feel bad, although it may be difficult at the time.

However, there is no reason for you to behave unkindly to yourself or to anyone else. Putting pressure on yourself to feel good all the time will not cause you to feel happy. In fact, it may implode, causing further pain, and possibly also explode, causing behavioural problems.

'Unexpressed emotions will never die. They are buried alive and will come forth later in uglier ways.'

SIGMUND FREUD

Orphaning the parts of ourselves that cause us pain does appear to work at the time and in the short term as we survive and continue to function in the world, whether that is going to school, playing with or meeting our friends, going to work, etc. On a longer-term basis, though, this is not the case. The unprocessed emotions transfer into feelings of anxiety, panic, anger and jealousy and behaviours such as comfort eating, drinking and other compulsive, negative habits. As you mature into a fully emotionally intelligent adult, you have a duty to yourself to understand the orphaned or cut-off parts of yourself. If you continue to ignore these orphaned parts they do not disappear, but rather they unconsciously affect each choice you make and your daily habits.

It is often easier to spot this mechanism at work in other people than in ourselves. Perhaps you have a parent who does not like to discuss their past and you know very little about their life before you were born. If you have the opportunity, ask them in a kind, non-confrontational way – not to cause them pain, but to show your desire to love and understand them. In doing so, you may also learn a great deal about yourself.

The extract below was written by one of my clients, who describes her background and journey to self-discovery, self-knowledge, self-acceptance and self-love.

> *In working with Fiona, we began to look at my early*
> *childhood, which was dominated by the sudden and very*
> *early death of my father. I was with him when he died, but*

as I was only 18 months old, I had no conscious memory of the event. We explored the very probable subconscious trauma of the actual process of his death – pain, crying out, putting me on the floor, my mother's shock and panic when she discovered us – him dead in a chair and me crying on the floor.

Growing up, I was always described by extended family as a 'bold brat'. I was definitely bolshie, strong-willed, demanding, mutinous. Fiona asked me to consider 'Little Kate' in a more compassionate light. I realised that I had been both neglected and spoiled as a child. Home life was quite cold. My mother was extraordinarily undemonstrative. There were no hugs, kisses, comforting. She carried a lot of baggage from her own upbringing and, perhaps, the shock of my father's death at 48 erased much of the warmth she was capable of. She was also struggling to raise five children on a very small income. She did her best and I always knew she loved us in her own way. However, the net result was that there was very little warmth in the house. As the youngest, I felt unheard, unimportant. I think I began to act up then as this 'bad' behaviour at least elicited a response. Negative attention was better than none. There was also a single incident of sexual abuse by a trusted non-family adult which I escaped but never told anybody about until I was in my twenties.

The more I thought about this little girl, the more I began to feel for her. She was a lonely little girl but feisty and determined not to be crushed by the coldness and judgementalism of both her home and the social environment of the time. I found myself quite admiring and fond of the 'little brat'!

Now I am also learning with Fiona to deal with the negative behaviours with which I have comforted myself over the years. I am developing a sense of wellbeing and positivity, which I have rarely felt before. I hope soon to be fond of and more compassionate towards the elderly adult that the little girl has become!

– KATE, 72, RETIRED, MOTHER AND GRANDMOTHER

As you begin to understand and love the orphaned parts of yourself using the four LOVE habits, you will notice how you can also extend this to your family and friends. Rather than focusing on how easy it is to love the parts that you like – the kind, fun and generous sides of them – you will gradually learn to accept their more difficult and challenging parts.

Just like the kindly and non-judgemental bachelor Mr Brownlow, who saves Oliver Twist from a life of hardship, you will provide a loving shelter to the orphans within yourself.

× × ×

The Malleable Self

ARE YOU THE same person you were one year ago, 10 years ago or 20 years ago? Do people remain *fundamentally* the same or do they change through time and experience? This is one of the big philosophical questions that David Hume, the Enlightenment Scottish philosopher, addressed in *A Treatise of Human Nature*.[31] Hume proposed that the mind is no more than a bundle of perceptions without a unified sense of self. If this is the case, who or what is the presence that observes these perceptions?

If we do change over time, what does it mean when someone says, 'I don't feel like myself any more', or perhaps, after a difficult period, 'I feel like I am finally getting back to myself'? Such expressions indicate an innate, unshifting sense of who we are. Let's examine it further.

DO WE REMAIN THE SAME PERSON PHYSICALLY?

We change continuously at a physical level over the course of a lifetime. We grow taller, we change body shape and size and eventually we get smaller again as we age. Humans shed molecules constantly – we lose 30,000 to 40,000 dead skin cells each minute, which is about 50 million cells every day[32] – so the answer is no, we are not the same person physically.

DO WE REMAIN THE SAME PERSON PSYCHOLOGICALLY?

We tend to see our behaviour as fixed and our memories as facts, but how true is this? We use terms such as 'always' and 'never' about ourselves, but they are rarely true. Can you think of any behavioural and emotional habits that you have changed over the years and what you once believed was an established fact about yourself that is no longer true? For example, I used to smoke, eat meat and believe I was unlovable.

The pre-Enlightenment British philosopher John Locke proposed a theory, 'personal identity over time',[33] that suggests we naturally presuppose that we are the same person throughout our lifetime with the same personality, likes and dislikes. According to the Lockean memory theory, our sense of self is a direct correlation with our memories. However, in most cases memory is fluid and behaviours and habits do change over time.

Linda Meyer Williams, an American sociologist, conducted one of the most revealing studies into memory loss and trauma.[34] The question the study posed was: 'Do people actually forget traumatic events such as child sexual abuse, and if so, how common is such forgetting?' Williams interviewed 206 girls directly after they had been sexually abused and interviewed 129 of them again, 17 years later. Williams wanted to see how close their memories were to the original account they gave. Thirty-eight per cent of these women did not recall the abuse at all. Women who were younger at the time of the abuse and also those who were molested by a family member were more likely not to remember. It appears that the earlier and deeper the trauma, the less likely we are to remember it consciously.

In Tara Westover's bestselling memoir *Educated*, she writes, 'My strongest memory is not a memory, it is something I imagined then came to remember as if it had happened.' Memories are highly subjective, to the point that if you were to ask your siblings (if you have them) to describe your childhood, it might sound radically different from the version you believe.

Locke proposed that our memories shape the continuity of the self over the ages. He postulated that if a person commits a crime and genuinely has no memory of this, they cannot be held responsible for their behaviour. In law, if a criminal has no recollection of the act, then the sentence can be lessened due to 'diminished responsibility'. Having no memory is a form of unconsciousness and is clearly dangerous, but as we know, memory alone is not reliable. I would argue that it is our duty to live as consciously, presently and alertly as we can to each moment. If we do not, the ramifications are often too great and cannot be undone.

Imagine a world where all people live consciously in harmony with themselves and others with no need to escape reality through addictive behaviours. A world free of hatred and violence. It may sound like a utopian dream, but one morning during the Extinction Rebellion climate change protest week in Dublin in 2019, I stumbled upon a meeting of the protestors in Merrion Square. I was drawn to the group by their positive energy and at how they conducted their morning meeting. They genuinely listened to and supported one another, working collectively for the greater good of all their members. It is extremely rare to witness a group with no need for hierarchy or ego power trips.

Of particular relevance that morning, they were discussing how the previous night there had been some drunken and rowdy behaviour by people on their way home from the pubs who had taken over their peaceful celebrations. As a result, they were discussing introducing a curfew that night as well as how to compassionately and collectively manage any late-night visitors on their way home from pubs and clubs. I should mention here that the group itself has a strict no drink, no drugs and no violence policy. As I reluctantly walked away that bright, sunny morning, I had a strong feeling of hope for mankind. Perhaps the 'new earth' that Eckhart Tolle speaks of is emerging – perhaps people are finally rising above themselves into a higher dimension and collectively saving the planet and its inhabitants through love.

You, too, have the opportunity to make a conscious choice to be more alert to life, to learn from all experiences and also to be fully responsible for your actions.

So if we accept that we do change both physically and psychologically over time, why do so many of us feel that we are fundamentally the same person? The answer is that we are both the same and different. The malleable self allows you to be at ease with yourself as you change aspects of yourself, including your likes and dislikes or your behaviours (for example, smoking). However, you are the same presence, the same soul, the same pure, unconditioned self that observes. You are the Beholder. Remember the equation for love?

The Beholder (conscious presence) + Energy = Love

The malleable brain enables you to learn the art of love, both showing and receiving it, and that is what this book is about. When you change your thoughts and experiences, you literally change the physical shape of your brain. This is known as neuroplasticity and it is the brain's capacity to rewire itself.

Internationally renowned neuroscientist Professor Michael Merzenich has been working on brain plasticity for five decades. He says, 'Your brain – every brain – is a work in progress. It is "plastic". From the day we're born to the day we die, it constantly revises and remodels, improving or slowly declining, as a function of how we use it.'[35]

In 2014, the Dalai Lama (who has long had an interest in neuroscience) met Merzenich, along with other leaders in the field, at a symposium to discuss neuroplasticity and healing. The Dalai Lama commented, 'Training the mind is not for the next life or heaven, or what Buddhists call nirvana. These things are simply for our present life.'[36]

> **You are the fixed continuum of presence and love and the rest is malleable.**

While we now know more about the workings of the human brain than ever before, we are probably still only on the cusp of understanding its true capabilities.[37] Neuroplasticity demonstrates scientifically the flexibility of the brain as it relates to personality, life choices, thoughts, moods, energy and behaviour. By realising this, you become empowered to nurture habits that serve you and the rest of humanity to the best of your ability. You are ready to become the united self.

✕ ✕ ✕

How to Unite the Self

'The game is not about becoming somebody, it's about becoming nobody.'

RAM DASS

YOUR PAST SELF is gone. Your future self does not exist. Your 'now self' is all that you have and it is everything you need.

Perspective is paramount. Have you considered that how you look at the world is often what is reflected back at you? If you are in a bad mood the world looks grey, but if you are feeling happy the world is brighter.

Let's now examine four metaphorical lenses that will help you to see yourself, your loved ones and the world with increased clarity and compassion.

LENS ONE: LOOK AT THE WORLD LIKE A BABY

In your preverbal state as an infant, you automatically lived in the now. In Zen Buddhism this state is often referred to as the 'beginner's mind', where we consciously observe the world anew. We remove labels from both objects and people so that, for example, a tree becomes something magical. Alison Gopnik, professor of psychology at University of California, Berkeley, says in her book *The Philosophical Baby* that 'raising children is one of the most significant, meaningful, and profound experiences of our lives. Is this just an evolutionary illusion, a trick to make us keep on reproducing? I'll argue that it is the real thing, that children really do put us in touch with truth, beauty, and meaning.' Most of us are naturally drawn to babies and it is not just because they are so cute. Their presence also subconsciously reminds us what it feels like to be at one with ourselves.

It is possible to return to pure awareness, to find again that stillness in your mind? As we explored in the last chapter, the conditioned self (Part B) is predominantly created in early childhood by our parents and society at large. It is now generally accepted in psychology that our personality and level of resilience are impacted by the quality of care we receive in the formative years of life from birth to five years old.

When you dwell in the now, the internal battle between Part A and Part B ceases. Conflict with the challenges of reality as it presents itself also dissolves, for example the myriad of things that do not go your way, delayed flights, postponed meetings or cars that break down. Being present, however, takes training. It is the art of mindfulness and self-awareness that we must return to again and again and again.

The default mode network[38] is the neuroscientific term for the brain when it is supposedly at rest and not focused on a particular task. For example, when you are daydreaming or your mind is wandering while you are doing repetitive household chores, you are still thinking, pondering the past and fearing the future. In other words, since all your attention is not spent on doing the laundry, your mind is free to roam, to ruminate or to catastrophise. If you have a busy brain, you can probably relate to this.

One of the many aspects of my work that I love is to witness a client's mind gradually slow down. I can actually hear the space between their thoughts start to open up. It is like driving on a motorway at five in the morning as the sun rises – the road has been transformed from a noisy, polluted place to a calm, liberating space that is wide open. Like a contented infant, we see the world become a place of wonder, not woe.

LENS TWO: LOOK AT THE WORLD LIKE A MOTHER

'A mother's love for her child is like nothing else in the world. It knows no law, no pity. It dares all things and crushes down remorselessly all that stands in its path.'

AGATHA CHRISTIE

It is perhaps unrealistic and unhelpful to suggest that we love everyone with the intensity of a mother's love. As both a mother and a daughter, I know what maternal love feels like and how strong it is. It has the potential to transform the planet.

A grain of maternal love shared with our fellow human beings would end wars and conflict.

Harry Harlow (1905–1981) was an American behavioural psychologist and is most famous for his work on maternal love and attachment in rhesus monkeys. Harlow, keen to demonstrate that love could be measured or quantified scientifically, conducted a number of highly contentious research experiments during the 1960s known as 'the wire mother' experiments. These were controversial because of the cruelty visited on the monkeys and would almost certainly not be permitted today. Newborn monkeys were taken away from their mothers and put in the 'care' of surrogate mothers. The experiment examined the positive impact of receiving maternal love and the detrimental effects of omitting it. Up to this point, science had generally accepted that an infant's prime motivation for bonding with a mother was simply a survival instinct and was concerned with being fed. The infant rhesus monkeys were given a choice between two types of 'mother': one that was made of terrycloth and had no bottle; the second was made of wire but had a bottle of milk to nourish the baby.

Harlow discovered that the monkeys would spend the majority of their time snuggled into the cloth 'mother' and would dart over to the wire 'mother' only when they were hungry. He reported, 'These data make it obvious that contact comfort is a variable of overwhelming importance in the development of affectional response, whereas lactation is a variable of negligible importance.'[39]

The monkeys suffered greatly in later experiments when the cloth 'mother' was removed; they would cry and rock back and forth. Harlow's methods, however cruel, actually acted as a catalyst for change in orphanages and childcare facilities, which started to move away from the 'let them cry' mentality to one where they placed just as much value on affection and love as they did on nourishment.

LENS THREE: LOOK AT THE WORLD WITH NEGATIVE ECSTASY

'In love, one and one are one.'

JEAN-PAUL SARTRE

Another key aspect of uniting our many selves comes in the form of negative ecstasy, which may appear at first to be a contradiction. Nihilistic philosophers such as Sartre, Nietzsche and Camus, known for their existential angst and perspectives on the futility of humanity, seem at first glance to be entirely depressing, yet on closer examination we discover love and liberty.

Nihilists see the divine in humans, not in God, hence humans are free to live autonomously, free from God. Life is given meaning through your conscious awareness, not through an external power that is out of your control. Nihilism attempts to reach beyond content and form and is ironically positive in the sense that in nothingness, everything becomes flexible and within humans' own will.

In *Being and Nothingness*, originally published in 1943, Sartre referred to the habit we have of lying to ourselves as *'mauvaise foi'* (bad faith). We adopt false values in order to conform to society and hence live an inauthentic existence. As a justification, we claim that we do not have a choice, which is false (bad faith). For example, someone who is living in an untenable situation, be it a job they hate or a dysfunctional relationship, may tell themselves that they are stuck and that there is nothing they can do. The pressure to conform to societal expectations coupled with the fear to stand up for themselves is greater than the ability to choose to leave.

> **By not making decisions, you make the biggest decision of all and that is to turn your back on yourself.**

Have you ever woken up in the middle of the night with your heart beating fast and the realisation that perhaps you are more free than you tell yourself? That maybe you *do* have a choice? If so, then you are experiencing what is ironically termed 'negative ecstasy'. From the security of your bed, you promise yourself that you will be brave and take action. However, the next morning the overwhelming fear has subsided and routine takes over. The practical steps and responsibility required to make the change can be too great and the habit of 'bad faith' is re-established. You soldier on. Psychologists also refer to this as 'cognitive dissonance' – the conflict of knowing something is not good for you, but continuing to do it regardless. Smoking is an example of this. Each time you light up, you know it is slowly killing you. More widely, we continue to make excuses for ourselves, putting ourselves in an existential prison with the hope that somebody else will set us free.

Refusing to take responsibility for your life is like swimming against the tide and going nowhere. You feel totally stuck and hopeless, as no matter how hard you swim, you stay in the same spot. Perhaps you are swimming in the wrong direction and you need to trust that the sea of life will help to carry you forward. You may have heard of the idea that if you could just get out of your own way, you would be unstoppable. It is true, but it is less about getting out of your own way and more about loving the parts that stand in your way. The next time you wake up in the middle of the night, listen to the fear and anxiety, and when you wake again reassure them that they have been heard. Take them with you on your journey through life and with time, through the power of habit, they will start to swim with you.

LENS FOUR: LOOK AT THE WORLD FOR NOTHING

Samuel Beckett once said, 'Nothing is more real than nothing.' Looking at empty space is a surprisingly powerful way to still the mind. I recall doing this as a child but not realising it was a 'method'. Back then it was just called daydreaming and if you did it at school you could get in trouble. Sometimes I would stare out of my bedroom window at the empty space between the branches of a tree in my front garden. It was heaven. Now, when we have a spare moment we tend to stare at a screen, whether it is a TV, mobile phone or laptop, where there is no space, yet this innate desire to find stillness is ever present.

The Open Focus brain technique was created by Les Fehmi and Susan Shor to help people manage stress and cultivate space in their minds. The method asks you to examine the space between objects, the empty space that is without form. The idea is that by looking at nothing, you clear your mind. The method also asks guiding questions, such as, 'Can you imagine the distance or space between your eyes?' In doing so, you move smoothly from the compulsive attention we pay to thoughts that can cause emotional stress and into a wider dimension above thought, above yourself and with a sense of freedom.

Like many discoveries, the Open Focus technique was discovered by chance. In 1971, Les Fehmi was conducting a series of experiments to help his clients reach the desired alpha brain wave state. This is an optimum state to be in during our waking hours, as we are relaxed yet alert.

In the alpha brain wave state, you are calm, present and highly efficient.

Fehmi was monitoring brain wave activity using an electroencephalogram machine, commonly known as an EEG, while his volunteers experienced different forms of relaxation, such as imagining beautiful scenes or listening to their favourite music. While these prompted a marginal shift towards the appealing alpha state, as soon as he asked the question 'Can you imagine the space between your eyes?', the EEG pen recording the brain waves immediately started to scribble the high symmetrical wave patterns that indicate a high amplitude of alpha.

Fehmi says, 'Nothing is not merely nothing. Nothing is, in fact, a great and robust healer ... space is unique among the contents of attention because space, silence, and timelessness cannot be concentrated on or grasped as a separate experience.' This immersion into empty space enables you to become whole. All your parts merge into a blissful state and you return home to the stillness of your heart and soul. Experiencing this is much more tangible than reading about it, which is why listening to your 'Love to Rise' and 'Love to Sleep' audios is so beneficial on both a conscious and a subconscious level.

× × ×

Join the Dots

ON 14 FEBRUARY 1990, a photograph of the Earth was taken from space by NASA's *Voyager 1* space probe at a distance of about 6 billion kilometres. Our entire universe looked like a speck of dust in the infinite space of the cosmos. Dr Carl Sagan, the famous astronomer, cosmologist and astrophysicist, coined the term 'the Pale Blue Dot' to describe it and this later became the title of his 1994 book. Sagan's quote from his book below perfectly captures humanity's need for perspective.

> *Look again at that dot. That's here. That's home. That's us. On it, everyone you love ... every saint and sinner in the history of our species lived there – on a mote of dust*

suspended in a sunbeam ... The Earth is a very small stage
in a vast cosmic arena. Think of the endless cruelties
visited by the inhabitants of one corner of this pixel on the
scarcely distinguishable inhabitants of some other corner.
There is perhaps no better demonstration of the folly of
human conceits than this distant image of our tiny world.
To me, it underscores our responsibility to deal more
kindly with one another, and to preserve and cherish the
pale blue dot, the only home we've ever known.

Imagine the perspective you could gain from seeing the Earth from 6 billion kilometres away! Would it change your attitude to life? From this heightened perspective, boundaries between gender, race, sexuality and religion pale into insignificance and our interdependency shines bright.

Perhaps it is time we all joined the dots between ourselves and saw the oneness in the multiple. Can you imagine truly no longer 'sweating the small stuff' or fretting over something someone said or did not say to you?

The Earth began without boundaries. Pangea is the name of the supercontinent that was the world when it was a single landmass over 299 million years ago. I believe it is time for the mass of humanity to join together, to become one, united by our love for one another and the planet.

The time has come for you to join the dots (to connect the parts) within yourself, to gently give space for all the parts of you to live under the same shelter: love. When you live as the unified self, you live in peace, at home with yourself.

We are ready now to move into the second part of the book to explore the four LOVE habits and the interviews with four well-known wellness leaders. The first habit we will explore is Listen and it is the beginning of love in action. But before that you will read my first interview, with Dermot Whelan, Irish media personality, meditation teacher, practitioner and a person I admire greatly.

LOVE INTERVIEW #1: DERMOT WHELAN, MEDIA AND MEDITATION EXPERT

Westbury Hotel Bar, Monday 6 January 2020

Ten years ago, Dermot was struggling. On the outside, everything looked fantastic. He had his own TV show, a hit radio show, and his stand-up comedy career was taking off. On the inside, though, it was very different. He was anxious, stressed, not sleeping properly and lacking in self-esteem. The only coping mechanism he had been using to handle stress was alcohol, so he was tucking into the pints to find comfort, but not surprisingly, that was not working. One panic attack and a drunken fall later and Dermot knew that something had to change.

Since 2017 I have had the privilege of working with Dermot Whelan and Dave Moore on their hugely popular radio show *Dermot & Dave* on Today FM. Dermot is one of the most uniquely talented people I have ever met. He somehow manages to be funny and profound at the same time. I was walking on air after this interview – pardon the not-so-funny pun!

Fiona: *Einstein once said of himself, 'There is a grotesque contradiction between what people considered to be my achievements and the reality of who I am' and how he privately felt. Do you relate to this?*

Dermot: I definitely relate to it because on a professional level, my job is I'm a performer and I wear a mask every day. I go into work and I literally have an on-air persona, you know, who is not necessarily me. It's an exaggerated version of myself. So I'm probably more positive, funnier, lively, cantankerous than I would normally be myself. The 'me' that gets into my car after work is a very different individual. I have found that over the years they have merged a bit more.

Our definition of success changes drastically in the decade from thirties to forties and I think this is why men and women have midlife crises. It is why I went out and bought a classic Saab earlier last year! I think you literally can wake up one day and say wow, the perceived me is the one that goes out and shuts the front door every morning but has nothing to do with the inside me and the most frightening thing is that we've no idea what the 'real me' is. It is why people go off on these mad journeys of travelling or buying cars or having an affair. They are all about people desperately trying to claw back a sense of self.

Do you find it easy or difficult to hold on to a core sense of yourself that is not identified with your ego?
I think I'm still drilling down into the space where I need to be. Because the nature of your ego and life is that you get pulled out of that serene space, you know, you have amazing intentions and some days I feel exceptionally connected to my true self or source or God or whatever name you want. And one email later I could be completely knocked off track. I don't think you can really talk about ego without looking at how we define success for ourselves. So much of what we think we want for ourselves is wrapped up in ego.

I was driving last night from Clare to Dublin in the car with my three kids and I was just listening to music and they were all sitting there quietly and I thought to myself, 'This is success, this moment is success. Not that you've managed three beautiful children and they're all going to school. It is this moment right here.' You are with people who you love more than anything and you have just realised in that moment you've got that sense of gratitude and awareness, that is success. The more open to those moments, the more able you are to soak them in, the better. It's like learning – it's like going to school to learn a new language because we have never been trained to talk to ourselves the way we're meant to talk to ourselves.

Do you believe human beings are born naturally loving themselves? You've had three kids – do you think when we come into the world do we know how to love ourselves, and when I say love, I mean to accept ourselves? There is no inner war, which leads on from that idea you were saying, about an innate trust in children.

Yeah, I think as we get older we just collect more stuff, you know, it's information, opinions, constructions, other people's perceptions, like when you walked through a bush when you were a kid and you came out with all those sticky bits all over your jumper. That's essentially life. We just get to the end of our lives with our jumpers covered. That's our garment for life.

I think in the beginning we are pretty much a clean slate. The wave analogy is one that I've always liked. I think you've used that yourself, in your book possibly, that we are all part of the ocean and then our individuality expresses itself as a wave that rises up but it's still very much part of the whole and we go through life as this wave and then the wave crashes and we've re-emerged.

I firmly believe that life itself, the purpose of us being here, is that journey away from the self and back to the self. It is the experience. We can make amazing accomplishments and strides in one lifetime or it may take us infinite lifetimes, but the journey here is to rise up as an individual wave. That's the essence of why we're here. Sometimes it's painful and sometimes it's joyful. All we can hope is that we become aware enough and don't beat ourselves up and that's kind of it. There'll be days when you forget, you know, I may be, yeah, giving a meditation talk and 10 minutes before the meditation talk I may have been full of anxiety and have veered off track, but I know that I have the tools and I have the awareness that I can help to bring myself back and if I don't get back straight away, that's okay too. That's the real thing; we're not designed to stay in a state of childlike wonder all the time. I really feel there are very few people walking around in a blissed-out state. Those people generally tend to be prophets or chancers!

What are the main reasons in your opinion why somebody would not love themselves?
It all comes down to a feeling of self-worth and for some reason feeling that you are not good enough. At some point either someone directly told you that you weren't good enough or you picked up on clues that you perceive to be evidence that you are not good enough. Or you learned that the road to success and achievements and getting on in life is a self-berating, like a dog, yeah, you know every now and again you need a good kick, or a horse you need to whip it in order for it to do what you need it to do. Certainly, in my experience. I grew up in a family where negative self-talk was almost a badge of honour, talking out loud aggressively to yourself was a sign of motivation and a sort of almost manliness or strength – you were showing that you were aware of your shortcomings. If you ever want to see how someone talks to themselves, play golf with them! It's very interesting, how I used to play golf to how I play golf now is extremely different and for me that's a great parameter. Some people will blame their surroundings, the stupid weather, the stupid grass, people who blame the things around them, yeah, then you have the 'oh my god I am an idiot' types and I was one of those for most of my life. That even if I hadn't played golf in two years I would be giving out to myself that I hadn't hit a shot like Tiger Woods. If you are a perfectionist, it will emerge on a golf course!

We can spend too much time trying to mine our inner underground to try to find the very moment where everything changed because it could be a perfect storm, it could be so many little small things and you could end up then just chasing the rabbit down the hole. All that matters is you become aware of how you are behaving and how you are speaking to yourself. And in my case I had to learn the language of speaking with love and kindness to myself.

To actually say to your heart and to your body and to yourself, 'I'm listening', and you'll find that you immediately become still and you might realise that your heart might have been pumping a bit louder or stronger than normal or you might have had a bit of an ache somewhere in your body. Our bodies are trying to give us messages the whole time. Our subconscious is trying to give us messages to actually connect and say I love you, everything's okay. I'm on your side and by the way, I'm listening.

Do you think it is necessary for people to love themselves before they can fully love others?
Yeah. I think there's different gradients. Do any of us really, fully love ourselves unconditionally? I'm in love with myself and not in a superficial kind of way. I definitely believe that the more you love yourself – the more time you dedicate to loving yourself, to showing positivity and positive feelings, not living in cloud cuckoo land, not refusing to face up to things – the more you can deeply love yourself, the more you can love someone else. But we're all at different stages on the scale and you know we may go through periods where we're quite far down that scale where we're not loving ourselves and we're bickering with people around us. And there may be times when we're feeling really good, really content within ourselves and our relationships benefit from that, but I think it's a sliding scale.

Do you see that in your own journey your relationships have improved?
Over the years, absolutely, yeah. It's not just the main players in my own personal drama like my partner, children. It's the doorman who works in the building, the girl in the shop, it's everybody you know, it's strangers – you'll find that people smile at you more or maybe you're just noticing.

A woman gave me the most gorgeous smile on the way here. She was an old woman with a woolly hat and an anorak and she just gave me this big flash of a beaming smile, that is so lovely. I then said a little mental prayer that her day would be fantastic. Never underestimate your own ability to energise someone with a feeling of goodwill.

Do you love yourself and if so, have you always?
I'm a stand-up comedian, of course I love myself! (*laughs*) I love myself, meaning that I have so much compassion for myself, even when I am getting it gloriously wrong. If I'm feeling stressed or anxious, instead of going, 'Oh my God, you idiot,' I say, 'You poor fellow!' I try to speak to myself the way I would with my kids, but sometimes I might snap but my overreaction is so short-lived now. My own dad was particularly short at times and he might snap if you sang while the news was on or something. I don't pretend I am a saint, but if I do overreact or if I am short, like if I'm packing the car for a weekend trip and I lose the rag about them jumping around, I will generally say, 'Hey, you know, sorry I was a bit short with you, I'm feeling a bit under pressure to get us all on the road. I'm going to go and do my meditation now and I'll be nice again!'

What one thing would you say to your eight-year-old self that you think they needed to hear back then?
I would put my arm around him and I would say, 'Well done for knowing what works for you, for getting out of the situation, finding your own space, keep doing that.' A big one is, don't let other people's opinions sway what it is you want to do. I was very good at impressions as a kid and as a teenager I made a demo tape which I was going to send into RTÉ because they had shown some interest and I played it for a friend and he said, 'Oh, I don't think that's very good. I'm not sure you should send that in.' And I remember feeling completely deflated and then thinking he is probably right, people who get on TV are much better than that; and it took me years to come full circle back.

Did you send it in?

No, I never did and it took me 10 years to get back into that frame of mind and do television, but that always stayed with me. You know, other people's opinions of you, they are exactly that: they are other people's opinions. Last thing ... yeah, don't eat so many sweets.

The Vietnamese monk Thích Nhất Hạnh once said that only love can save us from climate change. In essence, he suggests that if we are too consumed with our own suffering, we cannot help Mother Earth. Do you agree?

Yeah. Yeah, definitely agree. I mean, our natural environment is a reflection of how we treat ourselves. And it's indicative of the connection that we have lost with ourselves. I do think that our Celtic ancestors would have been appalled by what's happening because we had a really strong connection to the Earth because we relied on it so heavily to provide for us and we had a deep spiritual connection with the planets, the sky and the Earth.

Over time we have lost that because we were told that success was something else. It was accumulating and building big walls around your house and big electric gates. I think we're being shown both sides of the mirror at the moment and I think it's an amazing time to be alive because you have the darkness, organisations are stumbling, corruption being forced to the surface. There are so many exposés of things and people who are in positions of power. We are being handed this tray of darkness and nature is asking, 'What do you want to do with this?' Because at the same time I am showing you incredible moments of love, incredible inspirational people like Greta Thunberg. We have earthquakes, fires and we have flooding. We have all this exaggerated evidence of where we are as a human race and the options that we have. I do agree with Thích Nhất Hạnh that the journey to fix the outer us is the journey inward. The more comfortable we are with ourselves and the more empathy we create for other people and the environment around us, that's when things change. But we can't have empathy either for the Earth or for the people that we love unless we start to have empathy for ourselves.

1 You are already your ideal self. The ideal self is not perfect, it is proactive.

2 The malleable self is how you change physically and psychologically over time. However, the core of you – the Beholder – never changes.

3 Looking at the world from different perspectives will help you to unite your orphaned parts. While the external stays the same, how you look at it shifts entirely.

× × ×

The Self-Love Habit Tools

This is a gentle reminder to incorporate the following daily mindfulness tools into your every day. They are designed to be easy habit-building tools to make love your priority.

AUDIO MEDITATION

Listen to the 'Love to Rise' and 'Love to Sleep' audios every day. Record your progress in the chart at the back of this book.

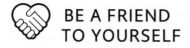

BE A FRIEND TO YOURSELF

Cultivate the voice of your inner critic to become your inner companion.

 THE DAILY PROMISE TECHNIQUE

Practise the daily promise technique: 'I promise to accept all the parts of MYSELF today to the best of my ability.' Write it down, if you have not already, on a sticky note and put it on the mirror where you brush your teeth. Repeat this promise every day and again if and when a fearful or negative thought emerges.

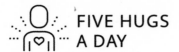 THE TWO-MINUTE MIRROR

Spend at least two minutes a day looking into your own eyes. Look beyond the physical, without judgement. Maintain eye contact until a feeling of calmness or ease emerges. This is something you can do last thing at night or first thing in the morning or both should you so desire.

FIVE HUGS A DAY

Don't forget to get your full five-a-day quota!

PART TWO

LISTEN

'*Le subconscient murmure sans cesse, et c'est en écoutant ces murmures que l'on entend la vérité.*'

('The subconscious is ceaselessly murmuring, and it is by listening to these murmurs that one hears the truth.')

GASTON BACHELARD

WHEN WAS THE last time someone really listened to you without interruption? If you shared a problem, can you recall someone listening without attempting to fix you or the situation? Did this person offer presence, not a solution?

Contrary to what you may believe, listening is a highly active skill, not a passive one. It requires both empathy and energy. Deep, active listening is, unfortunately, rare and many of us interrupt, often with the hope of making things better. However, by not giving the speaker a chance to fully say their piece and clear his or her mind, we are jeopardising the possibility that a solution may emerge organically. Frequently, we are not listening to understand, but to advise.

One of the main reasons people attend therapy is to be listened to without judgement, although the client may not realise this at first. Therapists are trained to do this and it is a real skill that can be learned to some degree. I for one am constantly honing this skill and, to be honest, am probably a better listener to my clients than I am to my loved ones.

In psychology, the closeness communication bias[40] is when we over-estimate how well the people close to us have actually understood us. We all use heuristics (mental shortcuts) to filter the avalanche of information we are exposed to every day, and the more familiar the person, the more likely we are to employ these shortcuts. With loved ones we make assumptions all the time and often only half listen, which can lead to misunderstandings and unfortunate and unnecessary disputes. For example, say a couple arrive at the airport without their passports and the stressed girlfriend says, 'I thought you said you would pack the passports!' She is probably making an assumption or prediction based on past experience because her boyfriend packed the passports the last time they went away. We often hear what we want to hear and so become complacent and make assumptions. Training yourself to listen to everyone equally will improve both your personal and your professional relationships and keep unnecessary conflict at bay. Interestingly, when someone truly listens to you, the same neural chemistry is activated in your brain as when you feel loved.[41]

Listening is therefore a profound act of love.

Someone who really, genuinely *listens* to you is showing that they care about you more than the sound of their own voice. Many of us eagerly anticipate a gap in the conversation so that we can interject with our own point of view. As the other person takes their time to get to the point, we can feel a similar impatience to when the wi-fi is bad and we see that annoying whirling circle that appears on a website that is slow to load. We demand to be heard and the reason for this lies in one of our most potent primitive needs: to belong. If we belong, we survive, and if we are not heard and acknowledged, how do we know we belong?

Painfully shy people are often mistaken for being good listeners, but in many cases they may be more concerned with how they are being perceived than actually paying close attention to what the speaker is saying.

In order to be heard, you must first listen.

Listen wholeheartedly and stay curious and present. According to the Vietnamese monk Thích Nhất Hạnh, 'Understanding is love's other name.' The soul-searching work you completed in Part One is designed to help you understand yourself and to prepare you to listen with love.

× × ×

The Self-Love Habit Tools

This is a gentle reminder to incorporate the following daily mindfulness tools into your every day. They are designed to be easy habit-building tools to make love your priority.

 **AUDIO MEDITATION**

Listen to the 'Love to Rise' and 'Love to Sleep' audios every day. Record your progress in the chart at the back of this book.

 **BE A FRIEND TO YOURSELF**

Cultivate the voice of your inner critic to become your inner companion.

 **THE DAILY PROMISE TECHNIQUE**

Practise the daily promise technique: 'I promise to accept all the parts of MYSELF today to the best of my ability.' Write it down, if you have not already, on a sticky note and put it on the mirror where you brush your teeth. Repeat this promise every day and again if and when a fearful or negative thought emerges.

THE TWO-MINUTE MIRROR

Spend at least two minutes a day looking into your own eyes. Look beyond the physical, without judgement. Maintain eye contact until a feeling of calmness or ease emerges. This is something you can do last thing at night or first thing in the morning or both should you so desire. Write the word 'Listen' on a sticky note, then place it on your bathroom mirror so that you see it each time you are doing your mirror work. This acts as a friendly reminder to practise the LOVE habit of listening.

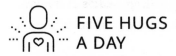

FIVE HUGS A DAY

Don't forget to get your full five-a-day quota!

LOVE LETTER #1: LISTEN TO ME

'To write a good love letter, you ought to begin without knowing what you mean to say, and to finish without knowing what you have written.'

JEAN-JACQUES ROUSSEAU

When was the last time you received a handwritten letter? Not an email or a text, but an actual letter written with pen and paper, in an addressed envelope, with a stamp and posted through your letterbox? What an effort to go to in this age of immediacy! How did receiving an actual letter (not a bill) make you feel? Most people truly love it. The effort, time and energy the writer has spent on the process equates to the level of warmth it brings to the receiver.

When I lived in Paris, I wrote letters every day, no exaggeration. Apart from the phone (not mobile), which was expensive, it was how we communicated back then (I realise I sound ancient, but I'm accepting it!). It was part of my daily routine, my therapy, and it really helped to soften my feelings of isolation. I felt very close to the people I wrote to. When you take the time to write a letter, even though you are not physically together, it can feel like you are. All your energy is consumed by the desire to connect in a way that a transient email rarely does.

Sadly, the art of letter writing is dying. Let's revive it!

My memories of coming down to my little post box in Paris and seeing a new envelope with my name on it will always remain in my heart. I could always identify the author before I opened the envelope just by the handwriting, a skill we are losing now as we rarely see other people's handwriting. Seeing your name and address written by someone you love really connects you to that person. Their energy is transported to you with each stroke of their pen.

You will write a total of four love letters, one for each habit. The first one is a love letter to yourself and it is the most important. This letter is divided into two parts and in each section you will answer five questions.

In answering the first five questions, I want you to imagine you are eight years old again. Most of us can just about recall being eight (it is clearer for some than for others), so try to tap into how you were at that age. The questions will help to spark your creative juices and once you start writing you may be surprised at how much will flow from your heart as you tune into yourself.

In answering the last five questions, switch to your adult self at the age you are now. This exercise is revealing and the insights you make can be transformative as you learn to listen to and understand yourself.

You will need at least 20–30 minutes of undisturbed time to complete this valuable exercise. Use some sheets of blank paper and a pen that you like to use. Take some deep breaths before you ask yourself the questions below. Simply listen to your heart as you write – the answers are already within you. If you can find a photograph of yourself around the age of eight, that might help; if not, a mental snapshot will work too, but do get an image in your mind before you begin. Don't be surprised if you shed some tears – I did. This is an emotional experience.

Start your letter with today's date and 'Dear Me'. Answer the first five questions as yourself at eight years old and last five as your adult self now.

1   **Ask your eight-year-old self if they are happy or sad.**
    (Listen and write their response. For example, 'I feel happy when I am skipping but sad if I hear my parents argue.')

2   **Where is their favourite place to be?**
    (Listen and write their response.)

3   **What are their favourite things to do?**
    (Listen and write their response.)

4   **What makes them laugh?**
    (Listen and write their response.)

5   **Who or what helps them to feel safe?**
    (Listen and write their response.)

Now switch to your adult self and write what you would like to say to your eight-year-old self. Write from your heart to theirs – this is an opportunity to become a parent to yourself.

6 How can you help them?
   (Listen to your heart. If you have a child, this might help.
   What would you say to them? If you do not have kids,
   then imagine a younger sibling, a niece or a nephew.)

**7 What one thing can you say that will help them to
   feel loved?**

**8 Tell them the story of what is to come in their future.
   How best can they manage the good times and the
   hard ones?**

**9 Reassure them that you are really proud of them,
   that they are resilient and strong. Tell them what is
   important and true.**

**10 If they hold on to blame and guilt for things that
   are not their fault, reassure them that it is time to
   let these feelings go. Tell them that you are always
   here and will never let them go. They are safe in
   your heart.**

*Now put the letter away somewhere safe. It is for you. It is inspiring to
read it at times when you feel vulnerable.*

What Kind of Listener Are You?

'Never miss a good chance to shut up.'

WILL ROGERS

MOST PEOPLE CONSIDER themselves to be good listeners, but this may not be true. Listening properly with presence and compassion is a skill we generally overestimate in ourselves. The science of listening helps us to understand why. Heuristics (mental shortcuts) are a protective mechanism of the brain designed to deliver the results we seek. Here's an example of how this works. Imagine that you need an umbrella and are in a busy shopping centre. The bright artificial lights, the noise of kids playing, babies crying and the latest pop song blasting out are all vying for your attention. In order not to be overwhelmed, you home in on the task at hand, blocking out all the external stimuli as much as you can, so you can exit the building quickly with your newly purchased umbrella in hand.

The same mechanism applies when we are listening to other people. We have an objective we want to achieve and we filter out the rest. Just observe a work meeting where two teams meet, each with different objectives. They bypass words they do not like, make assumptions, react and jump in, finish other people's sentences, attempt to speed people up and push others to the point quickly so they can get on with their day.

Have you ever had the experience known in French as *'l'esprit de l'escalier'*, which literally translates as 'the staircase mind' and originates from the long spiral stairwells you find in Parisian homes? It is used to describe that feeling of finding the words you wanted to say or 'should have/could have' said only when you have reached the bottom of the stairs – in other words, when it is too late. This understandable yet uncomfortable feeling can emerge when we have not been listening to someone properly. When we are actively engaged and compassionately listening to each other, the words flow more naturally when you need them, in the room at the top of the stairs, metaphorically.

On a personal level, our lack of real listening is a block to love and most of us are guilty of it a lot of the time. Much of this comes down to the simple fact that we do not know what being a good listener actually entails.

In her book *You're Not Listening*, journalist Kate Murphy, whose profession requires her to listen a lot, identifies that 'hearing is not listening'. She recommends we practise a support response instead of a shift response. By way of an example, let's imagine a friend is telling you about her recent holiday. A support response will ask them to elaborate ('Oh wow, that sounds amazing, what was the pool like?'), as opposed to a shift response, which is connected but is actually about your own experience ('I went there in 2017 and our pool was amazing').

A support response is an offer of interest in the other person, signifying that you genuinely want to hear more. A shift response brings it back to you, conveying the indirect message that you are more important than the speaker, that you are more interested in yourself than the speaker. This cuts off empathy and connection and leaves the speaker struggling to remember where they were in their story.

Can you identify with the shift response? Can you see it at work in yourself and others? Can you think of an occasion when this has happened to you? It is not pleasant and can be tiring as you need to backtrack on your story and reiterate its subject. The next time you find yourself about to use a shift response, resist the urge, allow the other person to finish and then share your experience. Your story is not more important, but is equally valid. You will feel more connected and your friend will feel genuinely listened to.

The *Harvard Business Review* conducted a listening experiment on 3,492 participants in a development programme to help managers become better coaches.[42] Contrary to what people believed to be good listening skills, it found that the top 5 per cent of those assessed displayed the following qualities:

1 They were **not silent** when the other person was talking and asked many probing questions, illustrating both that they had understood them so far and had a desire to know more. Listening is in fact a two-way dialogue.

2 The top listeners **helped** to build the self-esteem of the other person by displaying active listening skills with feedback.

3 They had a desire to help, **not to judge**, and did not use their silent listening time as a way to look for errors.

4 They offered positive suggestions **without the urgency** of trying to fix the situation.

Ditch the Digital Habit

WHEN I WAS A TEENAGER my parents put a lock on the phone to stop me and my sister making incessant calls to our friends, calls that I admit lasted hours and must have cost a fortune back then. To add insult to injury (to my parents), the lock was totally ineffective and easily picked – sorry, Mum and Dad!

My sister and I would often say farewell to our friends at the bus stop, go home and call them as if we had not seen them in years. The race to get on the phone first was part of our lives. It was fun and the connection to my friends meant the world to me; it still does. Nowadays, however, it is not just teenagers who are addicted to the phone. Most of us are, but I am not sure it is as much fun any more. Today's smartphones are not used very much for listening to one another, which was the original intention that Alexander Graham Bell had when he invented the telephone. Usage is now often less about a connection to genuine friends and more about checking social media and comparing ourselves to people we might not even know. In addition, constantly checking work emails is about keeping up, always being contactable and overachieving.

Today, there are many modern alternatives to the locks my parents put on the phone, such as apps that kick us off social media after a certain amount of time and/or that tell us how much screen time we have spent on the phone. However, they can be equally ineffective and easily hacked.

In the last few years, I have noticed in my clients, in my friends and in myself that the

level of smartphone use is one of the biggest threats to our mental health today.

Constantly checking our phones leads to dopamine overload while the lack of *real* connection is isolating, overwhelming and ultimately unsustainable. Noticing these trends in myself and after reading Marie Forleo's book *Everything Is Figureoutable*, I quit telling myself that I had to be on my phone all the time 'for work', 'because I have an online business'. Consequently, I have transformed how I use my phone and I want to help you do the same.

If you already have a healthy relationship with your smartphone, or indeed if you do not have one at all, then you are already my hero! However, if you are like most of us and want:

× More space in your mind

× A greater sense of inner peace

× To spend more quality time with loved ones

× To read more books

× To exercise more

× To be more creative

× To be more focused at work

× To have better relationships

× To laugh more

× To be more present with your loved ones

× And ...

× To become a better listener

– then developing a strategy for how you use your phone will help you to have more space in your mind so that you can listen from your heart.

The first step is to observe your phone habit as it is now. Notice how often you check your phone, where you are, the time of day and the impact it has on your peace of mind. Ask yourself what happens to you physically as you anticipate the next email or follow on social media. Is it social media, emails or news sites that you check the most? Which ones do you crave more? Observe how often the urge arises to check your phone. Do you do it in the car and/or anytime you are waiting for something, like a coffee or a bus? It is embarrassing to admit, but I lost a perfectly good iPhone to the toilet bowl once at the height of my addiction. I am not alone, as apparently one in five of us admits that they have suffered the same unseemly experience![43]

The simplest and most loving way to improve our listening skills is to put our phone away when in the company of others. Meeting a friend for coffee? Leave the phone in your bag or jacket pocket. Even the presence of a phone on the table sends a signal that we are not wholly present. Each time you pick up the phone when engaged in a face-to-face conversation, you chip away a little bit of trust within the relationship. The subconscious message is that the other person is not as important and/or that there are other people you would rather be with. If you do have to check on a child or a work situation, wait for a natural break and inform your friend or partner before you do so. Do one thing at a time. If you are having a conversation, have one. If you are on your phone, be on your phone.

Nowadays my 'digital habit' looks like this:

- ✖ 8:30 a.m. – check email and respond, check and post on social media some days.

- ✖ 12 p.m. – check email and respond.

- ✖ 5 p.m. – check email and respond.

- ✖ 7 p.m. – check social media and post on some days.

- ✖ Saturday morning – check emails and social media once in the morning.

- ✖ Sunday – no phone at all (I will talk about this more in the 'Sunday-somnia' section in the Energise habit).

I have found that this really works for me. I am much more effective at responding to people quickly and I have not lost another phone to the toilet! Could you find a similar strategy that works for you? If so, it can help to write it down on a sticky note and keep it where you can see it as a reminder. As this is a new positive habit you are creating, it does take time to become reinforced, so please be patient with yourself and acknowledge that some days it will not work due to the nature of your schedule, which may require immediate responses. If you can, try to make it your default state on most days. It will work and you will reap the rewards. Your peace of mind and productivity levels will increase massively. Having specific times for checking email clears space and time for you to focus on other aspects of your work. Show yourself the love you deserve and set digital boundaries so that you can actively listen to yourself and to others.

Listen from Your Heart

'Only do what your heart tells you.'

PRINCESS DIANA

ONE DAY, while practising a heartful-ness meditation led by the eminent psychiatrist Ivor Browne, I had a profound experience. It felt as though my heart had left my chest and I was holding it in my hands. Since that moment and with continued heartfulness meditation practice I have felt a deeper connection to my heart and ultimately to myself. Now I listen to my heart and do my best to listen to others from my heart, especially when they are upset.

Browne and thousands of people from all over the world practise 'heartfulness meditation', an Indian spiritual practice that puts the relationship with the heart as its central focus. Kamlesh D. Patel, also known as Daaji among his followers, is an Indian spiritual leader, author and the fourth in the line of Rāja yoga masters in the Sahaj Marg system of spiritual practice. He believes, 'We can master our life by listening to the heart again and again.'[44]

The 'heart-brain'[45] has 40,000 neurons that can sense, feel and offer a world of intuition. Interestingly, the heart sends more information to the brain than the other way around. These signals are sent directly to the amygdala, the alarm system of the brain, and also to the thalamus, which is responsible for transmitting signals from the spinal cord to the cerebral cortex, which plays a critical role in attention, perception, awareness, thought, memory, language and consciousness. The quality of these signals has a direct impact on your brain's ability to function and focus as well as on your mood.

In the relatively new field of neurocardiology (which studies the interaction between heart and brain), science is catching up with what many ancient sages taught: that the heart is not just a mechanical pump, but a crucial organ that communicates with your brain directly. The heart is an infinite source of wisdom, spiritual insight and emotional intelligence.

Aligning the heart and brain allows you to live in harmony with yourself and others.

Alison Canavan, the fourth LOVE interviewee in this book, introduced me to the HeartMath technique, a science- and evidence-based technique that helps people to reduce stress and anxiety. The technique trains us to self-generate heart and brain coherence, which is an optimal state for our body and mind. When our heart, mind and body are in sync, all our systems (respiratory, digestive, hormonal and immune) work coherently together. The HeartMath Institute, a non-profit organisation, has conducted over 300 peer-reviewed or independent studies using HeartMath techniques, such as breathing deeply and focusing on the warmth of a loved one, over the last 25 years. Out of a total of 11,903 people it has seen a 24 per cent improvement in the ability to focus, a 30 per cent improvement in sleep, a 38 per cent improvement in calmness, a 46 per cent drop in anxiety, a 48 per cent drop in fatigue and an impressive 56 per cent drop in depression.[46]

What seems clear is that emotions have a direct impact on heart rhythm. The two graphs in Figure 4 show the impact of negative and positive emotions on heart rhythm. The first graph (frustration) illustrates an incoherent heart rhythm, while the second (appreciation) shows a more coherent heart rhythm.

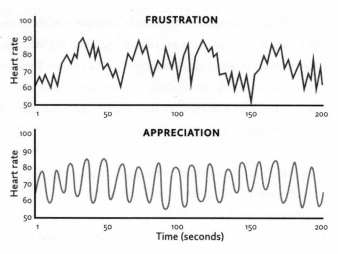

Figure 4 (*Source:* heartmath.com)

In order to create heart and brain coherence, you can self-generate heart quality emotions such as happiness, joy, gratitude, compassion and, above all, love. You can do this by breathing deep and focusing on the warmth of a loved one. Each time you listen to your audios or practise the exercises contained in this book, you are also doing this.

Scientists and doctors now know that our resting heart rate is not a monotonous beat, but it changes and shifts. When you activate your parasympathetic nervous system and the vagus nerve, you slow down your heart rate and reserve energy for when you truly need it. According to James Nestor in his book *Breath*, the most effective way to do this is slow, deep breaths – it has been shown that specifically breathing in and out of your left nostril activates the parasympathetic nervous system. A normal resting heart rate for adults ranges from 60 to 100 beats per minute.[47] Generally, a lower heart rate at rest implies more efficient heart function and better cardiovascular fitness. Some athletes have a normal resting heart rate of only 40 beats per minute.

A 2013 study in the journal *Heart* tracked the heart health of about 3,000 men for 16 years and found that a high resting heart rate was linked with lower physical fitness and higher blood pressure.[48] The higher a person's resting heart rate is, the greater their risk of early death. A resting heart rate of between 81 and 90 doubled the chance of death, while a resting heart rate higher than 90 tripled it. If, like many of us, you are not an athlete but consider yourself to be reasonably fit, you would hope to be in the region of the upper 50s to 60 beats per minute. If you would like to reduce your resting heart rate, then exercise more and manage stress with deep breathing and relaxation. The audios will help you to do this. It should be noted that smoking and excess weight are detrimental to heart rate, so you might also want to consider those if they are a factor for you. Like many things in life, it comes down to common sense and when you love yourself, you have the impulse to apply it.

THE SELF-IMPOSED PRISON

In 1959, Albert Camus, the French-Algerian philosopher, tragically died in a car crash at the age of just 46. Two years previously he had won the Nobel Prize for Literature, the second youngest recipient ever to win this prestigious award. In his moving acceptance speech, he stated,

> *Every man, and for stronger reasons, every artist, wants to be recognised. So do I. But I have not been able to learn of your decision without comparing its repercussions to what I really am. A man almost young, rich only in his doubts and with his work still in progress.*[49]

Camus's speech reveals a man who had been bestowed with one of the greatest honours in the world, yet he was consumed with self-doubt. Failing to listen and understand yourself keeps you stuck in what Camus refers to as the 'self-imposed prison'.

In his most famous novel, *L'Étranger* (known as *The Outsider* or *The Stranger* in English), the protagonist, a laconic, young Algerian man, Meursault, is so disconnected from his emotions that at the funeral of his mother, he displays no sadness. The opening line of the book, 'Today mother died, or maybe yesterday. I don't know,' captures the essence of anomie, a state of mental isolation where one feels completely disconnected from both the self and other people.

L'Étranger is regarded as an existentialist classic and a comment on the meaningless of existence. Yet Camus himself lived life to the full. He dressed and ate well, socialised a lot and had many lovers. His life was a bit like the script of a Hollywood film – it had drama, romance and a tragic ending. Therefore, on a personal level Camus accepted that while life might be a struggle, it is certainly worth living and we must be open to the joys it can offer. Camus certainly understood and experienced love. In a letter to his lover, the actress María Casares, in February 1950 he wrote, 'Tied to one another by the bonds of the earth, by intelligence, heart and flesh, nothing, I know, can surprise or separate us.'[50]

By listening from your heart and seeking first of all to understand that you are practising love both to the self and to others, you will illuminate negative thoughts and behaviours that are rooted in love but that need to change. Tune into your heart's wisdom when you need to make a decision and simply listen for it to guide you. If the conditioned mind is a prison, then your heart holds the key.

Exercise: Listen to Your Heart and Activate Heart and Brain Coherence

This short four-step exercise is incredibly powerful when you need to make a decision in your life, big or small. It will help you to literally 'get to the heart' of the matter. It is designed to tap into a deeper knowing of what is best for yourself and those who will be impacted by your decision – to trust your own instinct.

Take a few quiet moments with a pen and your journal.

✘ Write the decision in the form of a question that you need to answer, for example: 'Will I take the new job?' 'Will I go on a second date with X?' 'Will I send my child to this school or that one?' 'Will I tell my partner I want a break from the relationship?' 'Will I eat that second piece of cake?' Remember, it does not matter if it is a monumental moment in your life or something that seems small. If it raises stress or conflict, then we need to pay heed.

✘ Close your eyes. Take your gaze towards your heart and take seven deep breaths in and out of your left nostril. This will activate your heart and brain coherence by activating the parasympathetic nervous system. Take your time. Make each breath full. You can close your right nostril with a finger if it helps to block the air into that nostril. Make sure your mouth remains closed.

- ✖ Put your two hands on your heart and ask your question to your own heart. You can ask it with 'Should I ...?' or 'Is it best for me to ...?'

- ✖ Clarity will emerge almost immediately as a clear yes or no comes ringing through your mind. Just listen – there is no pressure here, but you will at least know that you have listened to the wisdom of your heart. Open your eyes and write down what comes to mind. Don't try to analyse it.

The more often you do this, the easier it will be for you to listen to others from your heart when they, too, have internal struggles.

✖ ✖ ✖

Listen to Understand

'Most people do not listen with the intent to understand; they listen with the intent to reply.'

STEPHEN R. COVEY

MANY OF US WORRY about being seen as stupid or not understanding something that everyone else appears to pick up easily, for example asking an 'obvious' question in a class or meeting. A deeper fear of being seen as uneducated or not smart enough is a common one and often stems from awkward memories of being in a classroom with the teacher singling you out to answer a question that you did not know the answer to. You may have tried to bluff your way out of it or perhaps it was painfully clear that you did not know the answer. Either way, the residue of feeling vulnerable at school can linger in your subconscious.

The Asch paradigm illustrates that the fear of making a mistake in front of our peers is so real that we may change our answer in order to conform. In the 1950s, the psychologist Solomon Asch conducted an experiment to investigate the extent to which social pressure from a majority group could influence a single person to conform.[51] Asch placed his subject in a room with a group of seven actors but did not inform the subject that the other people were actors. They were then all asked a very basic visual question: is the target line on the left the same length as option A, B or C on the right? Looking at Figure 5, the answer is clearly C. However – and this is the interesting part – when the seven actors all gave the wrong answer and were adamant that it was either option A or B, in over 12 trials, 75 per cent of the subjects conformed by also giving the wrong answer.

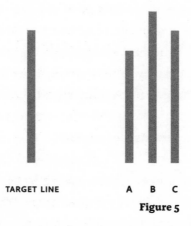

TARGET LINE   A   B   C

Figure 5

The fear of being 'wrong' is intense for many people. When your opinion is different from the group's, it is easy to fall into the trap of self-doubt.

This concern can contribute to what is known as imposter syndrome, which is relatively common and involves the fear of making a mistake at work and then being found out and regarded as a fraud or imposter. The sufferer feels that they are not good enough and questions their own abilities, thus eroding their confidence and self-esteem and giving rise to anxiety. The solution in this scenario is to actively listen to your colleagues in order to understand. Remove the focus on them being right or smart and you reduce the anxiety that can lead to imposter syndrome. When you really listen with the honest intention of understanding, you make a connection, not an assumption, and this leads to clarity.

If you do not know something or do not understand, it is important that you state this. It can take courage and confidence to do so, but honesty actually brings admiration, not criticism. In the case of the experiments conducted by Asch, many of the students, when interviewed afterwards, admitted that they did not believe the others were correct but did not want to be ridiculed for seeing things differently from the majority. Being true to yourself gives you the mental clarity to understand other people without the need to be right or to feel like an imposter.

Become curious, not critical.

Understanding is about looking at both yourself and others in the full context of life. If your partner is irritable, why is that? Instead of jumping into the defensive mode and retaliating with more negative energy, become super conscious. Take a belly breath and ask yourself what kind of day they have had. Is it possible that they are tired or overwhelmed? Are they worried about a parent or concerned about a child? Are they working too hard or having difficulties with their boss? *Seek always to understand before you engage.* After listening to your partner, it may transpire that he or she is taking out their frustrations on you, which then requires an open and honest discussion. It is more likely that a resolution can be found by proper listening followed by conversation.

Transform conflict into a conversation.

Trying to understand someone properly is like learning a new language. You need to invest time and energy in listening to their comments and colloquialisms, trying to appreciate their humour and observing their body language and behavioural patterns.

If you are experiencing difficulty in any relationship you have, it is most likely because there is a lack of understanding on both sides. You cannot control or change how a person behaves towards you, but you *can* control and change how you treat them. If you feel you are not being understood by someone close to you, first listen without judgement and try to understand them. This will aid the conversation and you can then explain your position in light of their comments. Before you can cultivate the necessary patience and energy, you must, as always, tend to your own heart and mind. You must continue to free yourself from the straitjacket of the conditioned mind.

The second habit in this book, Open, explores the importance of open speech, honesty, compassion, sexual intimacy and vulnerability (which is central to receiving love). Before addressing these issues, you will have the pleasure of meeting Roz Purcell in my second interview. She will inspire you to see the strength that lies in becoming comfortable with who you are, just as you are.

LOVE INTERVIEW #2: ROZ PURCELL

Royal Marine Hotel, Dún Laoghaire, 26 February 2020

Roz, a former model who won Miss Universe Ireland 2010, has battled with and overcome an eating disorder, one of the most difficult psychological conditions to tackle. The disorder stemmed from her hatred of her body and it wasn't until her sister was diagnosed with leukaemia in 2016 that she started her own journey to wellness.

Roz is now a best-selling cookery author and entrepreneur and has successfully launched a stellar media career. Her passion for healthy food and a healthy lifestyle, along with her authenticity and honesty, has earned her tens of thousands of followers on social media in recent years. She is now a role model for many, helping people to see past the filters of perceived perfection and into what it really means to be human, to be vulnerable.

Fiona: *Einstein once said of himself, 'There is a grotesque contradiction between what people consider to be my achievements and the reality of who I am.' In other words, he felt a divide between how he was received and who he really was. Do you relate?*
Roz: One hundred per cent. People assume things about other people. We especially do it about strangers and even with our friends we assume things. You only really, truly know another person if you live with them. I think achievements are something we are marked on. When you're describing someone, you describe their achievements and it really doesn't describe who they are. What we have done doesn't define us. I'm very separated from my past achievements.

They are not who you are?
No, they are not who I am. They are things that I went through and helped to develop who I am now, but they don't define me.

Do you find it easy or difficult to hold on to a separate sense of self that is not identified with your ego?

One of the most important things I've learned through going to counselling was losing my ego. Having such a big ego in my early twenties led to so many problems – in relationships, in how I looked at my own body and how I marked my achievements. I had to be the best at everything. I had to be the best model, I had to be the best food blogger, I had to have the best physique. I had to be the best at whatever I chose to do and that led to me not trying a lot of things, that led to me not risking for a fear of failure.

So perfectionism was an issue?

Hugely. My own ego stopped me from enjoying experiences. One of the most fundamental things I ever learned was letting go of my ego.

How did you do that?

(*Laughs*) I had a very good counsellor. I know this doesn't happen for many people in such a short space of time, but my priorities took a major shuffle. Self-awareness is a huge part of going and getting help and having that awareness changes everything.

Separating myself from having an ego and being able to look at things rationally and make decisions not based on my ego but instead asking the question, 'Is that going to give me fulfilment?' And also it's definitely made me a person who is not afraid to take risks and a person who if I get an opportunity, I don't I fear that I'm not going to do the best job at it. I'm just going to do it and give my best effort and that is okay.

Do you believe that human beings are born naturally loving themselves?

One hundred per cent. Not that I remember being a baby, but if you look at children looking in the mirror, they are touching their face or touching their belly and they're like in amazement of everything. When they are learning something new, they believe in themselves. They touch their belly and they love it. Do I think it's natural for human beings to love themselves the whole time? No, we're human beings, you know, we're going to have our ups and downs but I suppose it's being able to live with yourself happily.

In your opinion, what are the reasons why somebody would not love themselves?
I think society is the main one. I think we are conditioned to strive for one ideal body image. We are conditioned to feel like we need to be perfect physically and I think society makes us think certain things are bad, like gaining weight is bad, losing weight is good. Society is a huge factor. I think your environment growing up is another one. I think parents have a lot to do in terms of the language they use with their children. For example, if your parents don't like themselves and they pick out their flaws, you're probably going to do the same thing. Social media is a huge factor in terms of comparison. I think having the vast space just one click away and we can compare ourselves to absolutely every other person in the world, to their best photos.

Do you find yourself doing that?
One hundred per cent. I'm very positive, on social media I'm honest. And people might look at me and be like, 'Oh, you're so happy and you don't compare yourself to others,' but I do, I'm human. Sometimes I find myself on some stranger's page from a different country and I'm thinking, 'Oh my God she is flawless and she must live such a perfect life', and I can get off my phone feeling a bit grey about mine and thinking maybe if I change how I looked that would help. But then this side of me kicks in that has gone and sought lots of help and I start to rationalise. I think I'm seeing one moment of this random person's day and I don't know if this person is happy. So I'm gonna move on.

So you don't get sucked in like you once did?
No, but that has taken a lot of time.

Do you think it is necessary for people to love themselves fully before they can love others?

I can only really talk from experience, and for me, I definitely was, as I've heard you say, 'a wounded soul' for a long time and it wasn't until I really went and got professional help that that changed. I wouldn't say I loved myself but I started on the road to self-love when I met someone and I wasn't insecure.

I was ready to be present and I was ready to take down my walls and be open to the journey without any fear because I wasn't afraid of not being accepted. Everything about it was easier and you know I think at the time I was like, 'Oh my God, I just met the perfect guy, everything is so easy.' But I think I was easier to myself and I was easier to be in my own head. I felt I was worthy of being in a good relationship and treated well. I think I was just really happy and I was grateful and a huge part of relationships, I think, is being grateful for the other person. I feel like I returned to the person I was in my teenage years. I was jumping into rooms full of chats and energy, always wanting to be outside, being active, and I think that helps. Naturally I am positive. I of course have my times when I am down. I am always the person seeing the bright side of the situation or being able to flip something around. I'm practical also, like if I'm really late for something I won't get stressed about it. My dad used to say, 'It's better to be one minute late in this life than one minute early in the next.' (*Laughs*) I have really turned into an old person with all my old sayings.

Do you love yourself? And if so, have you always loved yourself? If not, why not?

I think it's really a big statement to say, 'I love myself.' I definitely am happy with myself and love myself enough not to hate myself and it hasn't always been that way. Growing up, I definitely loved myself and even as a teenager I oozed confidence. Many experiences I had growing up out-weighed anything I have done in the public eye. In my school I would go for different awards in competitions and I was not the brightest student at all but I would win them and even the teachers were surprised, they were like, 'You are really, really shit in school,' but I just went in with so much confidence.

Going into my late teens and early twenties, I lost that completely. It was a mix of adults telling me certain things about myself and then believing them and also about body image. It was a combination of being in a negative industry but also that comparing factor got worse being in a job when you are purely judged on aesthetics and just being wrapped up completely in diet culture. I think it happened to a lot of people at that age, like, late teens is when your weight can start to fluctuate. When you are a kid and eating all the chocolate, adults go, 'You enjoy that now because you won't be able to have it when you're 18.' I think it's like, as soon as you hit that age, food becomes good and bad.

But now there are days that I love myself. I'm in a really good headspace but I'd be lying if I said I was like that the whole time. I'm someone who does go up and down quite a lot. Fortunately, now I'm not like, people don't love me depending on my size. I think for a lot of time in recovery my biggest fear was people wouldn't like me if I wasn't the smaller version of myself and then I made the decision not to take other people into the equation, especially strangers.

When I am lonesome I'm not worried that other people don't like me. It's hard to explain, but when you are low, you are not thinking of anyone else, you are consumed with your own feelings. The thing that helps me to get to the other side is actually being active, so whether that's working with my hands, where, like going for a hike, doing something that makes me be present and not think about it. It's not that I'm avoiding it, but being present is the only thing that helps me to move on. Some people can meditate, I can't. For me, meditation is baking. Everyone is different.

What one thing would you say to your eight-year-old self that you think they needed to hear at that time?
I don't think it would be my eight-year-old self because I was loving myself

then. Oh my God! I would want to talk to my 14- or 15-year-old self. I found it really hard to talk to people and I didn't have any friends. I was that person who jumped from different groups because I never really fit in and people find that strange because I am very sociable now. My advice would not be for the future, but at the time not to feel like I had to fit in because being different is so unique and is going to help with whatever you do in the future because everyone wants to stand out and I spent so much of my teenage years trying to fit in and trying to just do what everyone else was doing rather than doing what I wanted to do.

I have this lovely image of this eight-year-old you and wouldn't it be lovely to say to her, you are doing everything right, you are amazing, always keep believing that?

I know. I look back on my younger self and I was doing things I wouldn't even do now. I remember I had to write this big essay about why you should represent Ireland to travel the world or something and I wrote this amazing essay and I was really bad at English! I got through to the top five in Ireland and went through more interviews and won a trip to travel to Ecuador for three months, at 14, by myself! And I wouldn't do that now. I would say my essay is not good enough. I went into the EU Parliament as a young inno-vator. I had to write an essay for that too and my teachers asked who had written it and I said, 'I did it myself!' I was just very honest. I said, 'I think most people would think that I'm probably not gonna be best suited to this because I am not the smartest kid in the classroom.' Honesty prevails and always wins above anything else.

It's the vulnerability.

Exactly, and I think it is something you lose. I became the image of what people expected me to be. I would say to my eight-year-old self, stay the same. To my teenage self, I would say don't forget who you are. I was so confident at eight I would do a one-woman show for my parents' friends. We need to empty the bucket and fill it with new ideas when we are conditioned, as we get older. I was really lucky to have a really good length of childhood with no worries. As adults we are so tired, we have so much to think about, so many responsibilities. Responsibilities are scary, it is important to balance that and not let fear outweigh them. I'm turning 30 this year, I still feel like I'm 24. I have grown up so much in the six years. I feel like age in society plays such a huge factor in how we treat ourselves.

I cried when I was 22 as I thought I was old, again at 30 and by my 40th birthday, I was so happy and knew I was actually young!
It's funny, I do feel younger now than when I was 22 or 23, as at that age I was so consumed by my image and eating disorders. I felt old inside. For me, it is constantly going to get help. I know it is a privilege to be able to afford to go and get help when I need it. I do a course of therapy every year because every year there is something new. And that is just life. Having a stranger point out what you already know inside is very useful and then giving you tools of how to manage is great.

Last question. The Vietnamese Buddhist monk Thích Nhất Hạnh once said, 'Only love can save us from climate change.' In essence, he suggests that if we are too consumed with our own suffering, we cannot help Mother Earth. Do you agree?
I think he is correct. We can be greedy and resist the need to change what's become comfortable for us. I feel really sad when I see people who have the resources not making an effort to help save the planet. I'm aware nowadays being eco-friendly in most cases is a very privileged thing to be able to achieve. I struggle on social media not to get angry with people and end up in arguments all day. When I see people online who are sharing anti-climate change conspiracies and believe it does not exist, I get that they are trying to hold on to some kind of reasoning that this must all be a mistake and that life itself isn't under threat. But avoidance and ignorance won't help.

I think Irish people are conditioned not to like to change – me included. We love a routine, but change is the only thing that is consistent in life. Nothing else is guaranteed.

Climate change needs to start at government level but that can take time, so starting with you is the quickest way to help. There is a huge amount of the population who can't make changes right now, but there are also those of us who can. Choosing to buy less, choosing carefully where and who to support, finding alternatives, being prepared, reusing, remodelling.

It all comes down to effort and a slightly slower lifestyle, one which we've strived for years to get away from. Will anyone ever execute it perfectly? Who knows? But I'll try to do what I can and have hope that innovations and collective effort will make a difference in time.

I look at kids now and think they are so lucky to be in touch with the world, yet they must hold so much worry and fear about the future. They have a mission that is bigger than themselves, which is something we got to grow up without, we just got to think about ourselves and our future. The schools movement has been incredible to follow. It is really connected to how we can unify as a species with so much energy and hope behind it. When you see people like Greta Thunberg, she is a perfect example of a child who went, 'I can do that, I can make a difference.'

OPEN

'Il n'y a pas d'oreiller plus doux qu'une conscience tranquille.'

('There is no pillow so soft as a clear conscience.')

FRENCH PROVERB

WHAT MAKES A PERSON 'open'? Is it their sense of ease, of fairness, of friendliness, of understanding, of acceptance? It is all these things and more. Above all, when you are with an open person you feel safe and you can trust that they will not judge you. Someone who is emotionally open has the courage to speak their mind, is able to have an honest conversation without entering into meaningless conflict and does not overshare. To be open is to accept yourself and other people as they are and the world as it is and not how you wish them to be.

Building from the Listen habit, where you sought to listen and understand, you are now ready to free yourself from the detrimental effect of 'shoulds', blame and chastisements. Being open to the world as it unfolds and relinquishing control of what is beyond your control allows you to enjoy life and to be naturally enthusiastic in all your endeavours. When you are eager to participate in life, you are present to it. Tasks that in the past irritated or bored you now become occasions to be open to gratitude. Developing appreciation and openness to life naturally prepares you to become emotionally resilient so that in hard times your mind will be primed to find solutions and to remain calm even in the most turbulent situations.

The Open habit is about moving gently from a state of being overly concerned about the opinions of others to one where you are entirely at peace with yourself. By non-identification with the ego, you become the Beholder and witness your thoughts, emotions and behaviours with an open, loving presence, free from judgement. If people judge you, that is their business and not your concern. By remaining open-minded you are flexible, tolerant and able to navigate through life's hurdles.

> **You cannot truly love unless you are open to acceptance, whether that is of yourself or another.**

Your confidence soars when you are truly open, honest and authentic with yourself. You have nothing to hide, nothing to fear. You provide for yourself all the acknowledgement and reassurance that you need. This chapter examines being open to honesty, vulnerability, sexual intimacy, compassion and the mental models through which you view the world. You will also write your second love letter.

✕ ✕ ✕

The Self-Love Habit Tools

This is a gentle reminder to incorporate the following daily mindfulness tools into your every day. They are designed to be easy habit-building tools to make love your priority.

 **AUDIO MEDITATION**

Listen to the 'Love to Rise' and 'Love to Sleep' audios every day. Record your progress in the chart at the back of this book.

 **BE A FRIEND TO YOURSELF**

Cultivate the voice of your inner critic to become your inner companion.

THE DAILY PROMISE
TECHNIQUE

Practise the daily promise technique: 'I promise to accept all the parts of MYSELF today to the best of my ability.' Write it down, if you have not already, on a sticky note and put it on the mirror where you brush your teeth. Repeat this promise every day and again if and when a fearful or negative thought emerges.

THE TWO-MINUTE
MIRROR

Spend at least two minutes a day looking into your own eyes. Look beyond the physical, without judgement. Maintain eye contact until a feeling of calmness or ease emerges. This is something you can do last thing at night or first thing in the morning or both should you so desire. Write the word 'Open' on a sticky note, then place it on your bathroom mirror next to the 'Listen' note so that you see it each time you are doing your mirror work. This acts as a friendly reminder to practise the habit of being open.

FIVE HUGS
A DAY

Don't forget to get your full five-a-day quota!

LOVE LETTER #2: OPEN TO LOVE

In writing this letter, choose a person you love, someone you would like to improve your relationship with. It may be someone you are currently experiencing difficulties with or have in the past. Choose a close relationship, perhaps with a parent, a sibling, a partner or an ex-partner.

Please note that you do not ever have to send this letter!

This is a very healing exercise and the relationship will benefit whether you decide to send the letter or not. The 'open' letter provides you with the opportunity to sweep away your pride and to be open to vulnerability. Through this technique, the honesty connection deepens and you will probably be amazed at what flows out once you start writing. Don't hold back!

Find at least 20 minutes of quiet time. Get a blank sheet of paper, take three deep belly breaths and use the guidelines below to help you.

1   Explain why you are writing this letter, why it is important to you.

2   Be open about your feelings concerning the relationship. Be honest – don't hold back; remember, you do not have to give or send this letter. Express all your feelings in the first person, for example 'I was hurt when ...', not, 'You hurt me.' This is a good tip for all communication.

3   Express your desire to understand how the other person feels about you. What are their thoughts about the relationship? Ask questions you may never have the courage or time to ask directly, for example 'Have you forgiven me?' or 'Do you really think I am not good enough?'

4   Express how important the relationship is to you. After all, if it was not important, you would not be writing the letter. Let your pen flow.

5   Now write down all the things you would love to hear them say to you to help heal or improve the relationship.

6   Now say those things back to them. For example, if you would like an apology, say you are sorry; if you long to hear that they miss you, say that you miss them.

7   Tell the person what you admire about them and what you are grateful for. Reminisce about happy memories and share future desires of times you would like to spend with them.

8   Finish by stating that no matter what has passed before, you love them.

Do not be surprised by the level of raw emotion that such a letter can produce. It is an amazing, powerful, sometimes hard exercise. But believe me, it is worth it in every way.

× × ×

Open to Honesty

'To be completely honest with oneself is a good practice.'

SIGMUND FREUD

SELF-HONESTY, like self-love, forms the basis of being truthful to others. If we are honest with ourselves, it is much easier to extend this out and to be honest with everyone we encounter. Many of us delude ourselves that we are not responsible for our own happiness. The discontent we feel is not our fault but is because of our job, partner, mother, etc.

Blaming others for our mistakes or shortcomings is a form of emotional dishonesty that causes conflict with those we blame and ultimately with ourselves. The problem is that we are often not even aware of this victim mentality – it is both unconscious and unintentional. However, when we are not accountable for our own actions or behaviour and seek instead to transfer blame to external sources, suffering is inevitable. The 'victim' (ourselves) feels that the world has a personal vendetta against them. Phrases such as 'Why me?' or 'Knowing my luck' are usually indicators of this unfortunate habit. Do you notice this pattern in yourself or in someone you love? Suffering becomes a way to guarantee attention and can become an addiction that constantly needs to be fuelled by fresh dramas and situations. There will always be a problem if you look for it and someone or something else is always the cause.

Such self-deception also puts an intolerable strain on many happy relationships, often causing them to crumble. A further but related neurosis is the martyr complex, where the 'martyr' will actually seek out suffering or people who do not treat them well. This then allows them to claim that they do not have a choice; they are suffering to help others. For example, a person who is in an abusive relationship but will not leave despite having the support to do so prefers to garner sympathy from others about how hard it is for them. Another example may be a mother who does all she can for her family but then complains that she has no time for herself. This evolves into a begrudging obligation and is a form of passive aggressiveness.

**The four LOVE habits require you to actively
apply them to yourself first before extending
them into your relationships.**

In order to progress and find emotional peace, it is essential to be honest with yourself. Start by asking yourself what the real motive is behind your behaviour. A client of mine – let's call him Paul – worked 12-hour days, six or seven days a week, and was on the brink of burnout when we first met. Paul worked for a charity and told himself that he had to work that hard in order to help people in need. However, the opposite was actually true – if he continued to work that hard, he would not be in a position to help anyone. Part of the problem was that Paul was afraid to delegate and allowed his ego to tell him that he was the only person who could do the job to such a high standard. Being dishonest to ourselves is a dangerous game to play and will have negative consequences – in Paul's case, burnout.

How honest are you with yourself? If you make a mistake, get irritable, blame others, cast judgements or make negative remarks, do you justify them? Do you feel that other people cause a lot of your suffering? Examples might include, 'If only my partner would listen more' or 'If only my mother was not so selfish.' Do you quickly go on the defence if you feel that you are being criticised? If so, you are not alone. Have you ever uttered the words 'he or she upset me', believing erroneously that your emotions are in the hands of someone else?

**Nobody can make you feel anything – you
choose your own emotional landscape.**

The hardest part of my job is helping people to be honest with themselves. I need to be cautious when I ask people to examine their own behaviour. As with the dynamics in any relationship, the timing has to be just right. I first need to build up a deep bond based on mutual trust and respect before I dare to enter the territory of truth and self-deception, but when this happens, and if it is executed with compassion, it can be an incredibly transformative time for the client and the therapy takes a significant step forward. A good therapist will never agree with everything you say, in the same way that a good friend will not. You need people to challenge you, to care enough to speak up.

It takes great courage to be open to self-honesty. It is usually much easier, in the short term at least, to continue with familiar patterns of subconscious dishonesty. Veracity creates solid, authentic and loving relationships that are built to last.

> 'I tore myself away from the safe comfort of certainties through my love for truth – and truth rewarded me.'
>
> SIMONE DE BEAUVOIR

Simone de Beauvoir, the long-term partner of Jean-Paul Sartre, was a feminist and existentialist philosopher whose famous book *The Second Sex* was banned by the Vatican. Like many before and after her, she found that she was losing herself in an obsessional love for Sartre. As a means of survival she created the theory of authentic love, which is similar in some ways to Alain de Botton's deliberations on romantic love (previously discussed). In essence, these are that infatuation and the romantic ideal are a mis-sold dream that ultimately cause us more misery than joy.

To love authentically, de Beauvoir states, we must offer three things:

1 **Freedom and equality:** Letting go of emotional or financial dependency on someone else and allowing that person freedom to explore their own path in life. To allow someone to be free, you need to be secure and to feel safe yourself. Let them find their own way.

2 **Be a great friend:** All through *The Self-Love Habit* I have asked you to be a great friend to yourself, but this needs to extend to all your relationships. Friends give each other space to breathe and can afford to be open and honest with one another. Hence, the relationship is one of mutual respect, trust and shared enjoyment.

3 **Share a common goal:** Having something that you are both working towards is incredibly uniting. Ideally, this might be a purpose that reaches far beyond your relationship and is for the greater good of humanity. For example, in de Beauvoir's novel *The Blood of Others*, Hélène loves Jean totally, although his love for her is not as strong until she decides to join his cause in the Resistance. When Hélène embarks on a life-threatening mission, Jean says, 'Now, nothing will separate us, ever.'[52] As a side note, I have found this really beneficial in my own relationship. A shared dream always brings people closer.

These three key points are crucial to authentic love and are mirrored in this book. It is really important to note that being honest with yourself does not mean being hard on yourself. Taking responsibility for your emotions does not mean blaming yourself for them. Rather, it provides an opportunity for you to observe and to align yourself with your heart, to be open to love and self-love.

✕ ✕ ✕

Open to Speech

DO YOU REMEMBER as a child really wanting to talk about something but holding back? For example, maybe you wanted to ask for a new bike or if you could sleep over at a friend's house. So great was your fear of the answer being no that you said nothing and/ or danced around the subject, perhaps even starting the sentence but not finishing it. That awkward feeling is familiar to me both as a child and as an adult. As a grown-up it is less about asking for something we want and more a fear of speaking our truth, having a different opinion, making a mistake or offending someone. The fear of expressing oneself is real for many of us and we can be terrified of the consequences. If we say what we feel, do we jeopardise our position or our relationship? However, what is left unsaid often causes more pain, both for ourselves and for others.

The courage to say what burns in your heart allows for authentic connection. Keeping your truth locked inside is a great disservice to yourself and to others.

My courageous clients share their innermost feelings and fears with me, but when I ask them if they have shared the same feelings and thoughts with their loved ones, they often seem shocked. 'Oh no, I don't want to burden them' or 'They wouldn't understand' are oft-repeated answers. However, the true burden comes from holding back and this can put serious strain on the relationship. Fear and tension are created each time words hang in the air unsaid. The hand that is not held, the fear that is not explained, the back that is turned in the bed all take their toll and can build a situation of damaged trust.

Having self-trust, loving and being honest will help you to find the courage to speak your mind in the moments you need it most, whether that is explaining to a loved one that you feel taken for granted or speaking up in a meeting at work. Be clear with what you say; do not be ambiguous. By being precise with your words, you build up inner trust with yourself. Choose your words carefully and honour what you say. Too often we use language flippantly – we gossip, complain or get sucked into negative spirals. It is also vital to examine not just what we say, but how we say it. While many of us may be aware of the importance of choosing our words carefully, we forget about getting the tone right and this can have a huge impact, either positive or negative. Getting it right helps the listener to feel safe and loved on an autonomic level.

THE PROSODY OF YOUR INNER VOICE

When your tone is kind and calm, people will respond to it accordingly. Knowing how you speak to yourself will help you to soften the way you speak to others. Let's examine this a bit further. The following questions will help.

✗ What tone of voice does your inner voice have?

✗ Is it high or low?

✗ Fast or slow?

✗ Is your intonation kind and patient?

✗ Is it irritable or impatient?

✗ Is it anxious?

✗ Is it relentless?

Imagine you could hear your inner voice out loud as if it were another person speaking. Would you want to spend time with that person?

When you speak harshly, what impact does it have on your family? If your tone is clipped in a meeting, what outcome does it produce? Sometimes when I am doing my best to be calm with my son (usually in the morning, trying to get out of the house on time to go to school) the words I use may be fair and kind, for example, 'Come on, love, we need to leave now if we don't want to be late.' However, it is my tone and intonation that he hears rather than the words. Read the sentence again with the emphasis on the words in bold. It changes everything,

'Come **on**, love, we **need** to leave **now** if we **don't** want to be **late**.'

Prosody is the rhythm and melody of how we speak and it provides clues to the true meaning of what is being said. When my son hears impatience in my tone, more often than not he will respond in an equally agitated tone, 'I'm coming!' In the rushed context of the morning routine, it is more likely to be,

'**I'm coming**!'

How I react to this is crucial. If it is calm and measured, then there is no bad feeling. Micro-moments such as these are common in most families, but they can create frustration and stress, which can build up over time and can erode the quality of our relationships.

> **Babies respond to prosody rather than words
> and so does your subconscious mind.**

Whether it is a mother speaking to her baby or someone having a conversation at work, tone and intonation will always have a huge influence on how other people feel about what they are hearing. If you have had an argument and you want to make things better, then pay as much attention to your prosody as your prose.

Open to Vulnerability

UNTIL YOU COME to terms with your own vulnerability (which is the essence of being human), you may live a life governed by fear and disappointment. A quick investigation into the etymology of the word 'vulnerable' may indicate why many of us do not embrace it so willingly; the Latin *'vulnerare'* means 'to wound, hurt, injure, maim'.[53] Who desires to be wounded or hurt? Who wants to feel weak or exposed? The truth is that our bodies are all fragile and vulnerable to illness, disease and eventually death, not to mention the ageing process. While one of the functions of the ego is to avoid this, the essence of who you are, the Beholder, is already at peace with how fragile life really is. On a spiritual level, this peace of mind liberates humankind to rise above physical circumstances and the inherent weaknesses of the body.

By becoming comfortable with your vulnerability, you are free to live and to love.

Imagine a page with Vulnerability = Weakness written on it. Now imagine putting a big cross over the word Weakness and putting the word Strength in its place.

VULNERABILITY = WEAKNESS

Compassion-based resilience is a concept I explored in my first book, *The Positive Habit*, the theory being that you replace pressure with kindness in order to build resilience. By using compassion you remove the pressure that the inner critic can put on you to push harder, work harder, try harder, which can actually be counter-productive. Instead, you protect your precious energy so that you have the resources to manage any situation calmly and without getting hung up on outcomes.

Those of you who have experienced loss, grief and pain will know what it is like to feel vulnerable, to be at the mercy of harsh conditions, a sick body or an abusive person. However, when you have a rich and loving inner life you are protected, safe, and you will find the resources you need to improve your external situation. Loving presence is a shield that will shelter you now and help you with the inevitable challenges that lie ahead in life.

Strength lies in the acceptance of being vulnerable.

At the time of writing this, Ireland and many other countries are in lockdown due to the coronavirus pandemic. If ever there was a time to feel vulnerable, it is now. Uncertainty is the only certainty we have. When we face dramatic change in a short period of time, anxiety is to be expected. As Viktor Frankl said in his iconic book *Man's Search for Meaning*, 'An abnormal reaction to an abnormal situation is normal behaviour.'

Perspectives and priorities have changed more quickly than a flick through Netflix. People are afraid of losing their parents and grandparents as older generations are being wiped out across the globe. It is beyond heart-breaking and while the statistics on the virus are changing constantly, they are still alarming. Isolation has become the new normal and it is only by staying apart that we unite in our fight against the virus. Threat brings us together in this individual and collective trauma – we as humankind are in this together.

Displays of love, care and compassion are abundant as people reach out to help the elderly, the sick and the homeless. At the start of the crisis in Europe in the spring of 2020, people in Italy sang from their balconies to remind one another that they were not truly alone. Many people contacted relatives they had not spoken to in years and grudges dissipated. Parents, many of whom were usually out working all day and with long commutes, now found they had more time to spend with their young children. Dogs were delighted that their owners were now almost always home. Feelings of both love and fear were palpable at this time.

How positive a person's mental health was before the virus struck is a strong indicator of how resilient they are now and how they will be going forward. That is why boosting your mental health and sustaining positive habits when life is relatively smooth is what helps you to navigate life when it gets hard.

Let's find out how comfortable you are with being vulnerable.

× × ×

Quiz: How Comfortable Are You with Vulnerability?

Answer yes or no to the following questions. I know it can be hard to be definitive when answering certain questions, so go for the answer that first springs to mind without analysing your thoughts.

1 Do you feel uncomfortable with uncertainty in general? Y

2 Do you feel uncomfortable with your mortality? N

3 Do you feel uncomfortable with the mortality of the people you love? Y

4 If you make a mistake, do you worry about what people will think of you? Y

5 Do you feel uncomfortable sharing your true feelings with your partner/close friends/family? N

6 Do you hold back professionally for the fear of sounding unprepared or stupid? N

7 Do you find it hard to try new things? N

8 Do you worry that if people saw the 'real' you, they would not love you? Y

Please give yourself one point for each yes answer you gave. The higher the score, the less comfortable you are being vulnerable. A score of more than four indicates areas that need love and attention, while a score under four shows a healthy relationship with vulnerability. Nevertheless, please note the questions that you answered yes to.

Our vulnerability is what unites us and allows us to rise above fear. As soon as you become comfortable with uncertainty, you become calm and strong, ready to embrace the world. It is within uncertainty that we find the incentive to continue to be open and excited to live. For example, imagine knowing how a film or book ends before you have seen it or read it. Would you be motivated to keep watching or reading? When someone reveals the ending, they take away the magic of the unknown. Imagine you knew exactly what was going to happen and when in your life. Would you feel excited to get up in the morning?

× × ×

Open to Sex

ONE DAY, as a child of 10 or 11, I stumbled across a copy of the 1970s classic *The Joy of Sex* in my parents' bedroom. I was repelled by the bizarre bearded man who appeared to be repeatedly torturing his 'friend' by contorting her body into shapes I did not know were feasible. Not even the strange yoga poses my mother practised looked like that! Curiosity got the better of me and I began to return often to the 'secret hiding place' where the book was hidden. I spent hours suspended between a state of horror and fascination as I sat staring at the multiple sketches of sexual positions. I was genuinely distressed by most of what I saw and also by the names of these positions, such as 'little death' and 'venus butterfly'. I even dragged various school friends in to have a look, thus shattering their innocence as well as my own. I secretly hoped that they could shed some light on what we saw, but of course, they were equally intrigued and horrified. I pondered endlessly, could people really do those things to one another? How vile. And above all, why?

Are you comfortable talking about sex? What about masturbation? Many of us cringe when these topics come up. Personally (perhaps it is the prude in me), I prefer the term 'love-making' to 'sex'. Somehow it seems more accurate, as it takes into account that mind and body are connected. However, *Love-Making and the City* does not have quite the same ring to it! We do not ask, 'How is your love-making life?' If they are going to talk about it, people generally use the word 'sex'. It is semantics; however, we need to be mindful of the connection of the heart to sex.

Both the TV show *Sex and the City* and *The Joy of Sex* manual now seem comparatively tame in a world where graphic hard-core porn is widely available. Research shows that the average age at which boys first view porn is 11 and there is evidence that some are as young as eight years old.[54] Estimates suggest that porn sites have more clicks each month than Amazon, Netflix and Twitter combined. What impact do these graphic images and films have on the role of love in sex? Is it even on the agenda?

I spoke with Dr Caroline West, a lecturer in sexual studies at Dublin City University, who recently completed a PhD in pornography and feminism. Dr West believes that it is not sex without love that is damaging to our psyche, but that sex without respect could potentially be emotionally damaging. 'When you have sex without respect, you run the risk of negative feelings afterwards, such as regret, especially if you are doing that on a constant basis without asking yourself why. You are caught in a cycle of build-up and beat-up.' She adds, 'The world of physiology and psychology through the lens of sex is often overlooked. There needs to be more research into the trauma of love, sex and respect.'

As previously referred to, the body holds on to emotions and it also does so in relation to sex. A sexual imprint, either positive or negative, is left on our hearts, bodies and minds from our past experiences. Do you know what your own imprints are? Are there unresolved issues that could be causing you physical and mental blockages? When we separate the mind from the body, especially in an intimate experience, we will inevitably struggle emotionally. Being open about sex is important. Expressing how you feel with a partner and explaining your sexual history to them could improve your love-making and bring you closer. A lot of undisclosed shame remains for people who perhaps were promiscuous in their youth. Teaching the younger generations to have a high sense of their own worth will mean they are less likely to engage in meaningless sex that is devoid of respect.

If you have suffered from sexual abuse, I am so sorry this happened to you. It is really important to seek the help of a trauma therapist to help you process the experience and allow you to heal.

Whatever your sex life is like right now, first and foremost it pays to connect to yourself. Solo sex is a wonderful way of building trust and love within your own body. Dr West believes that masturbation is an essential aspect of self-love and should be recognised as one of the most effective ways we have to relieve stress. However, due to social stigma it is unlikely to be mentioned in magazines as one of the top 10 stress busters. An orgasm releases a flood of positive endorphins that help build up the immune system and there is even some evidence to suggest that frequent ejaculation for men can reduce the risk of prostate cancer.[55]

Many women are not comfortable referring to their sexual organs, never mind touching them. In fact, it is relatively common for women not to know how their basic sexual anatomy operates. For example, it is in the vulva where the pleasurable nerve endings reside that allow a woman to orgasm; the vagina is 'just' a birth canal. Feelings of disgust about our own bodies are clearly self-destructive and can in turn cause sexual issues within a relationship. If a woman is repelled by her own vagina and does not know how to pleasure herself, it can make it difficult for her partner to do so.

Betty Dodson, now 90 years old, is the author of *Sex for One: The Joy of Selfloving* and has been teaching masturbation workshops since the 1970s in her New York apartment. Her Bodysex workshops are still running. Her website promises that these workshops are 'transformative and will help you to overcome negative body image and pleasure anxiety'. I had to read the 'pleasure anxiety' part twice. It seems a misnomer to have anxiety over pleasure, but in the context of female masturbation, it is clear that the fear is guilt. The iconic Dodson comments, 'Masturbation is a meditation on self-love. So many of us are afflicted with self-loathing, bad body images, shame about our body functions, and confusion about sex and pleasure, I recommend an intense love affair with yourself.'

Solo sex provides us with an opportunity to love our bodies and to give ourselves guilt-free pleasure. By building masturbation into your self-care routine, you will actually boost your self-esteem and relieve tension. Masturbating regularly will help you to be more relaxed and in tune with your body through experiencing pleasure and this in turn makes for better sex with a partner. When making love with your partner, if you have one, be sure to open your heart to the full experience by making eye contact. The soul mirror work will help you to have the courage to look directly into your partner's eyes.

To be open to intimacy, you need to feel safe and know that you are respected. Perhaps if someone had told me that the two figures in *The Joy of Sex* respected one another, I would have felt less terrified. On second thoughts, maybe not! Either way, embracing your sexual side will open up a deeper connection to yourself and your current or future partner.

Open to Compassion

'If you want others to be happy, practise compassion. If you want to be happy, practise compassion.'

DALAI LAMA

I ONCE GAVE a self-care workshop to a group of public health nurses who work in methadone clinics. The nurses witness desperate suffering up close every day. They see people die from overdoses, babies born with AIDS or addiction, children neglected and families torn apart by drug addiction. Despite their best efforts, they rarely see their patients get better and make a full recovery. Most nurses have an innate impulse to care for others, which is why they went into the profession, and very often they are also the carers in their families. They are the rock everyone turns to for support. They are in many respects modern-day saints, yet they are saints who often forget to care for themselves first.

Compassion fatigue is a syndrome whereby a person who is exposed to too much trauma or the difficulties of others loses the ability to feel empathy. They dissociate in order to survive. Many people in the caring professions suffer from compassion fatigue and often, to my mind, it originates in a lack of self-compassion, which in turn leads to a lack of self-care. When we do not meet our fundamental needs, we have no energy left to show compassion.

Compassion fatigue does not only affect those in the caring industries. It may be becoming a universal issue, partly because of a phenomenon known as vicarious trauma. Relentless exposure to bad news through the media is toxic and can leave even the most compassionate of us depleted and full of fear. An impending sense of doom suffocates compassion. Vicarious trauma can be hard to avoid as bad news travels fast, even when you try to avoid it. You can turn off your phone, but a friend may ask you if you heard about that shooting in … Or you go to the shop to buy milk and the headline 'Man Stabbed to Death' hits you as you reach for your carton.

Collective fear is all-consuming. This became even more evident with the onset of the coronavirus pandemic, when fear hung in the air like a thick fog. Eventually many people stopped listening to the daily death toll, as the number became just a number and meant little. It was all incredibly sad. Collective pain is a virus in itself. Without compassion, people feel hollow, like empty beings going through the motions of life.

> **When we fall out of love with the world and the shared plight of being human, we fall out of love with ourselves.**

If there is one thing you need to do, it is to be kinder not only to others but, critically, to yourself. Understanding your own private view of the world is one of the most compassionate things you can do for yourself. Be patient with yourself when you are feeling negative emotions. Give yourself permission to feel. Distress tolerance is the ability to accept emotional distress both in yourself and others. Without compassion, irritation and impatience seep into your relationships like a poison, eventually leading to arguments or manifesting as passive aggressiveness, whereby you unintentionally create an atmosphere that is far from loving.

Many people confuse self-compassion with self-pity, but they are very different. Self-pity is often about judging and blaming others and being a victim, whereas with self-compassion you take responsibility for how you feel without judging. For example, one of my clients, David, grew up with an alcoholic father who drank all the available money and left the family struggling. There was never enough money for David's football trips or new boots and his dad never came to his matches. David was understandably really hurt and carried this with him. When we first met, he was eaten up with anger and resentment towards his father. At the mere mention of his name, his body tensed, his jaw clenched and his hands closed into fists. He wanted nothing to do with his father, who at that stage was in recovery and had no contact with David or his grandchildren. We worked on moving away from the anger he held towards his father and towards developing compassion for his younger self. Gradually, while acknowledging it was hard and unfair, he came to realise that the past did not have to define him now. David was willing to work through his anger and sadness to cultivate understanding for his father, his addiction and why he had behaved the way he did. Curiosity replaces criticism and empathy softens blame.

Compassion-focused therapy was developed in the early 2000s by psychologist Paul Gilbert. In his book *The Compassionate Mind*, Gilbert writes, 'When we give up blaming and condemning ourselves (and others) for things then we are freer to genuinely set sail towards developing the insight, knowledge and understanding we need to take responsibility for ourselves and our actions.'

Carl Jung, the Swiss psychiatrist and psychoanalyst, believed that 'visiting the shadow'[56] within ourselves would help us to see the goodness in others. Jung suggested that those individuals who do not know or come to terms with the darker sides of their psyche are more likely to see only bad things in other people. Things that are disgusting or horrible are 'in the other' and never 'in the self'. Again, this is a characteristic of victim mentality and narcissism.

How good are you at recognising your Shadow Self (Part B)? The following 'parts therapy' exercise will help you to recognise your Shadow Self and then to show it compassion.

✕ ✕ ✕

Exercise: How to Show Compassion to Your Shadow Part

Internal Family Systems (IFS) was developed by psychotherapist Richard C. Schwartz. It is a model that identifies, explores and helps our multi-layered parts. Schwartz was a family therapist before he developed this model and used his knowledge and experience of families to develop it by drawing a comparison between the various roles in a family to the internal parts in an individual.

According to IFS, we all have multiple parts and when any of these parts becomes exaggerated, for example through trauma, multi-personality disorder occurs. Schwartz believes that each part of us is good and has natural talents and resources, but that the 'younger' parts can become frozen in time when their role is no longer necessary. For example, the part of 'fear' in a child who had to protect themselves from a parent's anger is redundant when they are an adult living in a loving home.

Our goal is not to get rid of these protective parts, but to enable transformation and to let go of the unnecessary burden they carry. As Richard Schwartz says in his audiobook *Greater Than the Sum of Our Parts*, 'Most of the world's problems arise from this misunderstanding about parts and burdens. When you assume the part *is* the burden, it makes sense to go to war against it, and when you go to war against parts, you go to war against people.' In other words, we must make peace with the parts of us we do not love in order to live in harmony with others.

The following steps are based on one of Schwartz's IFS exercises. They will help you to put into practice the idea of loving the more vulnerable, darker parts of yourself.

Take seven deep belly breaths and work through the following steps with your Shadow Self/Part B in mind. You can do this mentally, although I recommend doing it with your journal. The first three steps involve helping the different parts of you to become more easily identifiable.

1   **Locate where in your body you most feel the Shadow Self/Part B**. Is it in your chest? Stomach? Throat? The muscles in your neck and back?

   ✗   Is the **Shadow Self/Part B** carrying anxiety, stress, fear, doubt, anger or sadness right now? Be as specific as you can to name the emotion it is holding.

2   Concentrate on **staying with the physical feeling.** This takes courage, but it is the very thing that will help to ease the **Shadow Self's/Part B's** discomfort.

   ✗   Become quiet inside so that you can get closer to the **Shadow Self/Part B** *without the distraction of the outside world.*

   ✗   Breathe into the part of your body where it exists.

3   **Visualise** them.

   ✗   What does your **Shadow Self/Part B** look like? How does it hold itself? Is its head low, shoulders stooped? What energy would it bring into a room?

- ✗ If you can't visualise it, don't worry. What is it like to be in its presence?

- ✗ If it were a colour, what colour would it be?

- ✗ How well do you know it? Is it familiar to you?

4 How do you **relate** to **Shadow Self/Part B**?

- ✗ If there is acceptance and empathy, you can move to the next step.

- ✗ On the other hand, is there resistance towards it? If so, this is common. Do you wish it would go away or did not exist at all? Do you find it hard to have compassion towards it? If so, it is likely that a reactive (protective) part is standing in your way. Imagine asking that part to step back for a moment. For example, if you feel frustrated towards Anxiety, imagine asking Frustration to step back just for a moment. (The IFS model explains that parts often mirror family members that we do not feel safe expressing ourselves fully with. So this is like asking your mum or dad to step out of the room for a moment so that you can speak directly with your therapist.)

- ✗ It is important that you ask for and receive the permission of the protective part to give you some space just for a few moments.

5 Get to **know the part better. Become curious, not critical.**

- ✗ This builds the relationship between the Beholder and the **Shadow Self/Part B**.

- ✗ In his audiobook, Richard Schwartz says that some useful questions from the IFS model to ask are: 'How did it get this job, for example being the anxious part?' 'How effective is the job?' 'If it didn't have to do this job, what would it do?' 'How old is it?' 'How old does it think you are?'

'What else does it want you to know?' Apply the Listen habit here, listening with the desire to understand, not to fix or change. Remember, no pressure. I find it helpful to listen to my heart. The answers emerge naturally.

6 What is the **Shadow Self/Part B afraid of?**

   ✗ What does this part want for you? You may find that this is in line with what the Beholder/Part A (self) also wishes for you: to be calm, safe and happy.

   ✗ What would happen if the **Shadow Self/Part B** stopped doing this job?

7 The final question to ask is: 'What do you need from me in the future to **feel valued**?'

8 To finish, show the part compassion, gratitude and love.

   ✗ Now that you have got closer to it, extend your appreciation towards it and thank it for the weight it has been carrying all these years. Reassure it that your love for it is unconditional and that you are there for it any time it needs you.

Now shift your attention back to the external world. Any insights you have made from this exercise are really worth making a note of.

Soothing your Shadow Self is a profound internal shift, while opening to self-compassion is a habit that needs to be practised and built upon daily. Please notice and acknowledge when you choose to be kinder to yourself and others. Soak in compassionate moments and see them for what they are: precious shifts forward in the Self-Love Habit.

× × ×

Open Your Mental Models

I WENT TO A WELLNESS conference in London with a friend not so long ago. At the start of the weekend, my friend suggested that by the end of the weekend we offer the other a piece of well-intentioned advice about one thing we felt was limiting them. Believe me, I was on my best behaviour all weekend! What could possibly be limiting me? However, when we were back in Heathrow waiting for the plane back home, my friend said, 'It would really help you if you started to use more than just one or two mental models to look at the world.' 'Mental *what*?' I asked. I was aware of the principle but had never consciously considered applying it to myself.

A mental model is a subjective algorithm. It is a conceptual framework that can be applied to help solve problems and to aid decision-making. Most of us are probably not aware that we are applying a mental model right now and that these are often unconsciously inherited from family, society and our education.

Once we have an established mode of reasoning we tend to stick with it, even if it is holding us back.

For example, when raising children or managing staff, the incentive model is often used. This is based on reward and punishment – do well and you will be rewarded, but do something wrong and you will be punished. However, I know from personal experience that it is generally not fruitful to punish children, as it does not usually get the desired results, whereas rewarding effort, not results, does. Learning a new mental model provides you with a fresh outlook and opportunity to make better decisions and solve problems faster. Applying a new mental model can also help us to simplify complex situations.

Below I have identified four of the most established mental models that you can apply to your own life when making a decision or solving a problem.

'THE MAP IS NOT THE TERRITORY'

This phrase, coined by the Polish-American scholar Alfred Korzybski, distinguishes between what is real and what we believe to be real. No matter how detailed a map is, it does not capture the exact reality of the landscape. No matter how well you try to recount an experience, you cannot convey it exactly as it happened and someone else who has had the 'same' experience will most likely give a different account.

> **While the reality of a situation does not change, the witness's experience and understanding of it does.**

Have you ever read a book twice with a gap of several years in between? You may have felt that it was like reading a different book the second time around. The book has not changed, but your perception has. When we believe that the map is the territory, we make assumptions and apply principles that worked in one area to another. An example might be a pushy salesperson who always uses direct sales tactics; while this may work with certain clients, it does not with others. The ability to keep an open mind and not make assumptions is incredibly beneficial in finding solutions to problems and in not judging yourself or others. Falling prey to 'all or nothing' thinking can be very limiting. Someone who says 'I never feel self-confident' is projecting this into situations where he or she may actually be an expert and self-confident. The map is not the territory and your thoughts are not reality.

FIRST PRINCIPLES

First employed by Aristotle and now practised by Elon Musk of Tesla fame, the first principles model[57] is one you may want to employ if you wish to be a visionary in your field and your community. The basic premise is that just because something is 'known' to be true does not mean that it is true or that it is the only truth.

Elon Musk notes, 'The normal way we conduct our lives is we reason by analogy ... [With analogy] we are doing this because it's like something else that was done, or it is like what other people are doing. [With first principles] you boil things down to the most fundamental truths ... and then reason up from there.'[58] Musk used this principle to reduce the high cost of battery packs when designing his first SpaceX rocket. Refusing to accept the accepted norm that they cost $600 per kilowatt-hour, he discovered that he could get the materials (carbon, nickel, aluminium, polymers and a steel can) for $80 per kilowatt-hour and make his own batteries. As a result, he revolutionised the energy industry. Just because something has been accepted as the status quo for generations does not mean it always has to be like this, nor does it mean that the accepted method is the best or only way.

Consider how you could apply the concept of first principles to your own life. Always stay open to new ideas or ways of doing things and, above all, keep questioning. Persevere like a child who constantly asks 'Why?' until you get a satisfactory response.

SECOND-ORDER THINKING

Usually when we make a decision we consider the first consequence of our actions, but rarely do we go beyond that and think about the second, third and fourth consequences. If we fail to use second-order thinking, we can unintentionally create more problems than we had to start with. For example, if you are hungry, first-order thinking is all about solving the immediate issue. Eating a doughnut solves the problem in the short term, but eating doughnuts regularly has the potential to create serious health issues. Similarly, taking medication to solve one set of immediate problems can create more problems later on when the side effects start to show. Incorporate this powerful mental model into your life when making any decision, big or small, by pausing and then asking yourself what the consequences will be in 10 minutes, 10 months and 10 years.

Be sure to consider the impact of your decision on everyone involved, so ask the same three questions and imagine what it might be like from their perspective, for example choosing a school for your child that they do not want to go to. In 10 minutes they may hate you, in 10 months they may love the school and in 10 years they could have the benefit of a great education and lifelong friends. We can only do our best at the time of making any decision, but when we apply this model we take all the likely consequences into full consideration. Again, I find it useful to tune into my heart before asking the three questions.

HANLON'S RAZOR

Despite its harsh-sounding name, this is an incredibly compassionate tool for building close relationships. It was devised by Robert J. Hanlon and the basic premise is: 'Never attribute to malice that which is adequately explained by neglect.'[59]

The razor is metaphorically used to cut through the various levels of intention behind a person's behaviour. The concept asks us to consider if there is another valid reason for someone's behaviour beyond that which is immediately apparent. For example, if you wave at a friend in the street and they ignore you, you might conclude that they are annoyed with you and begin to fret about it. However, the truth may be that they simply did not see you. When you apply this model, you automatically give people the benefit of the doubt and are less quick to judge. It is especially helpful if you are overly concerned with what people think about you and often jump to conclusions.

Each of these four mental models shares a common principle: to remain open-minded and curious. Let's look at how we can apply this to the roles we identify with and use to judge others.

× × ×

Open to No Roles

IN HER BOOK *True Refuge: Finding Peace and Freedom in Your Own Awakened Heart*, Tara Brach, psychologist, Buddhist and meditation teacher, tells a story of a couple who bring their two kids to a restaurant on Christmas Day. Their youngest son happily calls out, 'Hi there,' from his highchair to a scruffy-looking man who is waving at him. The parents, judging the man to be a vagrant alcoholic, cringe in embarrassment as the man shouts, 'Hi there, buster, I see ya,' while the other diners look unimpressed at this disturbance. The atmosphere grows still more awkward as the man and boy continue their joyful exchanges and reaches a high point when they both start to sing 'patty cake, patty cake' and play peekaboo. The mortified mother tries desperately to distract her son and even turns his highchair away, to his loud displeasure. Eventually, the father, unable to deal with the chilling glances from the other diners, takes charge. Without waiting for the family to finish, he pays the bill and takes his older son out to the car. As the mother makes to leave, her baby son puts his two hands out to the man to be held. The man looks at the mother to see if this is okay, but before she even has time to answer, her son plunges forward into his arms. The man is so touched and with tears in his eyes he says to the mother, 'You take care of this baby. God bless you, ma'am, you have given me my Christmas gift.' The mother mumbles something in return, but with her head hung low, her only thought is, 'My God, my God, forgive me.'

One of the most profound and practical ways to achieve a state of peace and oneness with yourself and with others is to look beyond their adopted role, position, identity and social status. It takes practice to be able to look at a person and no longer judge them by their job or because of their appearance, as in the story above. Everyone, from the president to the person who serves you coffee, is entitled to respect and should be treated equally.

Being patient and understanding that many people are under pressure will help you to build and sustain harmonious relationships. Next time a bossy, ill-tempered security guard barks orders at you as you stumble through airport security, trying to remove your shoes and belt at the same time, smile and thank them. They have no personal desire to delay you but are likely to be under pressure themselves. You can make a difference and lighten their day. Don't take things personally.

Your ego may fight hard to hold on to the roles you have defined for yourself, seeing this as part of your identity. You may have worked hard to attain this role by, for example, studying and hard work and therefore you may feel that you can justify this role. Roles are not just identified with what you do for a living, but also within your family and social circle. Typical roles include the nurturing mother, the authoritative father, the always-available friend, the dutiful daughter. The roles we play are often unconscious and conditioned into the fabric of our personalities, yet, as we discussed in the introduction, they are not who you are.

Practise not defining roles for family and friends and you remove expectations too – for example, your mother is then no longer rated and judged on her maternal qualities. If you are a parent, can you stop regarding yourself as the 'all-knowing' figure? A child or teenager is often far better at identifying what they need. Young people generally have an innate ability to look at the world more simply; often it is adults who complicate things. Without roles, you begin to appreciate your loved ones in a new light. For example, you may find that your father is actually highly amusing rather than the serious, overly concerned parent you had previously believed him to be.

From this place of openness in our truth, honesty, speech, intimacy and compassion, we glide into our third LOVE habit, Value. Before we get there, though, my next interview is with Dr Rick Hanson, internationally celebrated psychologist and *New York Times* bestselling author who sheds a fresh perspective on many of the concepts in this book.

LOVE INTERVIEW #3: DR RICK HANSON

Zoom video conference, Monday 2 December 2019

Although Dr Rick Hanson grew up in a loving home, he was very young going through school (he started young and also skipped a year). Hanson says in his TEDx Talk that this 'combined with my shy and seriously dorky temperament – you know, skinny, glasses, picked last for baseball, the whole thing – led to lots of experiences of being put down by the other kids in school'. Many of us can relate to this.

Today, Rick Hanson is a psychologist, senior fellow of UC Berkeley's Greater Good Science Center and *New York Times* bestselling author. He's been a speaker at NASA, the universities of Oxford, Stanford and Harvard, and meditation centres worldwide. His books are available in 29 languages and include *Neurodharma, Resilient, Hardwiring Happiness, Buddha's Brain, Just One Thing* and *Mother Nurture*. His work has also been featured on the BBC, CBS and NPR.

Fiona: *Einstein said of himself, 'There is a grotesque contradiction between what people consider to be my achievements and the reality of who I am.' In other words, he felt a divide between how he was publicly perceived and how he privately felt. Do you relate to this statement?*
Rick: (*Long pause*) No.

Can you expand a little?
If I understand it right, you are raising the question of two disconnections. The first kind of disconnection is between our surface persona – our act – and the true self deep down inside. The true self, the false self, it's a classic distinction. There is a term I like from bodywork called 'sleeve' and 'core'. The sleeve is the external superficial presentation, and then there is the core of who we really are. So that is one kind of disconnection, and there could be a conflict between the false self and the true self.

Then there is the second kind of disconnection between the world's view of a person, let's say as very accomplished and worthy, alongside the person's internal view of themselves or sense of themselves. (Your *view* of yourself is your self-esteem, while the *sense* of yourself is self-worth.) So there can be a distinction between how the world sees you and how you feel about yourself deep down inside. I don't know exactly what Einstein was referring to, but it seems that this distinction is a common one and many people suffer from it. I would say for myself, when I was young these two distinctions were very relevant for me. My surface presentation was capable, rational and self-controlled, yet inside there was a lot of mess, not so nice. Also, when I was younger I would be praised for my achievements, especially at school, but deep down inside I still felt inadequate, so there was that disconnect as well.

Then over time, one of the greatest healings of my adulthood has been to gradually reduce these two kinds of disconnection. For example, I've tried to have the courage over time to lighten up about it all and be more willing for the messy innards to be more visible. I've also tried to let go of reactivity to the approval of the world; it can still happen, but it's gotten a lot, lot better.

Do you find it easy or difficult to hold on to a separate sense of self that is not identified with your ego?
I think that word 'ego' is really important to define very clearly and concretely. Otherwise it becomes a placeholder for a whole bunch of fuzzy ideas that expand and contract. The point for me is not semantics, but I want to know we are speaking the same language.

I agree. Perhaps it would be clearer if I said, do you find it easy or difficult to hold on to a separate sense of self that is not egotistical, because when I said ego there I mean it in the conceited sense.
I think that the identification with our persona, our act, is a big source of suffering for many, many people, and it certainly was a source of suffering

for me. In many ways, the purpose of practice is to come home to who we really are, our true nature. Awareness, wakefulness, lovingness, a kind of quiet joy and inner peace, calm strength, clear seeing, stability ... these are all personal attributes that people talk about when the war is over, when the noise stops, when they are no longer divided internally or feeling like they are running on empty. And so as we practise with meditation and other things, such as mindfully washing one dish at a time, we gradually train our bodies, our nervous systems and our brains and therefore our minds to become increasingly rested in ourselves as a *whole*, and less iden-tified with any part of it – including the egoic parts of ourselves.

Thanks for the clarity. Do you believe human beings are born naturally loving themselves?

What do you mean by loving yourself?

Well, it starts with the acceptance of the self, that is the beginning, then it is the sense of having that unity that you spoke of, that presence, that ability to feel that you are at one with the world, the universe, the ability to connect to others, that ability to see yourself as a valuable human being rather than to self-loathe. Do you think when we are born we have this innately and it is later on through experiences that we start to lose that ability to accept and to love ourselves?

Right, well (*pause*), just as a sidebar, I have found that people vary in the notion of loving themselves, including myself. I love my wife, for example, she is over there, I love her, that is part of what makes it work. As soon as I think of loving myself it means to turn myself into an entity that I am separated from, so I would say that loving myself, I don't feel that, I don't use that language, and I am not trying to talk you out of anything. But when you say acceptance, absence of self-loathing, absence of self-scoring, shame, guilt, being undivided, feeling whole, compassionate, tenderness for oneself – that is real for me. A sense of being a muscular ally for oneself, like I want to stand up for myself the way I would for another person, that all rings true.

In terms of infants, newborns, I think that what you are getting at is what is the natural condition, before we are disturbed or driven from home in one way or another or deformed by life? I think the natural condition of life is to be whole and to engage the world and be adaptive because that is Mother Nature's plan. From the beginning, children are vulnerable and open, they are eager to be lovable and they are loving themselves. I speak as a child psychologist. We are naturally lovable. In pure biological terms, children evolved in part to be lovable since that promoted their survival. In effect, Mother Nature's plan is for us to be very lovable in our core. In the hours, months and years of life children very rapidly internalise how the world treats them, so if the world treats them with dismissiveness or punishment or neglect – well, then they acquire the sense that they are not good, that they don't matter. They acquire certain acts that comprise the false self to enable relationships to occur with caregivers to keep them alive. So some children develop the act of being stoic and self-sufficient, otherwise their caregivers punish them for wanting too much. Other children develop the act of presenting themselves as being needy because that is how you keep the caregiver involved, and along the way there is an internalisation of what it feels like inside when you feel like you don't matter to other people, they don't care or they are critical of you, you are a bad boy or a bad girl and you take that in. All this is a kind of learning that is laid on top of our natural condition.

*What is/are the main reason(s), in your opinion, why somebody would **not** love themselves?*
As I understand it, you are asking: What gets in the way of a person really accepting themselves wholly and being compassionate to themselves, really appreciating their skills and talents, and being strong on their own behalf so that they think their life matters enough to stand up for? People vary in how resourced they are in those regards, people's life conditions sure make a difference.

First, the internalisation of how other people see us can have huge effects, shaped by individual differences. For example, some children are naturally more sensitive in their disposition, they can be more affected for better or worse. There are also large-scale macro factors, such as being someone in America who is a person of colour being discriminated against, being a woman, sexual orientation, how you look, being a child who's overweight in school or who has some kind of birthmark on their face that people make fun of. There could also be little support at home or at school. What matters is both the presence of the bad and the absence of the good.

And then I'd like to call out something here that is really important: an absence of growing. In other words, we are affected by the world for sure, but then the question is, *what do we do about it*? Some children and some adults become more resilient over time because of efforts they make in their own minds. Your sense of being, what it is like to be you, can gradually be healed and uplifted over time.

And the realisation for that ...
To be clear, I am in no way trying to minimise the impacts of the world or the weight of a person's medical issues. I am speaking to one of numerous factors that can get in the way of someone loving themselves: a lack of effort on their part to heal and release feelings of shame or worthlessness and to grow self-compassion, self-respect and self-worth.

Or a lack of awareness, support, knowledge ...
Yes, this is true. But even when there is awareness, etc., does the person persistently try to help themselves to grow and change over time? I'm focusing on something hopeful, that we can slowly but surely nudge our minds and our lives toward resilient wellbeing. Of course, I am not saying this to 'blame the victim'.

No, no, of course.
To put it bluntly, if someone says in mid-life, 'Well, I am not very fit, I weigh 10 kilos more than is good for me, I smoke cigarettes all day long,

I drink a lot of beer every night.' If that person wants to be healthier, there are things that person can *do* to be healthier. Much in the same way, if a person wants to feel more whole and adequate and have more of these aspects of loving oneself, then the opportunity is there to make little efforts each day that add up over time. And there is an inescapable personal responsibility for one's own life. Whatever happened in the past, still, every day a person can develop these qualities of self-love, as you put it, for their own sake and that of others.

Lovely, thank you. Do you think it is necessary for people to love themselves before they can fully love others?
No ...

Okay.
The tricky word in that question is 'fully'. There are many people who are loving towards others, they feel love and act loving ... yet also feel ashamed of themselves. They are anorexics of the heart. They don't take in the food of love for themselves, they deny it to themselves; they are capable of being loving to others without kindness to themselves. There is a cliché that we can't love others unless we love ourselves, and I just think that if you look out in the world there are many examples of this not being the case. Now, I think it is true that people can become even more loving if they increase their sense of loving themselves, with a sense of your own underlying inherent goodness, accepting yourself fully, feeling undivided, recognising your own virtues and talents and having compassion and being there for yourself. For example, as people increasingly accept themselves, they're usually more willing to accept others. I wouldn't put it in the frame of it's binary, you can love others or you cannot love others. People who do not particularly love themselves can still be very loving towards others. That said, when you love yourself in the ways you've talked about, you are going to have a lot more to give to other people.

Do you love yourself? And if so, have you always loved yourself? If not, why not? And we are back to your interpretation of self-love.

My earliest, earliest memories and my sense of myself deep down is a very palpable sense of a sweetness. I haven't always been able to stay in touch with this, but when I do, there is an inherent sweetness or goodness that moves the heart towards care and tenderness and appreciation. Perhaps it is a kind of loving oneself to bring awareness to an underlying sweetness and wakefulness and kindness deep down inside. And you can also relax self-criticism and open yourself to self-acceptance. These are the kinds of things we can practise.

That is, growing.

Yes. One key point, and I think you said it earlier, is loving yourself more is the result of two kinds of things: growing the flowers of self-acceptance, self-compassion and awareness of innate goodness ... and also pulling the weeds of self-criticism, self-scorn, self-loathing; you can let go of the heavy stone of shame. So if you ask me are you more able to love yourself over time, I think there are two aspects to it: one is harm yourself less, the second is love yourself more, and both are important.

Lovely, thanks, Rick. What one thing would you say to your eight-year-old self that you think they needed to hear?

Honestly, what rose in my mind and what would have been particularly useful for that kid, I would say, 'Dude, you are going to become quite a badass.'

(Laughs) He would have liked to have heard that, I think.

I was very young going through school so I felt shy and weak, like an outsider, so it would have been great then to have heard something like, 'You are fundamentally a warm, nice, conscientious person – and there is also a toughness in you and an independence and creativity and an undefeatable core in you that you can trust.'

Wow, I think every eight-year-old needs to hear this, Rick.

I guess so. I sure did. I'd add if I could to that kid: 'You've got some hard years ahead and you need to be smart about these bigger kids that you don't have the wherewithal to do battle with now, but deep down inside, you are strong and you are going to be okay.'

And the final question, Rick. Vietnamese Buddhist monk Thích Nhất Hạnh once said, 'Only love can save us from climate change.' In essence, he suggests that if we are too consumed with our own suffering, we cannot help Mother Earth. Do you agree?

I have a little saying for myself: recognise complexity, act simply. So when I hear a simple, clear statement from a great teacher, Thích Nhất Hạnh – that 'only love can save us from climate change' – I think there is truth in it. For example, loving our grandchildren, being horrified by what we are doing to the Earth they will live in. Loving the poorest third of the population on the planet that is going to be terribly harmed by climate change. This is love, loving each other enough.

But to be honest, it is also anger that can save us from climate change. I think most people are not angry enough or disgusted enough about what certain business interests such as the petroleum companies and their lobbyists and legislators are doing to our world. Human activity sends about 100 million tons of CO_2 each day into the atmosphere; in effect, we have been sending our excrement up into the sky, and the consequences are already raining down upon our heads, and will keep coming down for many generations to come. We are in the middle of a slow-motion emergency that is gradually accelerating. Do you know the book *Drawdown* by Paul Hawken?

I don't.

Check it out. Basically, if the human species said tomorrow we are going to deal with carbon emissions in a real way, aimed at quick results, we could make changes over the next 10 years. We could plant trees, shift technologies and stop businesses from freeloading by pushing the true costs of their business activities downstream onto the rest of us. There is a key term, 'externalising costs', such as when someone throws their own trash out the window for others to clean up. For example, the oil companies push their costs out into the world while keeping the profits for themselves. It's a kind of cheating to dump messes that are your own responsibility onto others to deal with. That is selfish, immorally selfish.

So I believe that we need to be angrier, we need to be out on the streets about this. Anger is not hate. We don't have to hate the people doing this, but we have to understand they are making so much money every day, why should they stop? They don't care, they are going to send their kids to air-conditioned schools in Switzerland or British Columbia, they don't care.

As a small point, sometimes we hear people saying that we need a new way of talking that is not divisive, that doesn't blame anyone, that involves a higher level of consciousness that transcends all differences, we just need to love each other, etc. I am wary of this because soothing sentimental rhetoric can be a refuge for progressives who feel helpless. It gives them the comfort that they seem to be doing something by adopting a new lingo. But actually what we need is fierce action – non-violent, of course – that imposes costs, real economic costs on carbon producers and real political costs on their enablers and allies.

Regarding climate change, the most consequential thing that people can do for the world is to help elect Democrats in America. Alone among all the world's democracies, America is the only country in which one major political party – Republicans – largely denies climate change due to human activity! To have America rejoin the Paris Accords, to respect science, to break the stranglehold of the oil companies on our government. That is what is going to change things, that is the kind of action that we need to take. We are in the middle of a crisis. We need to love ourselves enough to say fuck this, this sucks, this is insane, we *must* change and we must change immediately.

And that is the point, that when people are so consumed with themselves and their own suffering they just don't care – from the very simple things like putting the plastic in the right bin, they don't have the concept of care, it is irrelevant because they don't value themselves.

That is right. I am really glad we spoke, Fiona, I learned things speaking with you.

Well thank you, thanks so much.

Your project is great. I honour it, I encourage you to keep going. Don't let people like me who are generating certain complexities interfere with your straight shot. You have a real feeling for it. Trust that inner feeling you have for this topic, you are on good ground. Go the Irish!

(Laughs) Thanks, Rick. Thanks for your support. It means a lot.

VALUE

'*L'appréciation est une chose merveilleuse, elle fait que ce qui est excellent chez les autres nous appartient aussi.*'

('Appreciation is a wonderful thing, it makes what is excellent in others belong to us as well.')

VOLTAIRE

THERE WAS ONCE a strict Zen monastery where each monk had made a vow of silence, but there was one exception to this rule: every 10 years, the monks were allowed to utter just two words. After spending his first 10 years in complete silence, one monk went to the head monk to say his two words. 'What are the two words you would like to speak?' asked the head monk. 'Bed ... hard,' said the monk. 'I see,' replied the head monk.

Ten years later, the monk came back again. 'It has been 10 more years,' said the head monk. 'What are the two words you would like to speak?' 'Food ... stinks,' said the monk. 'I see,' replied the head monk.

Yet another 10 years of silence passed and the monk once again met with the head monk, who asked, 'What are your two words now?' 'I ... quit!' said the monk. 'Well, I can see why,' replied the head monk. 'All you ever do is complain.'

This story makes me smile. While there are many ways to interpret it, for me it is about two things: one, the lack of value and appreciation that the monk gave to his life; and two, the lack of value he gave to himself. I feel empathy for him, as he must have had 30 years of listening to the complaints in his mind; the head monk only had to listen every 10 years. If you are not happy about something, do not stay silent. When you fail to value your own worth, you will also not appreciate all that life has to offer. In this case, the monk found fault with his surroundings, his fellow monks and himself, but he did not appreciate being alive, having the opportunity to meditate and pray, nature and probably many other things.

Take a moment and consider what it is like *not* to be valued, not to acknowledge yourself or to be acknowledged by others. It is, of course, deeply painful. Many children and teenagers feel this if they are not part of the 'in crowd': their jokes go unheard, only to be repeated by someone else more popular a few moments later and met with peals of laughter.

An unheard voice is one that suffers.

To be unseen by others can lead to loneliness, which in turn can lead to depression and anxiety. To value and appreciate yourself is to value life itself. In this chapter, we will examine the importance of valuing other people's reality, trusting in yourself and in your own lovability. We will also look at the true value posed by life's challenges and hard times.

× × ×

The Self-Love Habit Tools

This is a gentle reminder to incorporate the following daily mindfulness tools into your every day. They are designed to be easy habit-building tools to make love your priority.

 AUDIO MEDITATION

Listen to the 'Love to Rise' and 'Love to Sleep' audios every day. Record your progress in the chart at the back of this book.

 BE A FRIEND TO YOURSELF

Cultivate the voice of your inner critic to become your inner companion.

 ## THE DAILY PROMISE
TECHNIQUE

Practise the daily promise technique: 'I promise to accept all the parts of MYSELF today to the best of my ability.' Write it down, if you have not already, on a sticky note and put it on the mirror where you brush your teeth. Repeat this promise every day and again if and when a fearful or negative thought emerges.

 ## THE TWO-MINUTE
MIRROR

Spend at least two minutes a day looking into your own eyes. Look beyond the physical, without judgement. Maintain eye contact until a feeling of calmness or ease emerges. This is something you can do last thing at night or first thing in the morning or both should you so desire. Write the word 'Value' on a sticky note, then place it on your bathroom mirror next to your 'Listen' and 'Open' notes so that you see it each time you are doing your mirror work. This acts as friendly reminder to practise the habit of valuing.

FIVE HUGS
A DAY

Don't forget to get your full five-a-day quota!

LOVE LETTER #3: VALUE LOVE

In this letter, your third, I want you to choose someone you love, feel close to and admire (a parent, sibling, partner, your child or a good friend) who has helped you in some way, big or small. They may not realise the positive impact they have had on your life, but they will be thrilled to receive your letter. As you write, observe the positive emotions that physically flood through your system and soak them in for maximum neuroplastic positive change. This is a task to really enjoy and you will feel amazingly close to the recipient after you have written it. As always, let it flow and come naturally. Please be sure to give this letter to the recipient.

GUIDELINES FOR THE LETTER

1 Tell the subject that you are writing to them to let them know how much you value them in your life.

2 Explain why you value them and what it is about their character that you are most grateful for.

3 Be specific. Think back over your lives together and choose moments when you feel they have helped you the most, when you have had the most fun together or special times you have had.

4 Finally, ask them what you can do to help them. Is there anything you can improve on in the relationship that would help them to feel safer or more valued? Above all, you want them to become aware of how deeply you value them and your relationship and that they can trust you to be there for them to the best of your ability.

× × ×

Value Others' Reality

THIS IS a highly beneficial exercise that I do with my clients to help them when they are feeling undervalued or taken for granted. It asks you to see the world through the eyes of the person who you feel does not appreciate your efforts. Often this can be with the people closest to us.

Let's use an example to illustrate how this works. Jane (name changed) works full time in a demanding role and is the main breadwinner in her family. Her husband is studying for a master's degree while also minding their three school-going children. Jane comes in from work tired but delighted to see the kids and although she would love to have time to play with them and to relax, she needs to help with the dinner, the chores and getting the kids to bed. Jane is frustrated, as she does not understand why the chores can't be done before she comes in; after all, her husband has had all afternoon at home. She feels he does not appreciate how hard she works or how guilty she feels being away from the kids all day.

I asked Jane to put herself in her husband's shoes and talk me through his day from the moment he wakes up until he goes to bed. It is essential to use the first person in this exercise. For example, 'I wake up at …, I have my breakfast,' etc. Again, being specific is very important. When you imagine the life of another person through their eyes, you begin to value all that they do and you begin to truly appreciate them for the effort they make. This exercise can be done with any relationship: an unruly teenager, a distant mother, a worn-out husband. As you look at the routine of their day, imagine what challenges they face and the impact this has on their feelings and energy levels. When I worked with Jane on this, she soon realised the pressure her husband was under to try to get enough time to study amid the busy afternoons as he picked the kids up from various activities. In fact, he was often home just before her. Thinking of all the school runs, the preparing of lunches and the supervising of homework, she began to value all that her husband did more and started insisting that *he* take a break! Needless to say, their relationship improved.

Please do this exercise with the people in your life regardless of whether or not you feel as if they take you for granted. Either way, you will have more understanding and as we know, that is always a positive.

✕ ✕ ✕

Value Trust

> 'Just trust yourself, then you will know how to live.'
>
> JOHANN WOLFGANG VON GOETHE

IMAGINE THAT your mind is like an orchestra and all the parts of you play different instruments, for example Fear is the violinist. An orchestra in sync is one organism, one symbiotic being, each player, each part present and attentive to the others. The Beholder presence is the conductor and both the strong and the vulnerable parts need to trust the conductor – you – to lead them to equanimity. Without a conductor an orchestra will produce a cacophony, but with one, something truly beautiful emerges.

The conductor is only absent in the moments, hours or even days when you drift away from being fully conscious to the moment.

You have unintentionally abandoned your integral location as the centre of awareness and have got caught up with the individual dramas of these multiple players. The conductor is giving the violinist all his attention and is not focused on the integral wholeness of the orchestra.

Our conductor going AWOL happens frequently to all of us. However, the second you notice that you are no longer present, the conductor returns. It is simple and hard at the same time. Once you have established the habit, the easy bit is gaining awareness; the hard part is trusting it. This is a slightly tricky concept to explain on paper, so please bear with me. I have included this concept in the 'Love to Sleep' audio that will, through experience, help to cement it for you. Essentially, once you become aware, you need to create a space from the thoughts that come with being aware.

For example, let's imagine someone called Katie is reading this book and is really engaging with the process. She is becoming more aware and, as a result, more loving. Observe Katie's thought processes after she bumps into a friend.

Katie's internal dialogue: 'It was nice to bump into Sarah. She is lovely, but why is she always complaining? I feel drained now. I could have done without that. She is so negative and she never once asked me how I am!' When Katie becomes aware of her thoughts, she says to herself, 'I shouldn't think that. I am being judgemental. I am supposed to be loving.'

In this example, Katie's awareness becomes just another voice to reprimand herself with. The thought is present that Sarah is always complaining and maybe that is true. Instead of feeling guilty for thinking this ('I shouldn't think that. I am being judgemental'), it is much more helpful to simply notice it. Becoming aware does not make any of us saints. We will all continue to have negative, unloving thoughts, but we can *choose* not to identify with them.

Being aware is enough in itself if you have a judgemental thought. Do not judge the thought. Observe it with compassion and it will dissipate in its own time. In other words, be kind to your own inner critic.

Making self-trust a habit takes time and energy, but the investment will pay off for the rest of your life. It is incredibly reassuring to know deep down in your heart that you can trust yourself to take care of your mind and body. You can then trust yourself to manage the chaos of life and to maintain loving relationships. You can trust that your own divine goodness will shine through in all your actions, that you are able to cope in the hard times and that you respond to life with presence and with love.

TRUST THAT YOU ARE LOVABLE

Have you ever given someone a hug and it felt stiff or awkward? It is not a great feeling for either party. In many cases, though, it may not be a rejection as such but simply that the person is uncomfortable receiving love so openly. We love others by allowing them to love us back. Knowing your own value and that you are indeed lovable is paramount to the success of the Self-Love Habit. It is easier for many of us to give love rather than to receive it and yet the natural flow of giving and receiving is essential for true love to flourish. When you give love and unconsciously block it being reciprocated, you can undo the good you have done. A good indicator of how lovable you feel is whether you find it hard to accept affection, compliments or gifts. Underneath such discomfort lies the belief that you are not good enough to receive them. Remember, having self-worth is not the same as having a big ego.

Receiving graciously is also an act of love.

In any healthy functioning relationship the energy must go back and forth, just as in a real conversation. This was previously highlighted in the Listen habit.

The roots of feeling unlovable are often deeply embedded in the formative childhood years (from birth to five years old). If your need for love and attention was not met at that stage, the painful imprint can remain in your neurochemistry. If you felt rejected often as a child, it is likely that your amygdala, the fear centre of the brain, was overstimulated. Memories of coming second to your parents' other needs or being ignored are recorded and are then sent out as a warning in any context where you predict similar hurt or rejection. The problem is that our brains often misinterpret situations so that we transfer earlier rejections from a parent to a partner later in life. So what can we do about it?

You can train yourself to feel lovable and valued.

Philip Shaver, professor of psychology at the University of California, and his colleague, Jude Cassidy, have expanded on John Bowlby's seminal 1958 attachment theory, which highlights that humans are predetermined to form attachments with their caregivers in order to survive. Shaver and his colleagues conducted further research that shows that when we prime our brains to feel safe by consciously recalling people who love us and intentionally holding on to the physical warmth of being loved, we can shift our neural networks to feel love more easily.[60] This is something you are doing each time you listen to the Self-Love Habit audios.

In addition, it pays to become hyper-aware of the micro moments of love every day and soak them in: the warm smile, the cup of tea, the lift home from work, the hand on your shoulder, the light-hearted text from a friend, the concern in someone's voice when you share a moment of vulnerability. If moments such as these are not available to you now, can you recall times in your life when you did feel loved? Also look for examples of love in your environment: your neighbours helping each other, parents hugging their kids, young couples kissing.

Open your eyes, your heart and your soul to the love that already exists in your world. Love is bountiful. It is everywhere.

To build on this, take a moment to do the following short exercise, which will support the work you have been doing on a subconscious level with your audios.

× × ×

Exercise: Wiring Your Brain to Feel Lovable

With consistent practice, applying positive, self-directed, neuroplastic training techniques, such as those I learned in my training with Dr Rick Hanson, will help to rewire old neural networks, like those associated with feeling unloved, and create new networks in which you feel lovable.

It helps to write down your thoughts when doing this exercise, but do it now. Do not defer it. This work is important.

The person you choose for this exercise does not have to be living. For example, I often choose my Aunty Lally, who passed away 30 years ago. It can help if you have a photograph of this person, but if not, a mental image works just as well.

- ✗ Bring to mind a person you love.

- ✗ What is it about them that you love? Be specific.

- ✗ Imagine them with you now.

- ✗ What is it like to be in their presence?

- ✗ Can you imagine the sound of their voice? What would they say to you if you were feeling anxious or sad?

- ✗ Pay attention to the physical sensations of being in their loving presence.

- ✗ What does it feel like to be valued, to trust that you are loved? Remain with this if it does not come immediately.

- ✗ Can you believe that you are as lovable as anyone else?

- ✗ Imagine what happens to them when you accept their love, when you surrender to it.

- ✗ Can you see how important it is to them that you accept their love?

- ✗ Soak in the mutual feeling of love for as long as possible.

- ✗ Take your hand to the place in your body where you feel this love (it is usually the heart).

Value Trust in Relationships

HAVING TRUST in all your relationships is crucial to emotional wellbeing. It is likely that at some point you will have experienced a breakdown in trust and although it can be regained over time, it takes considerable and conscious effort. This is equally true in a romantic relationship, in a family or in a friendship.

Esther Perel, a couples therapist and *New York Times* bestselling author, is known for her open and humanistic outlook on infidelity. She says, 'We need a new conversation and a new approach (to infidelity) that is more caring and compassionate for those who have experienced it.'[61] She highlights that frequently those who are unfaithful are not serial philanderers or narcissists, but have been in committed relationships for 10, 15 or 20 years. They often do love their partners but have lost the ability to show it and as a result they do not feel it and the relationship grows cold through familiarity. Perel also highlights that responsibility is the enemy of desire and that many couples in a long-term relationship find it hard to maintain a thriving sex life. Shared chores like sorting laundry or discussing the best life assurance policy to take out are not exactly conducive to erotic activities.

Perel also notes that after suffering the experience of infidelity, many relationships become much stronger and happier than they had been previously. The fault lines in the relationship that were being ignored are restored and love moves to a deeper level, where each party values the other.

Feeling and displaying no remorse in the case of discovered unfaithfulness makes it very difficult, if not impossible, for the romantic relationship to survive. It is essential when rebuilding trust that each party takes full responsibility for their actions and the consequences of them. This is true not only in the world of sexual infidelity, but is crucial to the success of any relationship. If a parent shouts at a child, they need to first acknowledge their actions and then apologise. If a child lies to a parent, they must admit their deceit and say sorry. If you have ever experienced a child admitting to a lie before you find out about it, you know that you are much more likely to be compassionate and the lie loses impact because of the subsequent honesty and bravery in admitting it.

> **The true damage to many relationships is less about the harm we do to one another in the heat of the moment and much more about the denial of the act afterwards.**

Feeling safe and valued are essential components in building trust, which might require you to adapt your behaviour towards others. For example, on the face of it being consistently late for social appointments may seem trivial, but for the other party it can be a big issue, especially if they suffer from social anxiety; they may feel that you do not value and respect them enough to be on time. Having the consideration and respect to send a quick message if you are going to be late will go a long way to reassuring and maintaining trust.

Value Challenges

'Real love is one that triumphs lastingly, sometimes painfully, over the hurdles erected by time, space and the world.'

ALAIN BADIOU

Simone George and Mark Pollock are a couple who have already endured more tests to their relationship than most of us will have to face in a lifetime. Simone is a human rights lawyer and activist and Mark, who sadly lost his sight aged 22, was an adventure athlete and is now a motivational speaker. They first met when Simone was teaching Mark to dance.

Mark says, 'When you can't see, there is something beautiful about the connection of dancing with someone in your arms. The fact that she is stunning isn't really relevant because I can't see her, but people tell me all the time how elegant and stylish she is. What attracted me was her perspective on the world, where she came from and the places she travelled. Her curiosity and passion.[62]

At that time, Mark was competing in ultra-endurance sports and was the first blind person to race to the South Pole. One night in England, four weeks before they were due to be married, Mark fell out of an open window – two full storeys. The friends who found him thought he was dead. Mercifully, he was not, but he had fractured his skull, had massive internal injuries and broken bones and had suffered a spinal cord injury. The doctors said that what movement and feeling he did not regain in the first 12 weeks he was unlikely to recover at all.

In the days just after the accident Mark questioned if living, blind and paralysed, was worth it. He also believed it was best that Simone get as far away from this as she possibly could, not for his sake, but for hers. But she refused to leave. Simone explained to me, 'I had the absolute privilege to be able to help save somebody's life, to help ease suffering for someone who had already gone blind and had to go through tragedy again. It was appalling. So painful. I couldn't just say, "This is really awful for me, I'll just pack my bags and go home." And what would I be doing at home, except thinking of him, of us? This thing had happened already, both our lives had changed utterly. Leaving him and this horrific situation we were in wouldn't have changed anything. It wouldn't stop me loving him.'

Since then the couple have worked on bringing people together to try to cure paralysis. This work led to a pilot study combining robotic legs with electrical stimulation of the spinal cord. Mark was able to recover some function and they are working to bring these therapies from university labs to those who need them most.

Their acceptance of the situation, not the doctors' understandably limited prognosis, coupled with their hope and determination, shows us that it's worth sticking in there. As Simone says in their TED talk, 'Acceptance is knowing that grief is a raging river. And you have to get into it. Because when you do, it carries you to the next place. It eventually takes you to open land, somewhere where it will turn out okay in the end.' If you would like to hear more about their incredible story, you can watch their TED Talk, 'A Love Letter to Realism in a Time of Grief'.

While most of us are not faced with such a challenge to our relationship, many of us do unintentionally give up on love, especially romantic love, far too easily. We can be quick to personalise what is not personal by being over-sensitive, defensive and quick to judge. Such behaviour often stems not from malice, but misconception (remember Hanlon's razor?). Pushing someone away before they have a chance to hurt us often ends with us hurting ourselves. Challenges in any relationship are not reasons for abandoning it, but rather are opportunities to deepen understanding and grow together.

> **Many perfectly viable loving relationships are cut short, which is a tragedy for love.**

I love all my clients, almost from the first consultation. I love them because I have the privilege to see the very parts of themselves that they so desperately hide from the rest of the world, the parts they fear will cause people to reject them. My faith in the goodness of humanity is high because by revealing their vulnerable selves, my clients enable me to help them. It is perhaps deeply ironic that when you show your full self to another, they love you more, not less.

Loneliness, which may be defined as an absence of meaningful relationships, is now a global epidemic.[63] Japan, with its ageing population, has a word specifically for old people who die from loneliness: '*kodokushi*'. In 2018, Britain appointed the world's first minister for loneliness, Tracey Crouch.[64] This was a response to a 2017 report that indicated that over 9 million people in Britain admit to feelings of loneliness.

Being lonely puts us at risk of high blood pressure and increases our chance of premature death by 45 per cent, with an accompanying 64 per cent rise in dementia.[65] The stress of being lonely increases cortisol, which causes inflammation, meaning our immune systems act to prioritise bacterial rather than viral threats. Learning to deal with the challenges in our relationships and so avoid loneliness is an act of survival.

Without loving bonds, we stagnate and eventually wither and die.

In *Lost Connections: Uncovering the Real Causes of Depression and the Unexpected Solutions*, Johann Hari writes that 'loneliness hovers over our culture today like a thick smog'. He disputes the commonly held belief that depression is caused by a chemical imbalance in the brain, arguing that depression is a perfectly understandable protective reaction to today's disjointed society where many people live disconnected lives. In many cases, community life has broken down on a societal level and this is one of the true reasons for increased levels of depression. In addition, Hari argues that the transient nature of employment today, with a zero-commitment policy to workers in many cases, leaves many feeling undervalued and with no sense of agency over their own lives.

A lingering feeling of being dispensable is toxic to our sense of self-worth.

Hari provides examples of the collective economy, where people dispose of hierarchies and band together to create communities where each individual is valued. These range from a housing project in Berlin to a group of gardeners in London to a group of bike mechanics who share the profits from their business equally. If coming together in pursuit of a common goal is so incredibly beneficial to our emotional, physical and mental health, why don't more of us do it? Why does it appear that Western societies in general are moving in the wrong direction?

In his book *Loneliness: Human Nature and the Need for Social Connections*, John Cacioppo, a neuroscientist and world expert on loneliness, believes we need loneliness to bind us together. Loneliness is a wake-up call to the importance of love. We are less likely to take each other for granted when we feel the pain of absence. It pushes us to consider others and to show that we care for others as much as we care for ourselves.

> **Loneliness, like hunger, is a signal that we need to respond to.**

Cacioppo scanned the brains of chronically lonely people and found that when they were shown pictures of people in distress, the visual cortex in their brains lit up with less activation in the areas of the brain that show empathy. Therefore, the more time we spend disconnected from others, the more easily we feel threatened. The result is that instead of pursuing friendships, we avoid them. The skill of reading social cues becomes rusty and an awkwardness develops. Being cut off from others often eats away at our sense of self-worth and when we value ourselves less, we hide away more.

If you feel lonely – and we all do sometimes – the challenge is first to acknowledge it (remember, the daily promise tool encourages you to accept all the parts of yourself). Secondly, gently guide yourself into situations where you may feel uncomfortable at first, but be aware that as you are primed to expect rejection, you will be quicker to go on the defensive. Knowing this will help you to lower your expectations of others and communicate with more ease. Valuing imperfection will help you to accept people as they are without pressure or intensity in your communication. It is also easier if you find a way to contribute and help others that also has a social aspect, for example if you are a parent, join the PTA; if you love sports, join a team; or volunteer for a charity that requires you to work in a group.

When I first began to write this book, it was a different world from the one we find ourselves in now – the term 'social distancing' did not exist. For many, physical distancing has strengthened empathy and emotional connection to the wider community. When we are all faced with the same challenge, like a global pandemic, there are two common responses:

1 React with fear.

2 Respond with love.

The coronavirus has provided the world with an opportunity to awaken to love. This 'opportunity' does not for a moment diminish the desperate sadness of the situation, especially if you have lost a loved one, but it can make it more bearable. We must find meaning in unavoidable suffering, otherwise it is truly tragic. This principle is explored in my final interview with the inspirational Holocaust survivor Tomi Reichental, who is a living example of this.

Please continue to listen to the audios and as you progress through the book you will begin to notice tender moments when you choose to value vulnerability and trust in the inherent goodness of yourself and others.

You are ready now to move on to the fourth and final LOVE habit, Energise. This one is my favourite – even the anticipation of it causes me to smile and feel full of joy. Life is energy. In the next chapter, you will learn to embrace forgiveness and allow your beloved Beholder to guide you with life-affirming energy though your life.

The penultimate interview is with Alison Canavan, international motivational speaker, transformation coach and author, who is truly full of loving energy. Be inspired and energised!

LOVE INTERVIEW #4: ALISON CANAVAN

Zoom conference call, Dublin–California, Wednesday, 6 May 2020

Alison Canavan spent 20 years on the catwalks modelling for some of the most famous designers in the world. However, behind her smile lay crippling depression, anxiety and addiction. She was immersed in the material world of worth: fashion and beauty. Despite being on the cover of numerous magazines, she still felt worthless. After years of study and a true journey of going inwards to heal from addictions, depression and anxiety, Alison has turned her life around and motivates thousands to do the same around the world. In 2019, Alison and her young son left Ireland to start a new adventure in America.

Fiona: *Einstein once said of himself, 'There is a grotesque contradiction between what people consider to be my achievements and the reality of who I am.' In other words, he felt a divide between who he was publicly and how he privately felt. Do you relate to this statement?*

Alison: Yes. I don't think you can but relate to the statement because we live in a world where we're not taught to connect with our authenticity when we're young. We're indoctrinated into a world of conditions first of all – conditioned thinking, conditioned habits, conditioned behaviours – and we're also taught to people please from a very early age. Do as you're told, show up a certain way, and when you tick all these boxes, then you'll be acceptable for society. And that's where people can get lost really, really early on.

A prime example for me was going into the modelling industry. Jesus, no one cares about what you have to say. And it really is just a world that is determined by your looks, you know, by how you show up physically every day. There's a difference between looking at someone who is beautiful and someone who is beautiful and shining from the inside out. There's a difference in the energy that comes through someone's eyes.

What I've learned over time is that we have been disconnected from ourselves at a very early age and we've been disconnected from our ability to imagine our life, which is done through a heart-centred connection. So I see the heart as being a portal, as being a door, and we actually have to connect with it each and every day and we have to open that door. That door then gives us access to parts of ourselves as yet undiscovered in a lot of people's lives. We get indoctrinated in a school system where our mind becomes the master and we have to try and figure out and solve all our problems, as you know, from the very place that created them: the mind.

Do you find it easy or difficult to hold on to a core sense of yourself that is not identified with your ego?
Yeah. These days, I absolutely have a great sense of myself. That is years and years and years of consistent hard work and it's daily. I don't start my day without connecting with my heart, without doing my heart-centred practice, doing my decrees, my praying. I live very differently to the way I used to live before and it's interesting – it's only the other day I said to a friend, 'I can't remember the last time I said something really nasty to myself.' That's huge.

That's lovely.
For someone who spent 20-odd years in modelling, never, ever, ever, ever uttering a kind word to myself. I mean, I always felt less than … I never felt good enough to be doing what I was doing. I always had this sense of anxiety. I felt like an outsider, do you know, that imposter syndrome?

And bit by bit, just practising the different techniques and tools that I have every day and leaning in to meditation and really kind of allowing myself to trust by opening my heart and allowing myself space to heal over the years as well.

Understanding that we're all born worthy of living an amazing life no matter what has happened to you. I truly believe that for everybody now. I don't wake up in the morning and look in the mirror and turn myself off the cart, and go, 'Look at your skin today. You look wrecked.' I live in the real world, where I'm like, 'Oh, God, your skin is a bit this,' but it's not in the debilitating, harsh, horrid way that I used to behave towards myself.

I really value myself. I really take care of my body. I really appreciate this life. I really appreciate this body. I feel deeply grateful today to be alive, to be happy, and I don't take it for granted, even for a second. I one hundred per cent believe that that is available for every single person if they so choose it. Every single person. I do.

Do you believe human beings are born naturally loving themselves?
I do. I think that children do know who they are, and I think we condition them away from that. I also believe, though, that a lot of kids are born with trauma through the birth process itself. Children need happy attachment and when they don't have that they can experience those traumas. So there are pieces of us that move in to help protect us from a very early age, but I do believe that ... our true nature is one of unconditional love.

What are the main reasons, in your opinion, why somebody would not love themselves?
Trauma, life experience, parts of them that shut down, a sense of deserving. We're not taught that. We're taught that we live in a limited universe with limited resources and limited abundance. It's a lie, and we're all taught that from birth, that there's not enough to go around. That's not true.

So we start to play within these kinds of limited worlds that we've been taught. I work with people all the time who have put down in their vision statement, 'I want to make three thousand dollars a month, just enough to pay my bills and afford my shopping.' I'm like, 'So you don't think you deserve to go out at the weekend or have a holiday?' Why do so many of us think we are only worthy of just surviving and not thriving?

So you can dream as big as you want to, but you never outperform your self-esteem. But you can increase your self-esteem.

Also, people always come to me and say, 'Oh, Alison, I can't manifest.' And it's like, 'But you're trying to manifest a dream that you're not an energetic match to.' So we're down in the lower vibrational emotions of guilt and shame, which Irish people have in abundance, by the way. We're born with it. We can't have it all and by that I mean that you can't have lack and abundance at the same time because they live on different frequencies. It's like you can't listen to 98FM and FM104 at the same time, they are on different frequencies, so you must choose one.

It's intergenerational, really.

If we don't resolve it, it gets passed down through our DNA. It's like I always say, it's like a film. It's like those old films strips that we used to have, and [if] we were to play it back over the years, it's playing out the same movie in a different way.

We need to decide to change that. What does the word 'decide' mean? The word 'decide' comes from the Latin root *'decidere'*, which means 'to cut away from'. So to cut away from the old to bring in the new. So we're cutting away from our old film, our old movie reel, and we're creating a new one. What you're doing then is you're creating a whole new way of being for the generations that are to come. So it's breaking generational patterns and it's healing itself.

Trauma doesn't have to be abuse or a car crash. Being part of a big family and your mum having kids very soon after you and you not getting that full attention, you experience that as trauma as a kid. We are a product of our pain and if that pain is not resolved and we don't allow ourselves to heal, then we start to live out our pain. Hurt people. The first person that you hurt is yourself, so not allowing yourself to go inwards and do the work and really show up for yourself each and every day creates these recurring passions in your life, and that's what creates the victim mentality.

Your point on childhood trauma is important. So many people think, 'Oh, my childhood was absolutely fine,' and once you start talking to them, you really start to see, 'Well, how was that from a child's perspective? Was it really fine?' The pain is buried deep.

If anybody ever says to me, 'Oh, my God, I had such a perfect childhood ...'

It's alarm bells.

Nobody's perfect and if we're a human being and we're breathing, we come across issues. I often say to people, it's not about pointing fingers or saying someone's to blame because everybody's doing the best with what they have. When your parents lost their job and it caused great stress within the family and you didn't have much money for a while, that's trauma. You experience that as trauma as a child, but that doesn't mean someone's to blame.

Do you believe it is selfish to look after your own needs first?

No, it is not selfish. I think it's our responsibility in this life to be the best that we can be. It's our birthright but it's also our responsibility. It's our birthright to live the life of our dreams and what I say to people is ... When people struggle with this whole selfish thing, I always say, 'There's a five-point rule that I would put dreams and tests through,' and one of the questions is 'Is there a point in this for others?' That's a question most people don't ask themselves. And that's an aspect of self-care, because we're emerging in a world where self comes first, and that's different from service to others. So, self-care with the primary goal of service to others is a completely different energy, a completely different consciousness and a completely different dimension and universe we're living in. We're moving out of the paradigm of service to self. You know, somebody said to me, 'Oh, yeah, but I mean if I'm looking for the love of my life, that's not really service for others.' And I'm like, 'Is it not?' If you're creating a beautiful, loving relationship that is serving humanity and operating at a high inspirational level, and you're inspiring others that they can have this, that is service to others. And the person you're going to get into the relationship [with] is going to benefit from it also! It's like a domino effect. I always say to people, 'Yeah, self-care is really important, but you always have to hold [on to] your dreams and make sure they align with your values and ethos that is there good in this for others.'

What's the base of it all, the foundational basis? Don't harm your-self and don't harm others. Are your actions each day harming anyone or could they harm anyone? If that's the only question you ask yourself, you'll probably be in alignment with natural law because as soon as you take an action that harms others, you're now out of alignment with your-self and with your authentic self and your true nature.

So, I think that's what we're beginning to learn and that's what's beginning to emerge at this time. We've been indoctrinated into a world where it's like, 'Look after yourself first of all costs.' You know, 'Me and my family come first.' That's not who we are as human beings. There's enough of everything to go around. There's just an unfair and unequal distribution of it and those decisions are made by other people.

Do you love yourself, and if so, have you always loved yourself? And if not, why not?
Yeah, I do, I really love myself now. I really just appreciate everything I have put my body through. And I just take care of my body so well now. I really treated myself so appallingly for so long, it's a miracle. Even my family says, 'We're going to put your body in science when you're done!' It's incredible what we're capable of doing when we abuse it so badly, but we're extraordinary beings and our bodies are very forgiving, and we can really go in and do that healing. You know the way people say, 'I've done so much damage, the damage is done.' That's just another excuse.

What I've learned is that each and every one of us deserves to feel amazing, we really do. Why not you? I always say to people I'm coaching when they tell me a story or whatever and they say, 'I just can't, I wish I could,' and I say to them, 'But what if you could? I just want you to hear that question. Why not you, and what if you could have this dream?' And I say, 'I want you to sit back when I ask you that question and take a deep breath: but what if I could? How does that feel?' The quality of the questions we ask ourselves determines the quality of the life we live, so we ask ourselves very limiting beliefs. My mentor, Mary Morrissey, always says to me, 'Stop with the "I can't, I won't, I could, I should" and always hold the question in your heart, what type of life would I love to live?' A whole different question. What type of life would I love to live? And now it's suddenly like, 'Oh.'

And now we're moving into what could be. What kind of life would I love to live? And then we take that 'how' out and leave it at the side and go, the 'how' is none of your business. Once you focus on the type of life you would love to live and you're consistent with the universe, the universe begins to co-create and open those doors for you.

Okay, the second last question: what one thing would you say to your eight-year-old self that you think they needed to hear?
You're safe. That's what I would say – you're safe. And everything's going to turn out okay. You're stronger than you think, yeah.

And the final question. Vietnamese monk Thích Nhất Hạnh once said, 'Only love can save us from climate change.' In essence, he suggests that if we are consumed with our own suffering, we cannot help Mother Earth. Do you agree?
A hundred per cent. Only love will save humanity. And you see, it's the misguided perception and understanding of love that we have in today's world, so we teach our children conditional love, we teach them that if they behave a certain way and say certain things and show up a certain way in the world, they're deserving of love. And actually, what's happening to each human being in the world is that every action is always either looking to give or receive love, and I firmly believe that. In all my work and my personal trauma, we're always just looking for love or we're looking to receive love and a lot of us don't know how to do that unless it's in a

manipulative, conniving way. Because very few of us understand what the energy of unconditional love really means, and it means accepting ourselves for exactly who we are in this moment, good, bad and indifferent, and also accepting other people for exactly who they are, and trying to hold space for others – this is where forgiveness comes in. Like the word 'namaste' means 'the divine in me sees the divine in you' and it's really trying to understand that human beings act out of their wounds, their wounded consciousness, and that's what the word 'shaman' comes from – wounded healer. Somebody who's gone in, dug deep and done the work and gone into those deep wounds and brought them up for healing.

But love is going to save us. But you see, love is not very well mobilised; hate is. So people often think that hate and fear have a lot more power than love, but love has a far, far greater power than hate or evil ever will. But it's just not organised. Imagine if love was organised. I did meditation online and there were well over a million people on the meditation. And the resonance which shows us the frequency and vibration of the Earth (the Schumann frequency) shot way off the charts, bigger than it's ever been before. If you want to understand the secrets of the universe, look at energy and frequency and vibration, as Nikola Tesla once said. Now, if a million people meditating can cause the human frequency to go off the charts, imagine seven billion people dropping down into their hearts and connecting with that aspect of themselves and helping to raise the consciousness of humanity. People would be able to breathe freely without anxiety and pain. Because evil feeds off fear, it needs that food to continue and to thrive. So the more of us that live from a heart-centred space and the more of us that drop down into our heart and truly begin to soften into our own true nature, and we begin to open up and even start allowing ourselves to see that aspect in other people too, no matter what they've done, through the act of forgiveness. Now we're beginning to change the world, now we're going to start to see things shift in a good, forward-moving direction.

I couldn't agree more, Alison. You've really summed it up there in terms of, I think, making love actionable. I think people know how to love but we don't know how to show it. It's like we've forgotten how to, actually.

We haven't been taught. We've been taught conditional love, so we can only act out what we're mimicking from our parents and they're teaching us what they've been taught. So unless we go inwards and connect and really unearth that for ourselves, so in that way we can be a little bit easy on ourselves, and realise that we weren't given the tools.

It was unintentional.

And then we can also give other people a break as well, people that we've blamed for things that have happened to us, or who have hurt us, because they're only acting out of their own limited paradigms. So we begin to understand what being human is a little bit more and forgive, which brings freedom.

ENERGISE

'*Un jour, quand nous aurons maîtrisé les vents, les vagues, les marées, la pesanteur, nous exploiterons l'énergie de l'amour. Alors, pour la seconde fois dans l'histoire du monde, l'homme aura découvert le feu.*'

('One day, after mastering the winds, the waves, the tides and gravity, we shall harness the energies of love. Then for a second time in the history of the world, man will have discovered fire.')

PIERRE TEILHARD DE CHARDIN

LOVE IS OUR authentic super-energy. As a species, we will survive only by being united. In order to save the Earth, humankind must collectively harness this energy to realise the interdependence of all beings, all cultures and all nations. The truth is that solidarity and collective action is our only hope of survival, both in the good and in the difficult times.

> **When you wake up in the morning you have**
> **only a certain amount of energy for that day,**
> **so how are you going to spend it?**

The amount of energy you have (as we discussed in Part One) will depend on how well you are taking care of yourself. It is a simple equation – how much you invest in yourself is how much you have to give.

Imagine a jug filled to the top with water. This water represents all the positive energy you have for the day. If by 10 a.m. you have already squandered two-thirds of your energy by, for example, getting stressed in traffic, becoming irritated with your family, mindlessly scrolling through social media, gossiping and getting lost in a stream of negative thoughts, then you will spend the rest of the day desperately trying to function from a dwindling supply of precious energy. By 4 p.m. you may be in the red, operating at a deficit.

In science, the term 'energy' is used to describe how much potential a physical system has to change. The fourth habit, Energise, is about how you can harness your own energy to transform the parts of yourself, your family, your friends, your work and ultimately the world into one of united peace. You will become aware of how to consciously choose how to use your energy and how to bring it to each moment, hour, day, week, month, year and indeed the rest of your life.

By now the subconscious, protective parts of you that need your love will be feeling safer, especially the more often you continue to listen to the Self-Love Habit audios. This chapter will help you to create the habit of energising your life with the most cherished fuel of all: love.

✕ ✕ ✕

The Self-Love Habit Tools

This is a gentle reminder to incorporate the following daily mindfulness tools into your every day. They are designed to be easy habit-building tools to make love your priority.

 **AUDIO MEDITATION**

Listen to the 'Love to Rise' and 'Love to Sleep' audios every day. Record your progress in the chart at the back of this book.

 **BE A FRIEND TO YOURSELF**

Cultivate the voice of your inner critic to become your inner companion.

THE DAILY PROMISE TECHNIQUE

Practise the daily promise technique: 'I promise to accept all the parts of MYSELF today to the best of my ability.' Write it down, if you have not already, on a sticky note and put it on the mirror where you brush your teeth. Repeat this promise every day and again if and when a fearful or negative thought emerges.

THE TWO-MINUTE MIRROR

Spend at least two minutes a day looking into your own eyes. Look beyond the physical, without judgement. Maintain eye contact until a feeling of calmness or ease emerges. This is something you can do last thing at night or first thing in the morning or both should you so desire. Write the word 'Energy' on a sticky note and place it beside the other words ('Listen', 'Open', 'Value') on your bathroom mirror so that you can see it each time you are doing your mirror work as a friendly reminder to practise all the habits. The acronym LOVE is now complete.

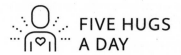

FIVE HUGS A DAY

Don't forget to get your full five-a-day quota!

LOVE LETTER #4:
ENERGISE YOURSELF NOW

Your fourth and final love letter is to your future self. The purpose of it is to help you to realise that *now* is the only moment you have to live your life full of loving energy. Too often we delay our happiness into the future. By choosing to write to your future self, you are closing the gap between your imagined future self and who you truly are now. You may notice that by writing this letter you become nostalgic for the moment and actively grateful for what you already have in your life.

This letter helps to eradicate 'I'll be happy when ...' thoughts. Happiness is NOW!

There is, of course, no certainty as to how many days any of us have left, but this exercise will help to wake you up to cherishing each day, full of loving energy.

Set aside at least 20 minutes of quiet time. Get a blank sheet of paper and take three deep belly breaths before you start. You can use the guidelines below to help you or just let it flow.

1　Decide how far in the future you want to read this letter. Is it one year, five years or 10 years? Figure out how old you will be at that stage. Personally, I find five years helpful because it is not too close or too far away. Write the future date at the top of the page.

2　Start with 'Dear Future Me' and wish yourself to be well, healthy and happy.

3　Summarise how things are for you now and what is going on in your life. Remember to focus on what you

appreciate, what is positive and how you are feeling. Identify any fears or worries you have about the
present moment and the future. Do not hold back – no
concern is too petty.

4 Let your future self know what is important to you
right now and what your key values are.

5 Express your desires, intentions and goals, including
what you would like to achieve between now and the
age your future self is in the letter.

6 Tell your future self the areas you want to improve on
or habits you need to do more or less of, for example
concerning exercise and diet.

7 Pinpoint emotional habits that need your attention, for
example listening more or being more patient.

8 Determine what you can do to build resilience in your
emotional habits now and in the future.

9 Finish with a genuine desire to be there for yourself
(present and future) at all times.

*Put a reminder in your online calendar for the future date or schedule
an email reminder to alert you to find the letter, stating where you have
hidden it. I hide the letter in a treasured book. Just make sure you do not
give the book away!*

× × ×

Energise Forgiveness

'The weak can never forgive. Forgiveness is the attribute of the strong.'

MAHATMA GANDHI

WHEN I WAS about 18, I borrowed a good watch from my dad without asking him. In hindsight this does not seem like a huge crime, but at the time it really felt like it. We were in Greece, just the two of us, and I spent my days going to the beach while he stayed at home writing. I was driving a moped for the first time and I was pretty anxious about it. On the day I borrowed the watch I ended up in a ditch after having an accident. Fortunately, it was not serious, just a bruised knee – and a lost watch. Although I looked high and low, I could not find that watch anywhere. My dad is incredibly generous but dislikes his things being moved, perhaps the result of being an only child. Anyway, I said nothing about the disappearance of the watch as I was afraid of his response. My dad had employed an Albanian labourer to help him do some renovations and when he could not find the watch, he thought the man might have taken it. Rather than accuse him of stealing, my dad let it go, saying that the man must have needed it more than he did.

His compassion compounded my shame.

I remained silent for years about the watch until one day my dad was telling the story to someone and reflecting on the hardship for Albanians in Greece during that period. The guilt was too much for me, so I confessed. I have to say, he took it very well. He was grateful for my honesty and most of all that he had chosen to say nothing to the innocent man. In the scheme of life this was a small incident, but for me it was profound. I learned to understand that one (my father in this case) could forgive another (the labourer) for a perceived wrong. I also realised that by being honest, forgiveness and love would triumph.

When I suggest to my clients that they forgive the people who have hurt them, I am often met with resistance and confusion. For many, it is a threat to their pride. Our ego demands us to be 100 per cent in the right and someone else to be 100 per cent wrong, yet we know deep down that this is rarely the case. We fear that if we forgive too easily, we will be emotionally or otherwise wounded again.

Our resistance to forgiveness is therefore entirely understandable.

Understandable, perhaps, but not very helpful. By withholding forgiveness, the original hurt is replayed many times over in our hearts and minds. We ruminate and are unwilling to confront our own pain or the situation. For example, feuds over inheritance are commonplace in families, with property and money issues dividing relatives for generations. Holding on to a grudge carves a hole in the heart that grows bigger with each passing year. While many justify their anger, and perhaps they have been wronged, they often fail to realise that anger hurts the person who carries it more than anyone else. Acknowledging that we have caused ourselves pain, for example through anger, is extremely hard, and even if we manage to do this the next part is to work out how to forgive ourselves. This is where parts therapy is very useful, as it can provide the stimulus for you to forgive the inner critic (Part B, the Shadow Self). This is self-love in action.

Exercise: How to Energise Self-Forgiveness

If, like me, you have memories that you are less than proud of – things you said, did or did not do – now is the time to forgive yourself. Do not be tempted to use such memories as further ammunition against yourself, but rather as an opportunity for self-compassion and forgiveness. While this may not seem easy and can feel as if you are dragging up the past, tread gently and start with something small. Remember, your processed past becomes your present and your future.

To energise forgiveness, follow these steps:

1 Take seven deep breaths.

2 Place your hand on your heart.

3 Listen, Open and Value how you feel right now.

4 Ask your heart, 'Is there anything I have done that you need to forgive me for?'

5 Listen carefully.

6 Make a mental note, or even better, write down what you hear.

7 Stay with the first memory that comes up.

8 Seek to understand the behaviour. What was happening, how old were you?

9 Identify the part that needs to be forgiven, for example Fear.

10 Breathe into your heart and repeat, 'I forgive you. I understand. My love is here to stay.'

You may need to repeat this exercise many times and it can be tiring, so work with only one memory at a time.

Forgiving yourself creates a powerful energy that transforms your internal relationship as you learn to trust yourself deeply. As with many aspects of the Self-Love Habit, if you can find it in your heart to forgive yourself for past or current behaviours, it is time to extend forgiveness outwards to others. Identifying whether you are holding on to any bitterness towards others is the first step.

× × ×

Energise Your Family

'Love is the ability and willingness to allow those that you care for to be what they choose for themselves without any insistence that they satisfy you.'

WAYNE DYER

RELATIONSHIPS WITH THE PEOPLE who are closest to us – our partners, parents, children, siblings – are often the most difficult to navigate, as both parties unintentionally take frustrations out on the other. The more history you share, the more likely it is that you will experience conflict, irritation and hurt in your relationships. This is because the more familiar something or someone is, the less present we become. In the same way, when driving a familiar route we go into automatic pilot (and hence are less present) and are more likely to have an accident. According to an article in the HuffPost, 50 per cent of car accidents happen close to our homes.[66] While most people want their family members to be happy, this is not usually just for altruistic reasons.

We want them to be happy so that we can be happy.

A subconscious concern about our own wellbeing comes into play. When the people we spend most of our lives with are lighter, kinder and more fun, we feel better too. Energy is contagious and we do not want to be infected with other people's negativity.

The two most common ways for dealing with the unhappiness or negativity in those close to us are:

1   We suppress and ignore their pain and say nothing; or

2   We over-identify with their feelings and thus get too involved in trying to 'fix' them or the situation.

If you are too attached to the people you love, their bad mood becomes your bad mood while your good mood is dependent on theirs.

Finding balance between these two states is worth cultivating. Accepting and allowing other people's existing emotional states is an act of love; behold their bad mood rather than react to it. For example, if your partner snaps at you over a minor issue and you know they are worried about work, then their irritability lives in an understandable context and it would be better to simply observe them without the need to defend yourself. This does not mean that you put up with unfair behaviour – you can choose to discuss it later if you feel the need. Your acceptance and non-defensive reaction will help to defuse your partner's frustration and make them less likely to snap at you in the future.

> **Trying to control the people we love is one of the most damaging things that we can do, both to ourselves and our loved ones.**

The desire to control stems from fear. Closer analysis indicates that the fear is often about being abandoned. Since, in general, nobody wants to be abandoned, attempts to control the people we love serve to make sure that this does not happen. Suffocating them with intense love leaves them without the capacity to breathe and operate freely and independently. This type of control is most often seen in the parent–child relationship, where the parent makes all the decisions: what to eat, bedtime, what school to go to, where to go on holiday, etc. Younger children will often attempt to assert some independence over their food and sleep and in many cases the stage is set for a power struggle. A battle of wills is not desirable or profitable for either parent or child. One of my clients who was despairing about her son's refusal to study for his final school exams said, 'Even if we chain him to his table, we can't make him study!'

Do you try to control or manipulate your partner, children or siblings? It may not be an easy question to answer honestly, but it is necessary. When I first met my husband, my own insecurities caused me to possessively monitor his every movement, which was not fun for either of us. Do you use control and manipulation to soothe your own inner fears and perceived inadequacies?

Using words like 'always' or 'never' to describe partners and family members is limiting and removes the belief in transformation, letting relationships stagnate. Examples include comments like 'my mother will never change' or 'my brother always criticises me'.

We constantly need new energy moving through our relationships to keep them healthy.

You can create that energy through your presence and love, which can soften the hardest of hearts. Waking up from unconscious habits, like using the words 'never' or 'always' about people, is a worthwhile investment. Encourage those you love by osmosis, not force. For example, if you choose to no longer get irritated with your kid's messy room, they may eventually tidy it themselves (without your nagging). It might not be perfect or to your standards, but making them responsible is more important. Believe me, I am talking from experience on this one! Relationships that do not change for the better occur when both individuals remain trapped in an unconscious dance, acting out the same patterns of behaviour that they have 'always' done.

Accept your family members as they are and relinquish the desire to mould them into how you would like them to be.

Each time you feel like criticising a family member, it is far more fruitful to turn your attention towards yourself and ask, 'What energy am I creating?'

× × ×
Exercise: Energise
Challenging Relationships

Is there a relationship in your life that is causing you pain? Do you keep arguing with someone or find it hard to let go of past hurts? If so, the following reflective exercise is invaluable in transforming negative energy into loving energy.

1 **Release:** Write down all the negative memories in the relationship that you are still holding on to. Do not hold back – get it all down on the paper! Examples might include the time this person let you down, shouted at you, forgot your birthday, etc.

2 **Understand:** What is the personal history of this person? What was their childhood like? Write down everything you know about them and what you imagine their life to be like.

3 **Appreciate:** Write down all the positive memories, all the times you felt close to them and all the times they have helped you.

4 **Transform:** Write a short letter or email to the person. You do not ever have to give it to them, but if you choose to they will be happy to receive it. Either way, the act of writing it is therapeutic. In the letter you need to write the words you long to hear from them. For example, if you have fallen out with your mother and you wish she would say that she misses you and is always there for you, write to her, starting with, 'Dear Mum, I miss you and I am always here for you.'

The humanistic approach in psychology teaches us that all behaviour, even negative behaviour, has a valid purpose. With this in mind, try to understand your loved ones as you are currently learning to do with your own protective and vulnerable parts. Your familial relationships will become a source of joy, not conflict.

✕ ✕ ✕

Energise Your Friends

True friendships are magnificently unique in their ability both to maintain closeness and at the same time relinquish expectations and judgement. When two good friends spend time together, they are at ease and their purest self is presented to the other. We often save the best of ourselves for friends and focus on how to create new positive activities and experiences. We may even reminisce about shared experiences, many of which are by their very nature pleasurable: dinners, country walks, concerts, holidays, baking a birthday cake. The bond of friendship grows stronger over time and tears and laughter are accepted in equal measure.

In his most famous work, *Confessions,* St Augustine, the fourth-century Christian philosopher, reflects on the death of his childhood friend: 'To discourse and jest with him; to indulge in courteous exchanges; to read pleasant books together; These and similar tokens of friendship, which springs spontaneously from the hearts of those who love and are loved in return – in countenance, tongue, eyes, and a thousand ingratiating gestures – were all so much fuel to melt our souls together, and out of the many made us one.'

Finding even one such friend in your life is rare. If you have a handful, you are truly blessed! Bear in mind that your partner, sibling or an adult child can also play the role of a close friend.

The love of a friend is fuel for life.

Ultimately, what makes a quality friendship so precious is the level of respect it entails. When respect is lost or when boundaries become non-existent, the relationship will suffer.

In his book *Friendship*, the British philosopher A.C. Grayling explores the hypothesis that friendship is one of the finest forms of love, if not *the* finest. He also stresses the importance of self-respect and of being a friend to ourselves: 'If we have no self-respect, how can we expect our friends to respect us, and in that case to be our friends at all?' The job of friends, according to Grayling, is not to boost your self-esteem or provide never-ending shoulders to lean on. Conversely, if you have a friend who drains you with their constant need for reassurance, then be cautious that you are not being taken for granted. To be clear, I am not implying that a friend in need is to be ignored. The opposite is true, but you must establish healthy boundaries that are based on respect.

Can you recall the top five regrets of the dying that were discussed in Part One? Losing touch with friends is one of them and is something that many of us can relate to. As teenagers and young adults our friends become our family, offering a support network where we feel we belong. Many look back on their school and college days with fond memories of fun and laughter being the highlight of their day. As we get older, our responsibilities generally increase and consequently many of us lose touch with friends. We become consumed with the responsibilities of family and work and as a result, we usually laugh a lot less. If you want to be energised, seek out positive friends and make spending time with them a priority. In fact, make it a habit by, for example, meeting up with a group of friends on the first Saturday of every month and/or going for a walk every Monday with a friend who lives locally. If you have fallen out of touch with old friends and have not made any new ones, you are not alone – this happens to many people. However, it is never too late to build new bonds if that is what you would like. Perhaps you could consider getting involved with a community project or join a walking or sports group. There is no shortage of potential friends and ways to meet them once you make the effort. Always remain open and approachable.

When you demote the integral role that friendships have in your overall happiness, you are also neglecting parts of yourself. A variety of close bonds helps you get in touch with the different parts of yourself. Have you ever noticed that certain friends bring out different parts of you? For example, you will be funny with one and more contemplative with another. Your tone, language and gestures will change depending on whose company you are in. You will have established patterns of communication that work and help you both to feel secure in the relationship.

Throughout this book I have asked you to treat yourself as a friend because when you do so, you are consciously energising and illuminating respect, kindness and lightness in all your encounters, both the fleeting and the more permanent.

Energise Your Work

'À vaincre sans
péril, on triomphe
sans gloire.'
(To win without risk is a
triumph without glory.)

PIERRE CORNEILLE

DO YOU LOVE what you do for a living? If your work does not make your heart sing, you are not alone. According to a 2018 *Forbes* article, nearly 70 per cent of people are actively disengaged with their work.[67] Many managers like to believe that their employees leave for financial gain, but chasing more money is only the case in 12 per cent of those who leave to work elsewhere. A *Harvard Business Review* survey reveals that 58 per cent of employees trust complete strangers more than they trust their boss.[68] This speaks volumes about where leadership is going wrong: if your boss is untrustworthy, then this will affect your performance as an employee. Recognition is the one thing that motivates people more than any financial reward or perk. It is free, yet it is in such short supply that 53 per cent of Americans are not happy at work because they do not feel they get the recognition they deserve.

These statistics probably do not surprise you. Most days, I meet clients who are on the verge of burnout due to overwork in jobs they do not like. The consequences for their physical and mental health, not to mention for their families, are substantial.

**People will sacrifice so much for their work
– too much, in fact. This needs to end.**

I have seen too many highly capable people cry with the fear that no matter what they do, how hard they work or how late they stay in the office, it is not enough to keep up with the demands of their career. The to-do list and emails never end. Many of us will go to our deaths with a to-do list that has not been completed. Does it really matter? On your deathbed, your to-do list will probably be the furthest thing from your mind. If you feel you are one of those people who work too hard at a job you no longer enjoy, then let's take a closer look at what is really going on for you. What motivation lies behind your daily slog? If it is financial gain, are you sure it is worth it? The Dalai Lama, when asked what surprised him most about humanity, answered:

> *Man. Because he sacrifices his health in order to make*
> *money. Then he sacrifices money to recuperate his health.*

Energise your work by being true to yourself. Find the courage to create work that is meaningful to you, that allows you to be of service to the world. Many people think that they must find something entirely new to energise their work. Clarity is key here. The most important question is:

Is it the work you are in that is causing you stress or is it your attitude towards it?

If your workplace or corporate culture is toxic and you cannot find the purpose in your work, then you need to consider finding a new position or even changing career entirely. However, often the meaning we are seeking in our lives is already there. As you awaken to love, you will begin to see more meaning in what you do and what already exists.

To help you gain more certainty on how you feel about your work, please consider the following questions:

1 What do you love about what you do? It does not matter how small it might be – make a mental note or write down everything that you enjoy.

2 Who do you like being around at work? Name all your colleagues who have a positive energy.

3 Why did you first start to do this work?

4 How can you improve on your work?

5 What effect do you think you have on people in your work?

6 Can you be more compassionate and understanding towards your colleagues/bosses?

If you are struggling to come up with much, perhaps it is time to consider a change. At least now, as with any relationship, you are doing your best to work it out before you consider leaving.

Whatever decision you make, ensure it is not driven by fear, which is one of the most common reasons why people stay in jobs they do not like and that drain them, sometimes for a lifetime.

'SUNDAY-SOMNIA'
Take a moment to consider the following:

✗ How do you generally feel on a Sunday?

✗ Do you experience an uneasy feeling if there is no set plan?

✗ Do you develop a feeling of dread of Monday morning as the day progresses?

- ✖ Is your sleep worse on a Sunday night than the rest of the week?

- ✖ Can you identify what emotions arise for you?

- ✖ Do you become more irritable with your family?

'Sunday-somnia'[69] is the name given to the common phenomenon of not sleeping properly on a Sunday night. According to an article about this phenomenon in *Forbes* magazine, as many as one in four people experience the 'Sunday blues', which affects their ability to sleep peacefully. Thoughts of the commute to work coupled with work-related anxiety keep many people awake when they need their rest the most, at the start of a busy week. If this is the case, it could be worth looking at how your job impacts you. We will examine this area further in the fourth LOVE habit, Energise.

Generally speaking, Sunday is a day of rest when we know we 'should' stop working and rest and have fun, but for many of us it actually highlights our restlessness.

SACRED SUNDAY PLEDGE

Can you create a day of total rest for yourself? A day to share with family and friends with a to-do list that has only rest, recreation and connection with loved ones on it? Can you set boundaries for yourself, such as no social media on Sundays, and make a vow not to check emails? If you have young kids who wake you up early or older ones that need to be driven to sporting events, is there anything you can do to share the load, such as take it in turns with your partner to lie in or start a rota with other parents to share the drop-offs?

A lie-in, a leisurely brunch while you read a book, a (family) walk or planning and preparing a Sunday feast are some of the activities that were revived for many during the Covid-19 lockdown. Our 'normal' whirlwind of activities was curtailed and only what was truly important remained.

The following pledge is also a practical way to create space and to avoid digital burnout and screen fatigue. By creating a 'Sacred Sunday', you are loving yourself in a practical way. The ritual of total downtime is not a luxury just for holidays, but an essential part of your weekly routine. This positive habit ensures you do not overwhelm yourself during your busy week and provides you with the energy you need. Make Sundays a time to cherish.

Are you prepared to make and commit to this pledge for yourself? I have been practising this for over a year now and it has really helped me to be calmer and more centred during my busy week.

✕ ✕ ✕

The Sacred Sunday Pledge

I, ... ,
pledge to create a Sacred Sunday practice, to switch off my phone and my mind, to be present and loving to both myself and others, to create meaningful rituals that nourish my heart and soul, to rest.

Signed: ....

Energise Consciousness

IN THE *New York Times* number one bestselling book *Proof of Heaven*, the American neurosurgeon Dr Eben Alexander strengthened the connection between science and spirituality following his near-death experience (NDE). He contracted bacterial meningitis and the deadly virus shut down his brain and sent him into a deep coma for seven days. The vivid level of consciousness he experienced while in the coma does not seem scientifically possible given that his 'entire neocortex, the outer surface of the brain and the part that makes us human was entirely shut down, inoperative'. The clichés of seeing white lights and feeling an all-encompassing loving presence were exactly what he experienced. It is difficult to shrug this off as hallucination when it comes from a renowned Harvard brain surgeon. In his follow-up book, *Living in a Mindful Universe: A Neurosurgeon's Journey into the Heart of Consciousness*, he suggests that the brain does not create consciousness and therefore it does not end when the body dies.

Have you ever experienced an NDE, an out-of-body experience or a psychic moment? Despite advances in brain-scanning technology, so much of how the brain functions still remains unexplained by rational, scientific analysis. On a personal level, I often dream of someone who I have not seen in ages and the very next day I will randomly bump into them; or sometimes I will have a fleeting thought during the day and later on the thought I had becomes a reality. I have noticed that these always occur when I am in a particularly open and positive frame of mind.

Energy and 'Vibrations'
Are Not Just for Hippies!

TAM HUNT and Jonathan Schooler of the University of California, Santa Barbara have developed the resonance theory of consciousness, which relates to synchronised vibrations. They believe that feeling 'vibes' is not just hippie talk and that vibrational frequencies have a basis in neuroscience, the study of human consciousness and biophysics.

For centuries, scientists have been grappling with the 'hard problem of consciousness', that is, determining what consciousness actually is. According to Hunt and Schooler, the 'easy part' in understanding consciousness is that the key component behind all physical reality is vibration. Everything is constantly in motion. Nothing is static, even if it looks like it is. Even objects have an energy field that causes them to oscillate beyond the visible eye.[70] When different energy vibrations come together, they sync, they work together. This can be seen when certain types of fireflies flying in large groups start to flash in sync. In a similar way, migrating birds often fly in perfect synchronicity.

What kind of energy do you exude? All vibrations are a form of energy and are contagious. For example, imagine you enter a room where two people have just had an argument and there is tension in the air. Your brain may be unconsciously hijacked by the associated low energy frequency and when you go home, you unintentionally snap at your partner. An unfortunate domino effect is in play. You need to cleanse negative energy, otherwise you leave yourself open to infection. Being aware, being compassionate and taking deep breaths will help you to accomplish this.

In contrast, high vibrations lead to feelings of being lighter, happier and more energised. Often the last thing we learn about ourselves is the effect we have on others. Davidji, an international meditation teacher who trained with Deepak Chopra, tells us that 'the highest vibration will always win'.[71] When you consciously choose to create, sustain and share your positive energy and higher vibrations, the more awake you are to life. The energy you create is magnetic and empowering for you and those around you. Higher vibrations allow you the energy to choose to see the good in everyone.

Before I conclude, I invite you to read the fifth and final interview that I conducted with Tomi Reichental, Holocaust survivor turned educator. This man's positive energy is truly incredible.

✕ ✕ ✕

Exercise: LOVE Interview with You

Before you read the final interview, I would like you to take a moment and revisit the eight questions that you were asked in the introduction and that Dermot, Roz, Alison and Rick have also answered. Now that you have read the book and listened to your love to rise and sleep audios, have any of your answers changed?

1   Einstein said of himself, 'There is a grotesque contradiction between what people consider to be my achievements and the reality of who I am.' In other words, he felt a divide between how he was publicly

perceived and how he privately felt. Do you relate to
this statement?

2 Do you find it easy or difficult to hold on to a separate
sense of self that is not identified with your ego?

3 Do you believe human beings are born naturally loving
themselves?

4 What is/are the main reason(s), in your opinion, why
somebody would NOT love themselves?

5 Do you think it is necessary for people to love
themselves before they can fully love others?

6 Do you love yourself? And if so, have you always loved
yourself? If not, why not?

7 What one thing would you say to your eight-year-old
self that you think they needed to hear?

8 Vietnamese Buddhist monk Thích Nhất Hạnh once said,
'Only love can save us from climate change.' In essence,
he suggests that if we are too consumed with our own
suffering, we cannot help Mother Earth. Do you agree?

LOVE INTERVIEW #5: TOMI REICHENTAL
Dublin, Friday 17 January 2020

I had the honour of interviewing Tomi Reichental, one of the few
living Holocaust survivors, who has lived in Ireland since 1959.
Tomi was nine years old when, with his immediate family, he was
imprisoned in the Bergen-Belsen concentration camp, where some
70,000 people, including 50,000 Jews, perished. In total, 35 members of Tomi's extended family were murdered in the Holocaust.
In this interview, I asked Tomi a different set of questions from

the other interviewees because of the magnitude of what he went through.

Like many trauma victims, Tomi did not speak about the horror of his experiences for a long time. For 60 years, he remained silent. When he retired and his first wife died, he finally found the words and the courage and since then he has been sharing his message: to remember and learn from the Holocaust. Few of us can truly understand what Tomi went through, which is why meeting this wonderful man was one of the most uplifting moments in my life.

Fiona: *In my work, I see people at war with themselves. Do you believe we need to contemplate more on self-love, compassion and kindness to help save the world from external wars?*
Tomi: Absolutely, that is what I am always talking about.

Why did you not speak about the Holocaust for so long?
This is not unusual, there were many thousands of Holocaust survivors that did not speak about it. Basically, I kept it in my background. My wife never knew anything. I never told anybody, I never told my children, I just couldn't speak about it. I couldn't even open a brochure about Bergen-Belsen that my cousin sent me about the history of the place. I could not open it. If something came on television that showed old footage, I would turn it off. It was such a weight on me, although I did not suffer. I did not have nightmares, no flashbacks. I really survived the camp very well. It is the way of nature, we put it in the back of our minds, we don't want to face the pain.

Did the transition to speaking about it publicly help you to deal with the pain?
It was a very slow process that I began to speak about it, after my wife passed away, I retired. I thought, who am I working for? My children had good jobs, they were not in trouble, I had plenty for myself to live. My wife died in June and then I told my partner I will retire after six months.

I was always a dynamic person, doing things, developing things, and I thought, maybe now I can begin to think about what happened to me. I began to write, and I sent some of the articles to magazines and once they were published, I had the media on my doorstep. The Holocaust Education Trust never even knew about me. It was my secret that I carried with me. People at first could not believe my story, my children read it in the newspapers, the horrors that I went through. They knew I was in Bergen-Belsen, but that is all. One of my grandsons told the teacher that his grandfather was a Holocaust survivor and his teacher asked would I be prepared to come to the school. I said OK. I had no experience in presenting a talk. There were about 30 kids in the class and in no time as I was telling the whole story, it became very real to me and I broke down, then all the children were crying, the teacher was crying. I was really panicked, I thought that I would be in trouble over this. I have made everyone cry! But the opposite happened, the principal arrived and asked would I speak to the whole school.

Did that surprise you?
I couldn't believe it, but I was amazed at how little people knew me. The media then started to film me, and I felt it was too much, I ran away. But I realised that people's education of the Holocaust was so limited. Students would say that 'six million Jews were murdered', that was all they knew. I realised that I am one of the last witnesses to this horrific event. In 2019 in Israel, 180 Holocaust survivors are dying each week. All of the survivors are now over 80, 90 ...

The time is so finite and precious to spread your message.
Yes, I realised I had to speak. I am one of the people who remembers.

Where did you find the courage to speak?
It was very difficult. The Holocaust Education Trust came to speak to me, and we were both crying. It was so emotional for me. Every time I spoke

about it, it became very real for me. For 60 years I never talked about it. To nobody. Nobody asked me and I never told anyone.

And in those 60 years, were you happy?
Yes, it did not bother me. It is the way of nature, to protect me. It was like it never existed. Even with my brother and cousin who were in the camp with me, we did not speak about it, we would meet and speak about everything else. It was taboo. Until one time I was on holiday in Israel the family came together, with the children and grandchildren, not my children, they were not there, we spoke about it in Hebrew. We made a video. But here in Ireland I never spoke about it. Now when I go to Israel, we actually speak about it, especially when my cousin was alive – he died last year. We remember the conditions; how did we survive? What we take for granted today, everything was life-threatening. We lived every minute in fear of what was going to happen. Then I wrote my book, *When I was a Boy in Belsen.*

Wonderful. Do you find it helpful to talk about it?
It has become a life desire that I have to talk about it. I owe it to the victims that their memory is not forgotten. I myself lost 35 members of my family: uncles, aunts, grandparents, cousins, people I played with. They were murdered. Cousins who used to come to my village for holidays. I remember them so well. One day we said goodbye to them and then we never saw them again. We said when all this is over we will be reunited and everything will be all right. Within a couple of days, a week, they were murdered.

That is unbelievable. Do you have any regret that you did not speak about it sooner?
No, I'm glad I am doing it now. I always say I didn't speak for 60 years, but now I won't stop. Not only this, I am more busy now than when I was working. It is something I have to do, it has to be done, people have to know. In

years to come, it will all be gone. In 15 years or maybe 20, nobody will be left. This is the legacy that I leave behind that is so important. Wherever I go, I ask that as many people hear my story as possible, bring as many people as possible. I want them to know what happened.

Because you were a child when it happened, do you think the psychological impact was more difficult?

Absolutely. A nine-year-old then and a nine-year-old today ... we were so innocent, there is such a difference, you know. I did not know what was happening beyond the village, never mind the cities. Today, nine years old, they know what is happening all over the world! I have a granddaughter, 10 years old, she tells me of all the terrible things around the world, there is fire, there is flooding. We didn't know anything. My parents did not tell me anything, even before, when the hatred against the Jews began in 1939, they didn't tell me anything, they didn't want to frighten me. I was a kid; I was not bothered by anything. Today, of course, they are much more sophisticated. When I saw what was happening in the camp, I probably thought, that is how life is. I asked my mother, older brother, what I was like then, in the camp. What did I do? They told me I was very apathetic. Today, we call it depressed. But how could you say that back then, a child was depressed? When the other children played I really didn't want to, but because they played, I played as well. It bothered me what I was seeing, but I couldn't understand it. I can't imagine seeing this horror that we saw. It was overwhelming. Why were people dying and then people throwing them like a piece of meat onto piles? I shut down. My father and I were reunited afterwards and I never told my father what I'd seen. He didn't ask me. I went to school, why should I tell anyone? It was like it didn't happen. Finished.

As if nothing had happened?

Yes, it was finished. We belonged to a Zionist movement and nobody there spoke about the Holocaust. Still, today there was a big campaign in Israel to help people who had never spoken about it to come forth. I was invited to a seminar on trauma and they wanted me to give a presentation about the anxiety and trauma of the Holocaust survivors. I am not an expert, so I did some research, and I was absolutely amazed that in Israel they have institutions for survivors who are still not able to function in society. They are too afraid to shower, they hoard food, 75 years later. These people were adults when this happened.

With my own children, when they left food, I would say to the kids, 'I would have given anything to have that food,' or when I go to a hotel and at the self-service breakfast people pile up the plate with cakes and leave them. Why did they not take two cakes? They have to take six? It bothered me. I had this complex, I couldn't stand it as I had starved so much.

Would you say the physical abuse, the starvation, the living conditions, the cold or the emotional abuse and humiliation, which was harder?
The humiliation. You know, we had to wear the yellow star so we were recognised as a Jew, so when we went out we were abused. When I first started to talk about this publicly, I would put on a yellow star to show the audience, and I broke down. I said to myself, 'Why did you cry?' Because at the time when I had to wear it I did not feel the humiliation, but now I feel it! Before we were liberated the guards from the watchtowers changed, they were prisoners of war from Hungary, but towards the end, in 1945, the soldiers had gone to fight and these fellows were there instead. When they were eating the bread, they would cut the crust off the bread and we used to play near the watchtower and suddenly the guard would shout, 'Come, come.' As kids we were afraid because we didn't know what they wanted. We were afraid to run away also, as if we ran away they would shoot us. So slowly, slowly, we came to the watchtower and then they would throw us the crust and we were starving. So we jumped on it like little puppies, like dogs, fighting over this crust. When I spoke about it, I broke down. When I speak about it today, it is a humiliation, it is a pain in my body. Today it is not so bad because I have told the story thousands

of times. But Joy [Tomi's wife] comes with me sometimes and still sometimes I talk about how I saw my grandmother, her dead body thrown into a cart, and you can hear it in my voice, suddenly I am in trouble. People wouldn't notice it. But Joyce would say, 'You were in trouble,' and I would say, 'I was.' When you talk about these things, they become very real. It's my life, then I get emotional.

Has the talking helped you to heal?
I don't know. I wouldn't consciously know that I was waiting for this to come out. It was more of a persuasion that I had to do it for humanity. For the greater good. (*Tomi suddenly gets up.*) I have to show you I have some proverbs, I have to show you some proverbs that mean a lot to me ... (*Tomi leaves the room and returns with a file.*) One thing people notice when they read my book is that I don't carry any hatred for what happened, for people. They ask me how can I think like this?

> (*He shows me a file with three quotes that he chooses to live by:*
>
> '*I speak so that my past does not become somebody's future.*'
>
> '*Make peace with the past so it won't spoil your present.*'
>
> '*Life must be understood backwards: but it must be lived forwards.*' *– Kierkegaard*)

If you carry hatred, it is pain. Hatred is pain. I have made peace with my past. I speak so that my past does not become somebody else's future. You don't forget what happened to you in the past, but you create a good future. Hatred is a double-edged sword because you might hate somebody and that person doesn't even know you hate them, you feel the pain.

So what do you feel about forgiveness?

I can't forgive. It is the people who are dead that should forgive, but they were murdered. I wanted to make a reconciliation with one of the perpetrators. I made a film shown all over the place, it is called *Close to Evil*. Hilda was her name, she is still alive, she was 96 in January. She came to Bergen-Belsen when she was only 22 or 23 years old. She was very cruel, she murdered two people as well. She stood trial and was sentenced to one year. At the time that was the standard; today she would have gotten life or been executed. People say, like my brother and my cousins, why do you want to meet this murderer? But then, in my own mind, and it might be very naive that I say not everything is black and white, there is also a grey area and in my opinion she was a victim as well, a victim of her time. From the age of 12 she was being fed with propaganda, brainwashed. She thought what she was doing was the right thing. If I was born to a Nazi family, who knows what I would have done. So when I wanted to meet her, I said I don't want to know about the past, I want to speak about the future. I researched her life, I knew everything about her. One thing she did not do was to say she was sorry, she showed no regret. I thought if I met her after all these years, surely she must realise that what she had done was wrong and that would be something. I am not forgiving her, but I am making a reconciliation from a perpetrator to a victim, something that nobody had done before. They might have met in a courthouse, but never privately. She agreed to meet me. I said to my producer Gerry Gregg, I have been in contact with this lady and he said, 'Tomi, if you are going to meet her, I want to be there with the camera.'

I thought, she did murder two people, but the people in Bergen-Belsen were skeletons, they were hardly alive when they were alive, you didn't even need to hit them very hard and you killed them. Maybe she didn't want to kill them, I thought. But she hit them and they collapsed. There was nobody to help them and they died. Not everything is black and white. This is very important also about what is happening today. We need to help people to co-operate and to make the world better. This is the way we have to go, through compassion and understanding. This was the purpose of the documentary, but at the last moment she said she didn't want to meet me. Because she was really afraid that all the interviews she gave before there was nobody to correct her when she denied what had happened. If she met me she could not do that, I was there, I was a witness to it all. I was disappointed that she didn't meet me.

But it doesn't change how you feel?
No. It was sad that this woman, how can this woman still today think that what she did was right?

I hope I am not tiring you; only two more questions. After the Holocaust, did you find it hard to trust other people?
(*Laughs*) No. Actually, Joyce always tells me, you know you trust people too much! When I discovered that I had a very good friend who let me down, I was very hurt. I didn't expect that this person could do this to me. (*Laughs*) I don't like to talk about it because it is so silly, but today there is a lot of crime over the internet and telephones. Not so long ago I got a call that my account in the bank was being raided. This chap was so clever that I thought really it was a genuine call from the bank security and I gave him the details that I shouldn't have. He took a lot of money, but after I thought this didn't feel right after only 20 minutes I rang the real bank. They were able to get all the money back. I am so trusting (*laughs*) I had people coming to the door and one day a clever man came and he said that his car had been clamped and he said he needed €50 or €60 and even though I know it costs more, he was so convincing. I said, 'Look, I don't know who you are but I can see you are stressed, I give you the €50, if you bring it back to me, thank you very much, but if you don't, if you are lying to me, I know that you need it, it is a charitable contribution.'

He never came back?
No! (*laughs*)

I must be like you, too trusting!
He left a phone number and I called it, but it never answered. But I don't care, I thought in my mind, he is a beggar but he is a clever chap who could have a fiver out of me but he got €50! Thankfully that doesn't happen every day. I don't get excited, some people, they would say, 'Oh, bloody so and so.' I let it go ...

That's a good story.
I just hope he didn't go to the pub! (*Laughs*) I am very trusting, the same thing could happen and I fall for it.

You see the goodness in people, even after everything you have been through.
Yes, for me everybody is good. We are all born good. We are not born crooks, but unfortunately if you fall to the wrong company, if you get attached to drugs or something like this, it is a terrible tragedy.

My last question is about love. Did you notice that love was a driving force for survival in the camp?
Within our family there were very strong characters, my mother and my aunt. My mother in the worst times in the camp, she did not show it in her face, she didn't show distress, she always had a smile.

Incredible.
Every evening we went to sleep my mother would sit beside me on the bed and she would say, 'You just keep strong, we will get through this, everything will be all right, we will survive.' Because we lived really for the day, you didn't live for a month's time, a year's time, this time did not exist, we just wanted to survive the day and if we survived the day, we survived. The next day is another day to survive. Because you never knew what they wanted. For example, we were on the roll call and one day this high-ranking officer came, which never happened, and we had our supervisor, these women would come and this officer was standing

there smiling and joking. After the roll call, everyone questioned what was going on. Were they planning something for us? The anxiety was terrible. We liked the routine, every day the same thing and we knew everything was all right, but when something changed, this made us feel anxiety. What will happen?

When you spoke about your mother, I can see why you are the way you are – your compassion and love.
Thank God, my mother lived until 96, she had a lovely life, she had grandchildren, great-grandchildren, everybody around her. My father was much younger, he died from a heart attack. Today he would have survived. My mother was a very good example, we never saw my mother arguing with my father. We knew that it happened but we never saw it, we got a very good upbringing. We were taught manners; if we were on a bus and saw an older person standing, we would automatically stand up, always say thank you. I had a loving upbringing and thank God it paid back. I love it in Ireland, the people are so good. I have never experienced any discrimination. I like nature, forests, sea, you have everything that you want. You don't need to travel thousands of miles, you have it all here. We never have it too hot, too cold, no flooding or fires.

(Laughs) You don't need my book [I had given him a copy of my first book, The Positive Habit.*] You are so positive already!*
I always say to Joyce, I think this is the best country in the world, people just don't appreciate it, they only like to complain. I used to say it to people in work. They would be complaining and I would say, 'Why are you complaining?' You don't know what you have, people would give anything for what we have. I broke my hip a few months ago and now I am back again, I'm flying.

You have amazing energy, thank you so much. I am so grateful for your time, I truly am.

CONCLUSION

'La vie est un sommeil, l'amour en est le rêve, et vous aurez vécu, si vous avez aimé.'

('Life is a long sleep and love is its dream; and you will have lived if you have loved.')

ALFRED DE MUSSET

AND SO our time together comes gently to a close. I was lying in bed this morning as the first few moments of the day gently pulled me into full consciousness and you, my dear reader, came to mind. My awakening was not a rude one, but rather a polite reminder of the journey we have been on and my responsibility to you as your guide.

As the first soft light of day crept through my bedroom window, I considered, not for the first time, the somewhat monumental task I had undertaken – to write a book about self-love. When I started, people would ask, 'What is your second book about?' When I told them that it was about love and self-love, I was often met with a stolen glance of ... I am not sure what it was. Apprehension, perhaps? The unsaid words hung in the air: 'What makes you an expert on love?'

It is a good question. I was, and I remain, assured in my own mind that I am no more and no less an expert than anyone else. When it comes to love, we are all the same; we are all equal in our vulnerability. Like life itself, love is fragile. My intention in writing this book is to bolster that fragility, to help you, the reader, unite your divided self using the power of the four LOVE habits and to make self-love the ultimate act of resilience.

My 'expertise' in love was, I believe, born more from my understanding of the absence of self-love. I have learned so much by listening to thousands of courageous clients who have shared their stories and their pain with me. Their wounded hearts have reminded me of what I knew intrinsically at age 20: that the most important thing in the world is love. They have taught me that the desire to love and be loved is universal and unites humanity. Love makes life both bearable and blissful.

What gave me the courage to write this book is people like you.

I am eternally grateful to you, dear reader, for your time and for bearing with me as I have done my best to fulfil my promise to help you to love yourself and relieve anxiety. I have shared what I know to be true: that you are truly worthy of both giving and receiving love.

It is my hope that the four LOVE habits will remain with you long after you have put this book down. Let Listen, Value, Open and Energise become the very fabric of your heart. Live as a unified self with an unshakeable belief in all the parts of yourself. Be confident no matter what situation you find yourself in.

You do not have to be in the public eye to have a public persona – you have this by simply living in a society. When you take away the noise of life and strip away the conditioned layers you have added over the years, what are you left with? It is important that you relish and love being with your core self.

Richie Sadlier, the former professional footballer who overcame alcoholism and the trauma of being abused, is now a psychotherapist who helps young people to deal with similar issues and how not to fall into the same traps as he did. In his recent memoir *Recovering*, Sadlier wrote, 'There was no difference now between the public me and the person who lived his life away from the media ... I was, finally, comfortable just being myself.'

This is my hope for you – that you, too, can be at one, can be comfortable and at ease with yourself. Remember that if your mind gets too busy, drop into the serenity of your heart.

Each day *you* get to be with this incredible person – yourself – which is a privilege. You are in good company, perennially. When you rise in the morning you can choose to immediately think, 'I am alive, what a blessing. How can I make the most of this beautiful day?' And when you are going to sleep, if fear arises, let love come quickly to your rescue.

In the end, the choice is simple. Do you want to live from and with the certainty of love or suffer from a world of fear and anxiety? If life becomes difficult or you have a hard decision to make, you will need to pause, breathe deeply and ask yourself, 'What is guiding me right now? Is it love or is it fear?'

Let it be love. Always.

If you feel anxious, be kind and patient with yourself. Remember, self-love is a new habit and new habits take time to cultivate. I find it comforting to recall that I am still on a lifetime journey to loving myself, others and the world more deeply. It has been my honour to bring you with me this far. I hope my efforts have been fruitful, but now it is up to you to see if I have succeeded and time will tell. It always does. Either way, love is what endures.

× × ×

The Self-Love Quiz

Welcome back to the same quiz you took in the introduction.

Please remember to take this quiz after you have listened to your 'Love to Rise' and 'Love to Sleep' audios for 66 days. The brain needs repetition and time to change for new habits to be formed.

Answer 'yes' or 'no' to these questions and make a note of your score out of 20. Give yourself one point for each 'yes' answer. Do not think about your answers. Move quickly through the questions and let your instincts guide you.

1   Can you sit peacefully in silence alone, without distractions? |

2   Can you sit peacefully in silence with others? |

3   Do you cope well with uncertainty? |

4   Do you accept yourself just the way you are? /

5   Do you feel comfortable maintaining eye contact with yourself in a mirror? |

6   Do you feel at ease making eye contact with others? |

7   Do you listen to your (gut and heart) instinct? |

8   Do you have an inner voice that is kind to you? |

9   Are you patient with yourself when learning something new or adapting to change? |

10 Do you feel comfortable feeling vulnerable? /

11 Do you take care of your mind and body on a daily basis? \

12 Do you say no to other people if you feel tired or overwhelmed? \

13 Do you value yourself? |

14 Do you trust yourself to make good decisions? |

15 Are you at ease with your body and physical appearance? |

16 Do you feel connected to family and friends? \

17 Do you let go of the hurt from the past? /

18 Do you feel you have enough energy to help others? *1*

19 Do you mainly live in the present moment? *1*

20 Do you love yourself? *1*

Score 2 /20

What has changed? Look back to page 36 to see your earlier score.

The higher the number of 'yes' answers, the more you love yourself. However, remember that scores are neither 'good' nor 'bad', but are just a useful tool to show where you are right now. In fact, the questions that you answered 'no' to are the most interesting, as they provide insights into where you need to pay attention. For example, the question on vulnerability is one of the areas I need to continue to work on. Accepting where you are at this moment is exactly where you need to be, as outlined in your daily promise technique.

x x x

How to Sustain the Four LOVE Habits

'Love without action is meaningless and action without love is irrelevant.'

DEEPAK CHOPRA

THIS BOOK is a carefully constructed practical strategy for you to become able to show love to yourself and others – in short, to put love into action. To echo Dr Rick Hanson in his interview, it is my intention that you *make the effort to* practise the LOVE habits every day.

In order to sustain

Listening

Opening

Valuing and

Energising

both in yourself and in others, please remember the following key points.

1   **Feel the reward:** The most effective way of maintaining a habit is to be aware of the reward it gives you. In the coming days, weeks, months and years, take time to truly soak in the warm glow that you receive when you practise any or all of the LOVE habits. Notice the impact you have on others and watch your relationships flourish. Document these moments mentally or in your journal, as this will help you to see the benefits and rewards over time and encourage you to keep practising.

2   **Hypnotherapy:** It is so important to reinforce and sustain the loving shifts on a subconscious level and this is what makes the Self-Love Habit unique. Continue listening to the audios for as long as you like, but for at least 66 days. You will also find further resources on my website, www. thepositivehabit.com. You might consider registering for my five-star-rated online hypnotherapy programme that is helping people from all over the world to create and sustain a positive mindset.

Remember to subscribe to my weekly blog (on www. thepositivehabit.com), which is sent out by email every Monday morning at 7:30 a.m. It has thousands of readers from all over the world and is designed to help people begin their week on a positive and loving note.

3 **Trust your heart:** Tune in and listen. Any time you feel fear or anxiety rising, slow down, then stop, place your hand on your heart and ask your heart any questions you want answered. The solutions you seek are already within you.

4 **Spend time alone every day:** Carve out some quiet time for yourself every day. I know this is easier said than done, especially if you live with others, but this has to be non-negotiable in order for you to practise self-love. Shut the bedroom door or wake up an hour before everyone else. If you can't get space at home, go for a walk or drive to a nice quiet spot. Alone time should be a minimum of 30 minutes but preferably 60 minutes, depending on your responsibilities. As with any relationship, if you do not invest the time and energy, the relationship will flounder and you will not perform at your optimum.

It is a good idea to choose the same time each day and get into the habit of making this 'me time' your priority. Do not distract yourself with your phone or any other device. This 'me time' is for self-reflection, so listen to a guided meditation or read a book that helps you to grow spiritually and emotionally. Journal, listen to music or simply stare out of the window. The main thing is that you are not interacting with anyone else or distracted. Give yourself your undivided attention.

This 'me time' should provide the stillness you need to listen to yourself. If you are experiencing challenging events, such as the death of a loved one or a major change like children leaving home or a relationship ending, you will need to spend even more time by yourself in order to process the associated emotions. Let yourself feel, allow yourself to cry. There is no pressure on you to feel better until you are ready. Perhaps you could take a weekend by yourself and luxuriate in your own company without the need to compromise on anything.

5 **Surround yourself with loving people:** You deserve to be loved and appreciated just as you are. Make sure the people you spend your time with reflect the value that you have for yourself. A good way to measure this is to ask yourself how you come away feeling after meeting them. If you feel less good about yourself than you did before you met them, ask yourself why. Sometimes this can be hard to pinpoint and often it is as much about what people do not say as what they do. Either way, seek out people like you who listen, are open, who value and energise you.

6 **Remember the daily promise to accept all the parts of yourself:** This is particularly important on the days when you do not feel great. Accepting yourself just as you are will help negative feelings to pass. Acceptance is everything.

7 **Scan the world for LOVE:** Each day, whether you are waiting for a bus or going for a walk, look for examples of people who are listening to others in order to understand, who are opening to the world as it is, who are valuing and energising themselves and others. If you look for small examples of love, you will find them everywhere: in a mother holding her

child's hand, in friends who laugh together, in the person who holds a door open for you or lets you go first in the queue. As you scan the world for love, be sure to also carry it with you.

8 **Be ready for death at any moment:** If you knew you were going to die tomorrow, how would you feel? Are you ready to go? From the moment we are born, we are already preparing to die. Socrates was sentenced to death by the people of Athens for impiety and for 'failing to acknowledge the gods that the city acknowledges'. Legend has it that Socrates drank the poison he was administered as if it were a carafe of wine. In true stoic form, he accepted his fate.

Each moment we live could be our last. Rather than viewing this as negative or as an anxiety-inducing fact of life, turn it around and live this moment at peace with yourself, your loved ones, your world. When death comes – and it will – be ready. All that really means is to be at peace with it. Be safe in the knowledge that you have lived from love, not fear.

'It would not be much of a universe if it was not home to the people you love.'

STEPHEN HAWKING

PRIVATE DIARY ENTRY, AGE 42. SUNDAY, 15 OCTOBER 2017, CAFÉ, PORTE DE VERSAILLES, PARIS.

I've left everyone back in the apartment as I really wanted some space to come and write to you. It's bliss. This morning, I woke up early and Mum and I went on a huge walk to find the little blue studio I used to live in. It has literally been 20 years since I was there!

I wasn't sure I would find it. Honestly, if you had asked me for directions, I could not have given them to you. Yet my feet seemed to know the way without hesitation and once I saw the Métro stop, I was away. It was lovely to have Mum with me. I wanted to tell her how much I missed her back then, but the words didn't come. They will.

I had forgotten just how beautiful it was and I totally forgot the old church that was right outside my building. Ironically, it all looked grander than I remembered. I saw the tabac where I used to buy my 20 Benson and Hedges and timbres (stamps). I used to hate saying that word, as I could never pronounce it right! I saw the Monoprix where Ciaran went to buy 'food' and even took a picture for him. I was always amazed back then that he actually went to supermarkets. I called him 'Monsieur Monoprix'! I used to just grab a croissant or a McDonald's. It makes me laugh now. I had forgotten that.

Isn't it amazing how much we think we forget, but don't really? I mean, my feet knew the way. How is that? My subconscious guided me and as soon as I set foot in the area, all these memories came flooding back.

I feel sad for the younger me, she seemed so vulnerable and anxious. Yet I also feel love mixed with admiration and empathy because she was so sad and yet happy, so excited and yet afraid all at the same time. It was exhausting. I still feel like that today sometimes. I'm so happy my heart bursts and sometimes I'm so desperately sad for all the pain in the world. Now, though, I am no longer afraid. I think that is the difference.

I was braver than I gave myself credit for. I was kinder than I believed and the memory of my little blue studio with my French verb drills stuck on the wall beside my bed reminds me of my determination to always learn. The person I was is who I still am. I know that now and I love her. I mean, I love me.

DAY 1	DAY 2	DAY 3	DAY 4	DAY 5	DAY 6
DAY 7	DAY 8	DAY 9	DAY 10	DAY 11	DAY 12
DAY 13	DAY 14	DAY 15	DAY 16	DAY 17	DAY 18
DAY 19	DAY 20	DAY 21	DAY 22	DAY 23	DAY 24
DAY 25	DAY 26	DAY 27	DAY 28	DAY 29	DAY 30
DAY 31	DAY 32	DAY 33	DAY 34	DAY 35	DAY 36
DAY 37	DAY 38	DAY 39	DAY 40	DAY 41	DAY 42
DAY 43	DAY 44	DAY 45	DAY 46	DAY 47	DAY 48
DAY 49	DAY 50	DAY 51	DAY 52	DAY 53	DAY 54
DAY 55	DAY 56	DAY 57	DAY 58	DAY 59	DAY 60
DAY 61	DAY 62	DAY 63	DAY 64	DAY 65	DAY 66

NOTES

1   World Health Organization, 'Number of People with Depression Increases', who.int, 28 February 2017.

2   Brown, Brené, Unlocking Us podcast, 3 April 2020.

3   Tolle, Eckhart, 'What Is Self? Timeless Wisdom from the Archives', YouTube, 24 April 2019.

4   Le Roux, Gaëlle, 'Are French Students Taught to Be More Philosophical?', France24, 16 June 2011.

5   Neal, D.T., Wood, W., Wu, M. and Kurlander, D., 'The Pull of the Past: When Do Habits Persist Despite Conflict with Motives?', *Personality and Social Psychology Bulletin*, vol. 37, no. 11, 2011, pp. 1,428–1,437.

6   IPCC, 'Chapter 3: Impacts of 1.5°C Global Warming on Natural and Human Systems' in *Global Warming of 1.5°C* (ipcc.ch/sr15/chapter/chapter-3/).

7   Confino, Jo, 'Zen Master Thich Nhat Hanh: Only Love Can Save Us from Climate Change', *Guardian*, 21 January 2013.

8   Schwartz, Mildred A., *Trends in White Attitudes toward Negroes*, National Opinion Research Center, University of Chicago, 1967.

9   'Regrets of the Dying', bronnieware.com.

10 NHS, 'Maternity Staff Undergo Hypnobirthing Training to Help Parents', hey.nhs.uk, 16 April 2019.

11 Kubie, Lawrence S. and Margolin, Sydney, 'The Process of Hypnotism and the Nature of the Hypnotic State', *American Journal of Psychiatry*, vol. 100, no. 5, March 1944, pp. 611–622.

12 Tabaka, Marla, 'Most People Fail to Achieve Their New Year's Resolution. For Success, Choose a Word of the Year Instead', inc.com, 7 January 2019.

13 Economy, Peter, 'This Is the Way You Need to Write Down Your Goals for Faster Success', inc.com, 28 February 2018.

14 Anxiety and Depression Association of America, 'Understand the Facts: Body Dysmorphic Disorder (BDD)', adaa.org.

15 Dr Sue Carter, Polyvagal Theory, Oxytocin and the Neurobiology of Love conference, Cork, September 2019.

16 University of Rochester Medical Center Health Encyclopedia, 'Understanding the Teen Brain', urmc.rochester.edu/encyclopedia.

17 Rubin, Zick, 'Measurement of Romantic Love', *Journal of Personality and Social Psychology*, vol. 16, no. 2, 1970, pp. 265–273.

18 Wu, Katherine, 'Love, Actually: Science Behind Lust, Attraction, and Companionship', SITNBoston (sitn.hms.harvard.edu), 14 February 2017.

19 helenfisher.com/about

20 English, Jason, 'Odd Facts about Nobel Prize Winners', CNN, 6 October 2009.

21 Central Statistics Office, Life Expectancy Tables, cso.ie.

22 Orth, U., 'The Family Environment in Early Childhood Has a Long-Term Effect on Self-Esteem: A Longitudinal Study from Birth to Age 27 Years', *Journal of Personality and Social Psychology*, vol. 114, no. 4, 2018, pp. 637–655.

23 Black, M.C., Basile, K.C., Breiding, M.J., Smith, S.G., Walters, M.L., Merrick, M.T., Chen, J. and Stevens, M.R., *The National Intimate Partner and Sexual Violence Survey (NISVS): 2010 Summary Report*, National Center for Injury Prevention and Control, Centers for Disease Control and Prevention, 2011.

24 Exploring Your Mind online magazine, 'Donald Winnicott and His Theory About the False Self', exploringyourmind.com, 26 July 2018.

25 Selva, Joaquín, 'Shame Resilience Theory: How to Respond to Feelings of Shame', positivepsychology.com.

26 Swider, B., Harari, D., Breidenthal, A.P. and Bujold Steed, L., 'The Pros and Cons of Perfectionism According to the Research', *Harvard Business Review*, 27 December 2018.

27 Encyclopaedia Britannica, 'How a Rejected Block of Marble Became the World's Most Famous Statue', britannica.com.

28 Whitehead, Nadia, 'People Would Rather Be Electrically Shocked than Left Alone with Their Thoughts', *Science*, 3 July 2014.

29 France in the United States: Embassy of France in Washington, DC, 'Liberty, Equality, Fraternity', franceintheus.org, 30 November 2007.

30   McLeod, Saul, 'Carl Rogers', simplypsychology.org.

31   Pike, Nelson, 'Hume's Bundle Theory of the Self: A Limited Defense', *American Philosophical Quarterly*, vol. 4, no. 2, April 1967, pp. 159–165.

32   Yavorski, Kimberly, 'What is the Life Span of Skin Cells?', sciencing.com, 5 April 2019.

33   Gordon-Roth, Jessica, 'Locke on Personal Identity', *Stanford Encyclopedia of Philosophy* (plato. stanford.edu), 11 February 2019.

34   Williams, Linda Meyer, 'Recall of Childhood Trauma: A Prospective Study of Women's Memories of Child Sexual Abuse', *Journal of Consulting and Clinical Psychology*, vol. 62, no. 6, 1994, pp. 1,167–1,176.

35   Merzenich, Michael, 'How You Can Make Your Brain Smarter Every Day', *Next Avenue*, 2 August 2013.

36   Pang, Duanna, '3 Key Commitments of the Dalai Lama', storm-asia.com, 11 May 2014.

37   Green, C.S. and Bavelier, D., 'Exercising Your Brain: A Review of Human Brain Plasticity and Training-Induced Learning', *Psychology and Aging*, vol. 23, no. 4, 2008, pp. 692–701.

38   Andrews-Hanna, J.R., 'The Brain's Default Network and its Adaptive Role in Internal Mentation', *Neuroscientist*, vol. 18, no. 3, 2012, pp. 251–270.

39   Cherry, Kendra, 'Harry Harlow and the Nature of Affection', verywellmind.com, 5 July 2020.

40   Savitsky, K., Boaz, K., Epley, N., Carter, T. and Swanson, A., 'The Closeness-Communication Bias: Increased Egocentrism Among Friends versus Strangers', *Journal of Experimental Social Psychology*, vol. 47, no. 1, January 2011, pp. 269–273.

41   Wagoner, Heather, 'The Science of Listening', HuffPost, 17 July 2017.

42   Zenger, Jack and Folkman, Joseph, 'What Great Listeners Actually Do', *Harvard Business Review*, 14 July 2016.

43   Matyszczyk, Chris, 'Study: 19 Percent of People Drop Phones Down Toilet', CNET, 21 July 2011.

44   Heartfulness, 'Interview on Heartfulness, Lyon, France', heartfulness.org.

45   Alshami, A.M., 'Pain: Is it All in the Brain or the Heart?', *Current Pain and Headache Reports*, vol. 23, no. 12, 2019, p. 88.

46   HeartMath, 'The Science of HeartMath', heartmath.com.

47   Laskowski, Edward R., 'What's a Normal Resting Heart Rate?', mayoclinic.org.

48   Solan, Matthew, 'Your Resting Heart Rate Can Reflect Your Current – and Future – Health', Harvard Health Blog, 17 June 2016.

49   Albert Camus banquet speech, 10 December 1957, nobelprize.org.

50   Marlowe, Laura, 'Camus's Sizzling Letters to One of His Three Lovers', *Irish Times*, 25 November 2017.

51   McLeod, Saul, 'Solomon Asch – Conformity Experiment', simplypsychology.org, 28 December 2018.

52   Cleary, Skye C., 'What Is Authentic Love? Simone de Beauvoir on Romance', HuffPost, 7 January 2016.

53   etymonline.com

54   Coleman, David, 'Too Much, Too Young: Why We Need to Talk to Our Sons About Porn', *Irish Independent*, 9 April 2019.

55   Rider, Jennifer R. et al., 'Ejaculation Frequency and Risk of Prostate Cancer: Updated Results with an Additional Decade of Follow-up', *European Urology*, vol. 70, no. 6, 2016, pp. 974–982.

56   Henriques, Gregg, 'Can You See Your Shadow?', *Psychology Today*, 21 February 2017.

57   Clear, James, 'First Principles: Elon Musk on the Power of Thinking for Yourself', jamesclear.com.

58   Baer, Drake, 'Elon Musk Uses This Ancient Critical-Thinking Strategy to Outsmart Everybody Else', *Independent*, 9 October 2017.

59   Farnam Street, 'Hanlon's Razor: Relax, Not Everything is Out to Get You', fs.blog.

60   Cassidy, Jude and Shaver, Phillip R. (eds), *Handbook of Attachment: Theory, Research, and Clinical Applications*, Guilford Press, 2016.

61   Sweeney, Tanya, 'Esther Perel: "We Need a New Approach to Infidelity"', *Irish Times*, 9 December 2017.

62   Smith, Andrea, 'An Utterly Unbreakable Bond of Love and Devotion', *Irish Independent*, 3 October 2014.

63   O'Brien, Breda, 'Breda O'Brien: The World Must Tackle the Epidemic of Loneliness', *Irish Times*, 9 October 2016.

64   John, Tara, 'How the World's First Loneliness Minister Will Tackle "the Sad Reality of Modern Life"', *Time*, 25 April 2018.

65   Hello Heart, 'Loneliness Puts Your Heart at Risk', helloheart.com, 25 May 2020.

66 Partners Studio, '4 Reasons Why Over 50% Car Crashes Happen Closer to Home', HuffPost, 14 December 2017.

67 Sturt, David and Nordstrom, Todd, '10 Shocking Workplace Stats You Need to Know', *Forbes*, 8 March 2018.

68 Twaronite, Karyn, 'A Global Survey on the Ambiguous State of Employee Trust', *Harvard Business Review*, 22 July 2016.

69 DiSalvo, David, 'Why are so Many of Us Sunday Night Insomniacs?', *Forbes*, 8 August 2016.

70 Strogatz, Steven and Goldenfeld, Nigel, 'Sync: The Emerging Science of Spontaneous Order', *Physics Today*, vol. 57, no. 6, 2004, pp. 59–60.

71 Davidji, meditation retreat, Dublin, March 2019.

FURTHER READING

✖ Alexander, Eben, *Proof of Heaven: A Neurosurgeon's Journey into the Afterlife*, Piatkus, 2012.

✖ Alexander, Eben and Newell, Karen, *Living in a Mindful Universe: A Neurosurgeon's Journey into the Heart of Consciousness*, Rodale, 2017.

✖ Augustine of Hippo, *Delphi Collected Works of Saint Augustine (Illustrated)*, Delphi Classics, 2016.

✖ Aurelius, Marcus, *Meditations*, Everyman, 1992.

✖ Barrios, A.A., 'Hypnotherapy: A Reappraisal', *Psychotherapy: Theory, Research & Practice*, vol. 7, no. 1, 1970, pp. 2–7.

✖ Bernstein, Gabrielle, *Super Attractor: Methods for Manifesting a Life Beyond Your Wildest Dreams*, Hay House, 2019.

✖ Brach, Tara, *True Refuge: Finding Peace and Freedom in Your Own Awakened Heart*, Hay House UK, 2013.

✖ Cacioppo, J.T. and Patrick, W., *Loneliness: Human Nature and the Need for Social Connection*, WW Norton & Company, 2008.

✖ Carslon, Richard, *Don't Sweat the Small Stuff – and It's All Small Stuff: Simple Ways to Keep the Little Stuff from Taking Over Your Life*, Hyperion Books, 1997.

✖ Clack, Beverly, *Freud on the Couch: A Critical Introduction to the Father of Psychoanalysis*, Oneworld Publications, 2013.

✖ Clear, James, *Atomic Habits*, Random House Business, 2018.

✖ Cotton, Fearne, *Calm: Working through Life's Daily Stresses to Find a Peaceful Centre*, Orion, 2018.

✖ de Botton, Alain, *Essays in Love*, Picador, 2015.

✖ Dodson, Betty, PhD, *Sex for One: The Joy of Selfloving*, Random House Value Publications, 1996.

✖ Fehmi, Les and Robbins, Jim, *The Open-Focus Brain: Harnessing the Power of Attention to Heal Mind and Body*, Trumpeter Books, 2008.

✖ Forleo, Marie, *Everything Is Figureoutable*, Portfolio Penguin, 2019.

✖ Frankl, Victor E., *Man's Search for Meaning*, Rider, 2004.

✖ Gibran, Kahlil, *The Prophet*, Alfred A. Knopf, 1923.

✖ Gilbert, Paul, *The Compassionate Mind (Compassion Focused Therapy)*, Constable, 2010.

✖ Gladwell, Malcolm, *Talking to Strangers: What We Should Know about the People We Don't Know*, Hachette USA, 2019.

✖ Goldhill, Simon, *Love, Sex and Tragedy: Why Classics Matter*, John Murray, 2005.

✖ Gopnik, Alison, *The Philosophical Baby: What Children's Minds Tell Us About Truth, Love and the Meaning of Life*, Vintage, 2009.

✖ Grayling, A.C., *Friendship*, Yale University Press, 2014.

✖ Gunn, John Alexander, *Modern French Philosophy*, Pinnacle Press, 2017.

✖ Haig, Matt, *Notes on a Nervous Planet*, Canongate Books, 2018.

✖ Hamid, Mohshin, *How to Get Filthy Rich in Rising Asia*, Penguin, 2014.

✖ Hamilton, David, *I Heart Me: The Science of Self-Love*, Hay House, 2015.

✖ Hanson, Rick, *Resilient: 12 Tools for Transforming Everyday Experiences into Lasting Happiness*, Rider, 2018.

✖ Hari, Johann, *Lost Connections: Uncovering the Real Causes of Depression and the Unexpected Solutions*, Bloomsbury, 2018.

✖ Katie, Byron, *Loving What Is: Four Questions That Can Change Your Life*, Random House USA, 2011.

✖ Midal, Fabrice, *The French Art of Letting Go*, Seven Dials, 2017.

✖ Murphy, Kate, *You're Not Listening: What You're Missing and Why It Matters*, Harvill Secker, 2020.

✖ Nhất Hạnh, Thích, *How to Love*, Rider, 2016.

✖ Nestor, James, *Breath: The New Science of a Lost Art*, Penguin Life, 2020.

✖ Obama, Michelle, *Becoming*, Viking, 2018.

✖ Perry, Philippa, *The Book You Wish Your Parents Had Read (And Your Children Will Be Glad That You Did)*, Penguin Life, 2019.

✖ Rousseau, Jean-Jacques, *The Social Contract*, 1762.

✖ Sadlier, Richie, *Recovering*, Gill Books, 2019.

✖ Sagan, Carl, *Pale Blue Dot: A Vision of the Human Future in Space*, Ballantine Books, 1997.

✖ Sartre, Jean-Paul, *Being and Nothingness*, Routledge, 2nd edition, 2003.

✖ Sartre, Jean-Paul, *Sketch for a Theory of the Emotions*, Routledge, 2013.

✖ Schwartz, Richard C., *Greater than the Sum of Our Parts: Discovering Your True Self through Internal Family Systems Therapy*, Sounds True, 2018.

✖ Tolle, Eckhart, *A New Earth: Create a Better Life*, Penguin, 2009.

✖ Trombley, Stephen, *A History of Western Thought*, Atlantic Books, 2013.

✖ van der Kolk, Bessel, *The Body Keeps the Score: Mind, Brain and Body in the Transformation of Trauma*, Penguin, 2015.

✖ Ware, Bronnie, *The Top Five Regrets of the Dying: A Life Transformed by the Dearly Departing*, Hay House UK, 2012.

✖ Westover, Tara, *Educated*, Windmill Books, 2018.

✖ Winfrey, Oprah, *The Path Made Clear: Discovering Your Life's Direction and Purpose*, Bluebird, 2019.

✖ Wood, Wendy, *Good Habits, Bad Habits: The Science of Making Positive Changes That Stick*, Macmillan USA, 2019.

✖ Zaretsky, Robert and Scott, John T., *The Philosopher's Quarrel: Rousseau, Hume, and the Limits of Human Understanding*, Yale University Press, 2009.

ACKNOWLEDGEMENTS

Thank you to Ciaran – this book would not exist without your love and relentless support. Thank you to my very own 'Monsieur Monoprix' for looking after me in the little blue studio, from cooking food to listening to all my angst and dreams. Thank you for the time you have given to helping make this book clearer and for the hours you spent on it when you had already been staring at a screen all day! Thank you for 25 years of love.

Thank you to Luca for saying the kindest things that anyone has ever said to me in my entire life. I never knew such love was possible until you came into the world. Thanks for your patience in having a therapist as a mother who infuriatingly and constantly asks you, 'How are you feeling?'

Thanks, Dad, for your endless wisdom, support, honesty and genuine interest in making this book the best it could be.

Thanks, Mum and Orla, for all your support, love and laughter.

Thanks to my clients, each and every one of you, for giving me the opportunity to see into your worlds. This book would not exist without you and I remain eternally grateful.

My most sincere gratitude to Niall Breslin for his insightful foreword to this book. My heart lifted when I first read Niall's words. I knew my work had been understood and, more importantly, Niall's direct encouragement to the reader to do the work required to love themselves is paramount to the success of this book in helping people. Thank you for that.

Thanks to my editor, Sarah Liddy. Your faith in me as a writer has helped my confidence to grow.

Thanks to Aoibheann Molumby for her commitment and care in the editing. Thanks to Kristin Jensen for her very thorough copyedit, it really helped.

Thanks to the marketing and PR team, Teresa Daly and Avril Cannon, for their inspiring ideas, humour and kindness.

Thanks to the designers Graham Thew and Bartek Janczak for their ingenuity and for working with the cover until 'it was perfect'!

Thanks to the five main interviewees in this book: Dermot Whelan, Roz Purcell, Dr Rick Hanson, Alison Canavan and Tomi Reichental. I am so grateful for your wisdom and input, which has made the book so much richer.

Thanks to Keith Walsh, Dr Mary Ryan, Padraig O'Morain and Lorraine Keane for your support and kind words. Thanks to Vivienne and Terry in Head Office, you brighten up my days.

Thanks also to Dr Caroline West, Simone George and Mark Pollock for your insights and the generosity of your time.

Thanks to my family and friends for your loving support, in no particular order: Linda Gambrill, Caoimhe Jordan, Tanya Kerry Keane, Zara Griffith, Roisin Byrne, Jane McDaid, Lorraine Tucker, Suzanne Warde and Grainne Nugent. Thanks to Phoebe Crowe for our lockdown morning walks that helped to keep me sane as I finished this book. Thanks to Síne Quinn for your continued support and interest in my work. Thanks to Brian Pennie for the positive cheer you bring to my world. Thanks to my 'This Is Me' team and fellow Gill authors, Siobhan Murray and Allison Keating. Also, thanks to Taragh Loughrey Grant. Thanks to my mentor, Jean Callanan, I am so grateful for your amazing acumen; and to my clinical supervisor, Aisling Killoran, I owe so much to your guidance and hypnotherapy sessions.